Microsoft Works 4
for Windows 95

James E. Shuman

Bellevue Community College

Heidi Sewall

CTI

A DIVISION OF COURSE TECHNOLOGY
ONE MAIN STREET, CAMBRIDGE, MA 02142

an International Thomson Publishing company I(T)P®

Cambridge • Albany • Bonn • Boston • Cincinnati • London • Madrid • Melbourne • Mexico City
New York • Paris • San Fransisco • Singapore • Tokyo • Toronto • Washington

Managing Editor	DeVilla Williams
Product Manager	Lisa Strite
Production Editor	Nancy Ray
Composition House	GEX, Inc.
Cover Designer	Ark Stein, Studio Silicon

© 1996 by CTI.
A Division of Course Technology – I T P®

For more information contact:

Course Technology
One Main Street
Cambridge, MA 02142

International Thomson Publishing Europe
Berkshire House 168-173
High Holborn
London WCIV 7AA
England

Thomas Nelson Australia
102 Dodds Street
South Melbourne, 3205
Victoria, Australia

Nelson Canada
1120 Birchmount Road
Scarborough, Ontario
Canada M1K 5G4

International Thomson Editores
Campos Eliseos 385, Piso 7
Col. Polanco
11560 Mexico D.F. Mexico

International Thomson Publishing GmbH
Kônigswinterer Strasse 418
53227 Bonn
Germany

International Thomson Publishing Asia
211 Henderson Road
#05-10 Henderson Building
Singapore 0315

International Thomson Publishing Japan
Hirakawacho Kyowa Building, 3F
2-2-1 Hirakawacho
Chiyoda-ku, Tokyo 102
Japan

Trademarks

Course Technology and the open book logo are registered trademarks of Course Technology.

I T P® The ITP logo is a registered trademark of International Thomson Publishing.

Some of the product names and company names used in this book have been used for identification purposes only and may be trademarks or registered trademarks of their respective manufacturers and sellers.

Disclaimer

Course Technology reserves the right to revise this publication and make changes from time to time in its content without notice.

ISBN 0-7895-0649-1

Printed in the United States of America

10 9 8 7 6 5 4 3 2 1

Contents

Chapter 7   **Viewing, Enhancing, and Linking Spreadsheets   WK 133**

Chapter 8   **Working with Charts   WK 163**

Chapter 9   **Introduction to Databases   WK 177**

Preface

The Windows Workshop is a series of Windows applications books. Currently, the series includes Windows, Word, WordPerfect, Excel Quattro Pro, Lotus, Access, and Paradox. These books focus on the fundamental features of each application and provide a way for students to become fairly proficient within a short time. The emphasis is on how the application can be used to develop documents, analyze information, and solve problems. A case study, following a company called Adventure Tours Inc., is used to provide realism and continuity throughout the series.

TO THE INSTRUCTOR

The purpose of this text is to help students develop the skills necessary to create documents using Microsoft Works for Windows 95. As students create documents they learn the basics of working with word processing documents, spreadsheets, and databases. In addition, students learn about the most commonly used features of Microsoft Works for Windows 95.

The Windows 95 Workshop: Microsoft Works 4 for Windows 95 provides a practical, hands-on approach to developing skills in the use of Microsoft Works for Windows 95. The text requires active participation as the students develop real-world documents. The emphasis is on learning by doing, a process that is exciting and motivating for students as they learn Microsoft Works.

The text is designed as a self-paced tutorial to be used in a lab setting. A concept is presented, such as merging documents (mail merge) or creating database fields. The concept is then explained, followed by the actual steps so students learn the "why" along with the "how." In each chapter students work through examples so that new commands are practiced as they are presented. Exercises reinforce learning by requiring students to apply skills as they are learned. Figures duplicating the monitor display guide students through the operations involved in completing a particular exercise. This approach allows you, the instructor, to determine your level of involvement—from providing presentations that supplement the text material to acting as a resource person.

Chapters are organized as follows:

- Chapter objectives
- Self-paced tutorials to teach new commands and techniques
- Exercises to reinforce learning
- End-of-chapter Key Terms, Review Questions, and Projects

Features and Benefits of This Text

Explanation of Underlying Concepts Students gain an understanding of word processing, spreadsheets, and databases; how to create and save documents using each of these tools; and the Windows graphical environment used by Works.

Sequential Instruction Step-by-step instructions allow students to progress at their own pace. They learn basic commands first and then move to more advanced features. This approach allows students to redo a section for reinforcement or review. Chapters may be completed in an open lab setting where the instructor need not be present and where students can aid one another in the learning process.

Extensive Use of Figures Students can check what is displayed on their monitor with the more than 160 figures provided in the text. These figures guide students through the sequential instruction.

Exercises Once a command is learned, students are challenged to use the skill to complete a practical exercise.

Numerous Projects End-of-chapter projects provide practical applications to stimulate interest, reinforce learning, and test acquired skills.

Student-Tested Approach Students unfamiliar with computers are able to complete this text with minimal guidance. Students like the self-paced tutorial approach and the challenges provided by the exercises and projects.

Data Disk The data disk accompanying this text has several files used by the students to complete the tutorials, exercises, and projects. Use of the data disk adds realism to the business case and allows students to work on complex documents without having to spend time entering data.

TO THE STUDENT

The purpose of this text is to help you develop the skills necessary to create documents using the Microsoft Works for Windows 95 word processing, spreadsheet, and database tools. You will be developing commonly used business documents such as letters, memos, announcements, spreadsheets, form letters, and reports. You will learn how to enhance the appearance of these documents and to work with the special features provided by each of the Work tools.

This text provides a practical, hands-on approach to developing skills in the use of Microsoft Works for Windows 95. The text allows you to work at your own pace through step-by-step tutorials. A concept is presented, such as inserting a graphic into a document. The concept is then explained, followed by the actual steps. Throughout the text, figures show appropriate screen displays to help keep you on track. Examples, exercises, and projects will reinforce your learning.

To learn the most from the use of this text you should:

- Proceed slowly: Accuracy is more important than speed.
- Understand what is happening with each step before continuing to the next step.
- After finishing a process, ask yourself: Can I do the process on my own? If the answer is no, review the steps.
- Check your screen display with the figures in the text.

Enjoy learning Microsoft Works for Windows 95!

Introduction to Microsoft Works for Windows 95 and the Word Processing Tool

IN THIS CHAPTER YOU WILL LEARN HOW TO:

- Start the Microsoft Works program

- Develop documents using the Word Processing tool

- Make changes in a document

- Save and print documents

- Move and copy text

- Align paragraphs

- Open a previously saved document

WHAT IS MICROSOFT WORKS?

Microsoft Works for Windows 95 is an integrated software package that contains a word processing application, a spreadsheet, a database, and a telecommunications package. The **word processing application** is used to develop documents such as letters, memos, and reports. The **spreadsheet application** is used to create documents that use numbers and calculations such as budgets, sales forecasts, and inventory reports. The spreadsheet application also can be used to create charts. The **database application** is used to keep track of data such as customers' names and addresses, students' transcripts, and patients' medical records. Works also has a **communications application** that is used to link up computers across phone lines in order to share information.

Works is referred to as an **integrated program** because it contains four applications in one program and these four applications can be used together. For example, a budget could be developed using the spreadsheet application and then inserted into a report that was created using the word processing application. An advantage of an integrated program is that the skills you learn in one application are transferable to other applications. For instance, the process to print and save a document in the word processing application is the same process used in the database application.

STARTING WORKS

Before starting Works you must start the Windows 95 program. After Windows 95 is running, you will display a series of menus that lead you to the command for starting the Microsoft Works application. The first menu is displayed when you click on ![Start] on the taskbar. The next menu is displayed when you point to Programs on the Start menu. Next, point to Microsoft Works 4.0 on the menu that is displayed to the right of the Programs option. This new menu displays all options for the Microsoft Works program. To start the Works application, choose Microsoft Works 4.0 from the final menu. Figure 1.1 shows the Windows 95 screen with the Microsoft Works 4.0 menu displayed. Complete the following steps to start Works. (*Note:* The Microsoft Works 4.0 command may appear in a different menu, depending upon your computer setup. Also, there may be a shortcut icon on the Windows 95 desktop which will give you quick access to the application. In either case, your screen may differ from the one portrayed in Figure 1.1, and the steps needed to start Works may vary from those that follow.)

1. Start Windows 95.
2. Click on ![Start].
3. Point to <u>P</u>rograms on the menu that appears.

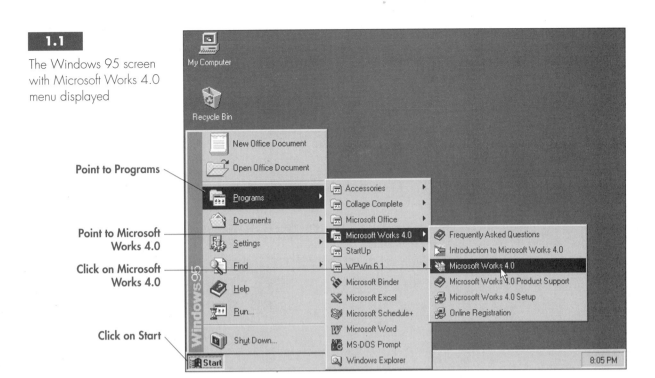

1.1

The Windows 95 screen with Microsoft Works 4.0 menu displayed

Point to Programs

Point to Microsoft Works 4.0

Click on Microsoft Works 4.0

Click on Start

4. **Point to Microsoft Works 4.0 on the next menu (see Figure 1.1).**

5. **Point to and click on Microsoft Works 4.0 on the next menu.**

(*Note*: Works may display a message box that allows you to see a short demonstration of the application. Click on Cancel to bypass this message.)

THE WORKS TASK LAUNCHER

Figure 1.2 shows the screen that appears after you start the Works 4.0 program. The dialog box in the center of the screen is called the **Works Task Launcher**, which is a gateway to the various parts of Microsoft Works for Windows 95. It allows you to create a document using the **TaskWizards**, a feature that helps you automatically create a document; to open a previously saved document by choosing the Existing Documents tab; or to select one of the Works application tools (word processor, spreadsheet, database or communications). The Works Task Launcher window will appear when you start Works or when you choose New from the File menu.

For now, continue by choosing the word processing application from the Works Tools index tab.

6. **Click on the Works Tools index tab (see Figure 1.2).**

This portion of the dialog box will give you direct access to the four Works applications: word processor, spreadsheet, database, and communications. Choose the word processor tool.

7. **Click on ▨ (see Figure 1.3).**

1.2

The Works Task Launcher

Click on the Works
Tools index tab

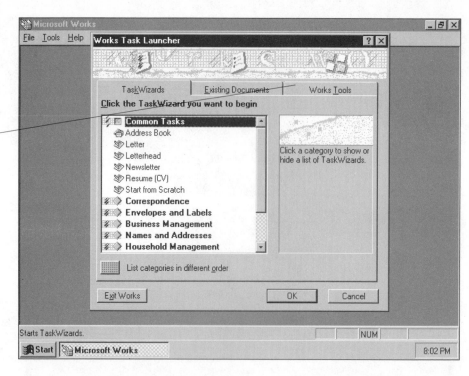

1.3

Selecting the Word
Processor tool

Click on Word Processor

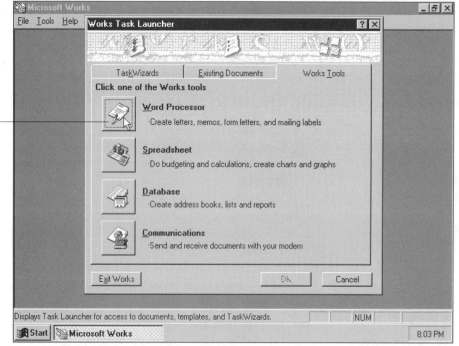

THE WORD PROCESSOR WINDOW

Figure 1.4 shows the Microsoft Works Word Processor screen. Refer to Figure 1.4 as you read the following description of each part of the screen.

- Title bar. At the top of the window is the application **title bar**. This bar displays the name of the program, Microsoft Works.

- Menu bar. The **menu bar** displays the menu names that contain the commands used to work with Works. For example, the File menu contains the Save and Print commands.

- Toolbar. The **toolbar** displays buttons that are used as shortcuts in carrying out various functions. For example, the is used to check for spelling errors in a document.

- Help window. Works displays a **Help window** that can be used to access information about using the word processor commands.

1.4

The Works 4.0 word processor screen

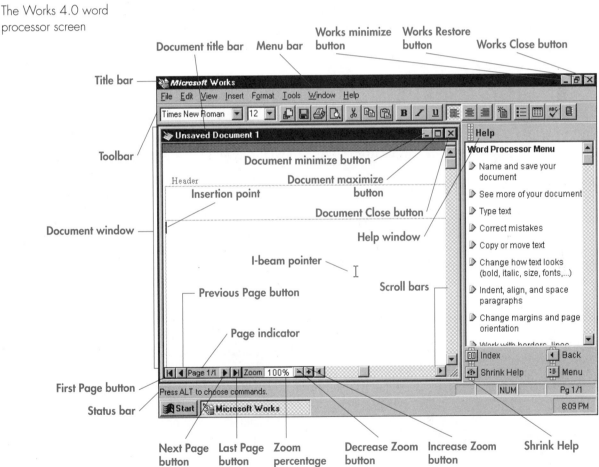

- Maximize, minimize, and restore buttons. The **maximize, minimize,** and **restore buttons** are used to resize the window. Notice that buttons appear on the Works window as well as on the document window. The maximize button becomes a restore button when the window is enlarged to full size. The restore button appears again when the window is reduced to a smaller size.

- Close button. The **close button** closes the window and any document or program that is displayed in that window.

- Status bar. The **status bar** displays information about the document or task you are working on. For example, it displays the page number where the insertion point is located. The status bar also displays different working modes. For instance, when you press the (CAPS LOCK) key, "CAPS" is displayed on the status bar.

- Document window. The **document window** is where the text appears as you type. The window can be enlarged (maximized) or reduced to an icon. The document window has the following parts:

- Document title bar. Works assigns a number to a document that hasn't been saved and the words Unsaved Document appear in front of the number. When you save a document, the name you specify replaces Unsaved Document 1 on the title bar. If you open another document, the title bar displays Unsaved Document 2.

- Insertion point. The **insertion point** is a vertical bar that acts like a cursor. It shows the location where the next keystroke will appear.

- I-beam pointer. The **I-beam pointer**, controlled by the mouse, is used to select text or to position the insertion point.

- Page buttons. The **first page**, **previous page**, **next page**, and **last page buttons** can be used to quickly move through a document. The **page indicator** between the buttons tells what page is being displayed.

- Zoom buttons. The **zoom buttons** allow you to reduce or enlarge the onscreen display of the document. (*Note*: Zoom does not change the way a document prints, merely the size it appears onscreen.) The **zoom indicator** tells what percentage the display is set at.

- Scroll bars. The **scroll bars** are used to view different parts of a document when it is too large to fit within the document window. For example, if you are working on a two-page document, you could use the vertical scroll bar to move to the second page.

At first, the Works application window may seem somewhat intimidating to you. However, after using the program for a short while, you will understand how intuitive the various menus, commands, buttons, and other elements are. You also will quickly realize that many of the items are just duplicate ways of accomplishing the same task. For instance, to print a document, you can use either the Print command from the File menu or the Print button on the toolbar. In most cases, the process you choose is a matter of personal preference.

In the following sections you will learn how easy it is to enter, edit, save, and print a document. You will be introduced to Adventure Tours Inc. (ATI), a travel agency that specializes in nontraditional excursions. ATI uses Works to develop an array of documents, including letters, memos, press releases, and reports. Figure 1.5 shows the first document you will develop, an announcement concerning the opening of a new ATI office. You will start by typing in the first paragraph. As you type text, you will notice that as you get to the right edge of the window, Works automatically moves the insertion point to the beginning of the next line. This is called **word wrap**. If you make a mistake while typing, use the (← BACKSPACE) key to erase the mistake, and then retype the text.

1. Make sure you are starting with a new document window, as shown in Figure 1.4.

Before starting the new document, shrink the Help window and maximize the document window to give yourself a larger view of the document work area.

2. Click on the [⬚] to reduce the Help window.

3. Click on the [⬚] to enlarge the document window.

4. Type the first paragraph (see Figure 1.5).

To create another paragraph, you need to press (← ENTER). Pressing (← ENTER) twice will insert a blank line between paragraphs.

5. Press (← ENTER) twice.

6. Type the second paragraph.

7. Press (← ENTER) twice.

1.5

An announcement

Adventure Tours is happy to announce the opening of a new office at Gillman Village. This office is specifically designed to serve our growing clientele living in the greater Eastside area.

The official opening will be on Wednesday, November 10th. There will be an open house reception on Tuesday at 6:00 pm. All our customers will be invited and door prizes, including an excursion to Tibet, will be given away. Please attend the reception and meet the new staff including the manager, Joanne Terry.

Works allows you to easily make changes in a document. Figure 1.6 shows the document with the following changes:

First paragraph:

- *Inc.* is inserted in the first line.

- *happy* is replaced with *pleased*.

- *Business Park* is inserted after the word *Village*.

- *specifically* is deleted.

Second paragraph:

- *an open house* is deleted.

- *customers* is replaced with *clients*.

To edit text, you first move the insertion point to the desired location. There are two ways to position the insertion point: with the keyboard and with the mouse. Following are the keys commonly used to position the insertion point:

Key(s)	Moves the insertion point
↑ ↓	Up and down one line
← →	Left and right one character
HOME	To the beginning of the line
END	To the end of the line
CTRL + HOME	To the beginning of the document
CTRL + END	To the end of the document
PAGE UP	Up one window of text (not up one document page)
PAGE DOWN	Down one window of text (not down one document page)

1.6

Changes to the document

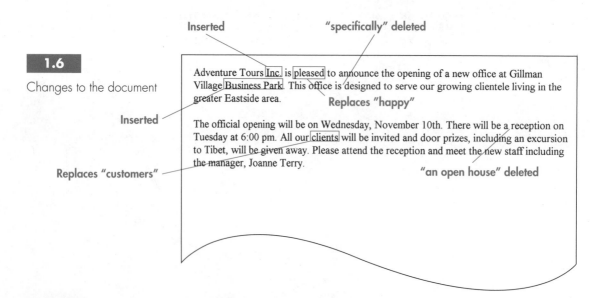

Inserted

"specifically" deleted

Inserted

Replaces "happy"

Replaces "customers"

"an open house" deleted

Adventure Tours Inc. is pleased to announce the opening of a new office at Gillman Village Business Park. This office is designed to serve our growing clientele living in the greater Eastside area.

The official opening will be on Wednesday, November 10th. There will be a reception on Tuesday at 6:00 pm. All our clients will be invited and door prizes, including an excursion to Tibet, will be given away. Please attend the reception and meet the new staff including the manager, Joanne Terry.

(*Note:* When two keys are shown joined by a plus sign (+), it means you hold down the first key while pressing the second key. Thus, CTRL + HOME means hold down the CTRL key while you press HOME.)

Take a moment to practice using these keys. Notice how the position of the insertion point changes after each of the following steps:

1. **Press** ↑ , ↓ , → , **and** ← **several times.**

2. **Press** END .

3. **Press** HOME .

4. **Press** CTRL + END .

5. **Press** CTRL + HOME .

To use the mouse to position the insertion point, position the I-beam on the desired location and click the mouse button. Use the mouse to position the insertion point, and then insert *Inc.* on the first line.

6. **Point the I-beam to after the *s* in *Tours* (see Figure 1.7).**

7. **Click the mouse button.**

8. **Press the spacebar.**

9. **Type** Inc.

Now delete the word *happy* using ← BACKSPACE .

10. **Position the I-beam after the *y* in *happy*.**

11. **Click the mouse button.**

12. **Press** ← BACKSPACE **five times to delete *happy*.**

13. **Type** pleased

1.7

Positioning the I-beam

Point here and click

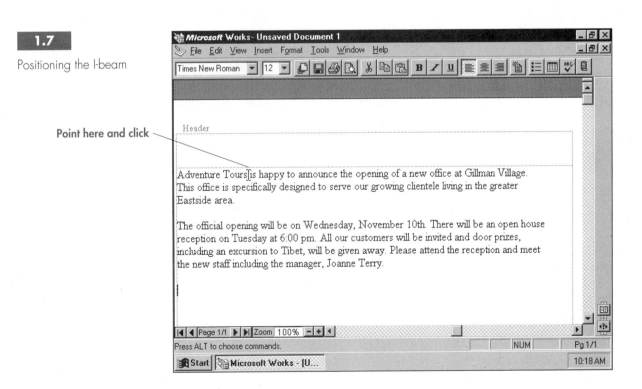

Now insert the words *Business Park* after *Village,* and delete the word *specifically.*

14. On your own, insert the words **Business Park** after the word *Village.*

15. On your own, use (← BACKSPACE) to delete the word *specifically* and the space preceding it.

Another way to delete text is to select the text and then press (DELETE). For example, you can delete the word *reception* by selecting it and pressing (DELETE). You can select a character(s), a word(s), a paragraph(s), even the entire document. The mouse can be used to select text by holding down the mouse button and dragging the I-beam across the desired text to highlight it. To select a single word, point to the word and double-click the mouse button. Start by selecting the words *an open house* in the second paragraph. To do so, position the I-beam in front of the *a* in the word *an,* hold down the mouse button, and drag the I-beam across the three words (see Figure 1.8). As you drag the I-beam, notice how the text is highlighted.

16. Position the I-beam in front of the *a* in *an.*

17. Hold down the mouse button.

18. Drag the I-beam to the *e* in *house.*

19. Release the mouse button.

Notice as you drag the pointer across *house* that the space following the word is also selected. You could perform any number of operations on the selected text, including replacing or deleting it. If you delete the text, the space will also be deleted. If you replace the text, the space remains in the document.

20. Press (DELETE) to delete the selected text.

21. Type a

22. Press the spacebar once to insert a space.

1.8

Selecting text

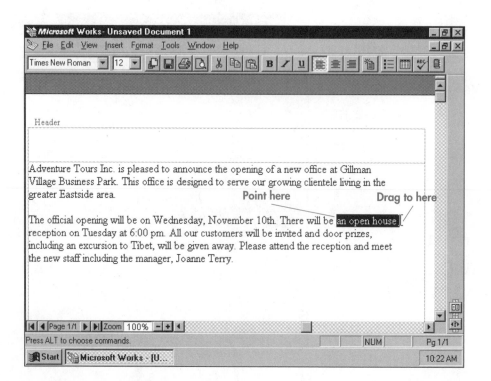

Continue by replacing the word *customers* with *clients*. This can be done by highlighting the word *clients* and typing *customers*. This time use the double-click method to select the word *clients*.

23. **Point to the word** *customers*.

24. **Double-click the mouse button to select the word.**

25. **Type** clients

26. **Press the spacebar.**

SAVING A DOCUMENT

In this section you will learn how to save a document, which involves choosing the Save As command from the File menu and completing the Save As dialog box. Menus, commands, and dialog boxes will be more fully explained in a later section. For now, you will use the two commands Save and Save As to save a document. The **Save command** is used when your document was previously saved and you want to save changes you have made to it using the same file name. The **Save As command** is used when you are saving a document for the first time or when you want to change the file name.

When you save a document, you must specify a file name. Because you are saving your documents to a data disk, the file name must be unique. If you try to use the same name for two different documents, Works displays a message asking if you want to replace the current document. Continue now by using the Save As command.

1. **Point to** <u>F</u>ile **in the menu bar.**

2. **Click the mouse button.**

3. **Point to the Save** <u>A</u>s **command.**

4. **Click the mouse button.**

The Save As dialog box appears, allowing you to tell Works where to save the document and what name to use. Documents are saved as files onto a disk such as the data disk that is used with this book. When you save a document, you need to specify two things: the disk drive that contains the disk you will save to and a file name.

Figure 1.9 shows the dialog box specifying the file a:\announcement. The file name is *announcement* and the document will be saved to a disk in drive a. (When you use a data disk, the drive is usually drive A or drive B.)

5. **Place the data disk that is used with this book in the appropriate drive (A or B).**

6. **Type** a:\announcement **(or** b:\announcement**).**

7. **Click on Save.**

The document is saved to the data disk in drive A (or B) with the file name *announcement*; the title bar displays the name of the saved document.

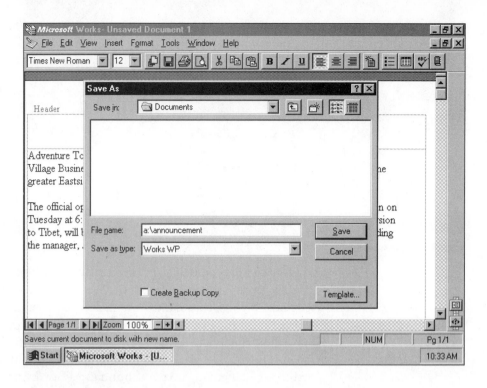

PRINTING A DOCUMENT

The Print command is found in the File menu. Before printing, make sure that your computer is connected to a printer and that the printer is ready.

   1. **Click on File in the menu bar.**

   2. **Click on Print.**

(*Note*: When you choose the Print command, a dialog box titled First-time Help may appear. This dialog box can be used to get instructions on printing a document. You will bypass this dialog box by clicking on the OK command button at the bottom.)

   3. **If necessary, click on the OK command button in the First-time Help dialog box.**

The Print dialog box appears, specifying the printer being used and allowing you to change settings such as the number of copies to print.

   4. **Click on OK.**

In just a short time you have learned how to start Works, enter and edit text, and save and print a document. You now have the skills to create simple word processing documents. In the following sections you will learn more about menus, commands, and dialog boxes.

The menu bar displays several menus (File, Edit, View, and so on). Each **menu** has several commands, such as Copy and Print. To display **commands**, you choose a menu name by pointing and clicking on the name or by holding down (ALT) and pressing the underlined letter in the command name (for example, F for the File menu).

1. **Click on File in the menu bar to display the File menu commands.**

A pull-down menu appears, displaying the File menu commands. Many of these commands are self-explanatory, such as Save and Print. The status bar at the bottom of the window gives a brief description of the highlighted command. You can highlight commands by dragging the mouse pointer slowly down the list, or using the (↑) and (↓) keys. Do not click the mouse button until directed to do so.

2. **Point to New.**

3. **Read the description on the status bar.**

4. **Point to Open and read the description.**

5. **Point to Print Preview and read the description.**

6. **Point to File in the menu bar.**

7. **Click the mouse button.**

The File menu is removed from the screen. You can also close the File menu by pressing (ESC) or by clicking on the document. Now choose the File menu again.

8. **Click on File in the menu bar.**

Once a menu has been displayed, there are four ways to select a command:

- Point to the command and click the mouse button.

- Drag the pointer to the command and release the mouse button.

- Press the underlined letter (for example, S for Save).

- Use the arrow keys to highlight the command and press (↵ ENTER) to select the highlighted command.

The method you use to choose these commands is up to you. In this book we use the mouse and the point-and-click method. However, commands can also be given using shortcut keys. **Shortcut keys** bypass the menu and directly execute the command. Some of the shortcut keys are listed next to the command in the pull-down menus. For example, the shortcut keys for the Save command are (CTRL)+(S).

Several commands have ellipses (three dots) following the command name. Ellipses indicate that choosing the command will display a dialog box that is used to give Works additional information. For example, the Save As... command displays a dialog box asking you to specify a name to use when saving the document.

9. **Click on Save As.**

A **dialog box** prompts you to provide information that Works needs before continuing. For instance, when you save a document for the first time, you must specify two things: the disk drive that contains the disk you will save to and the file name. These are specified using a dialog box. Figure 1.10 shows the Save As dialog box. (*Note:* Your screen may not look the same as this figure.) In Figure 1.10 the disk drive is set to a:, and all the files that are on the disk in drive a are listed. The Save As dialog box has the following parts:

■ Save in box. This list box allows you to choose a drive and directory (including subdirectories). Figure 1.10 shows the current drive is drive a. Beneath the Save in box is a list of the files stored on the selected directory.

■ File name box. This box allows you to type in the file name (currently the file name is *announcement*).

■ Save as type list box. This list box allows you to select a file type other than the one used by Works. For example, if you wanted to use this document with another word processing program such as WordPerfect, you could choose to save it in that format.

Take a moment to see how you could change a setting in this dialog box. Start by displaying the list of disk drives in the Drives box. Figure 1.11 shows the list that is displayed by clicking on the down arrow ▾ in the Save in box.

1. **Point to the down arrow ▾ in the Save in box (see Figure 1.11).**

2. **Click the mouse button.**

1.10

The Save As dialog box

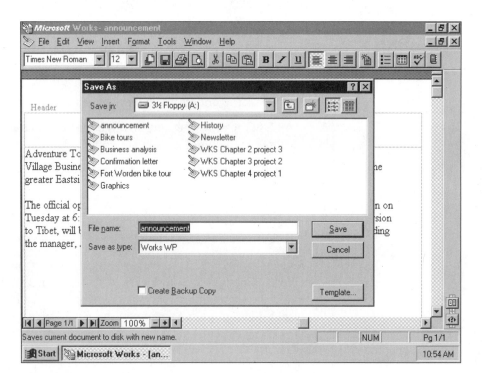

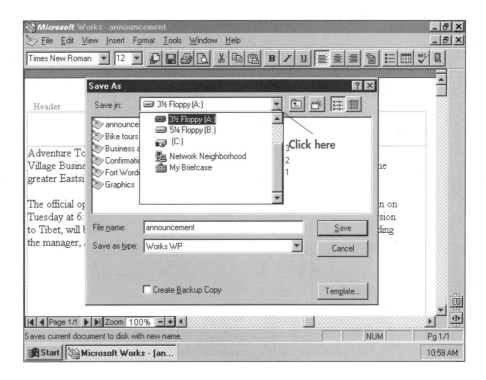

The drop-down list appears, showing the available disk drives to which you can save. To select a disk drive, click on it. To return to the document without saving it a second time, click on the Cancel button twice or press (ESC) twice.

3. **Click on Cancel.**

4. **Click on Cancel again.**

WORKING WITH PARAGRAPHS

In this section you will learn how to insert, combine, and move paragraphs. Before working with paragraphs, you need to understand how Works defines a paragraph. A paragraph is created when you type text and then press (↵ ENTER). As little as a single character followed by (↵ ENTER) or as much as an entire document followed by (↵ ENTER) will be defined as a paragraph. Figure 1.12 shows the announcement document with two additional paragraphs. Paragraphs can be inserted by positioning the insertion point and then typing the paragraph. When done typing, you press (↵ ENTER). If you want a blank line between paragraphs, as in the announcement document, you press (↵ ENTER) again before typing a new paragraph.

1.12

The announcement document with two additional paragraphs

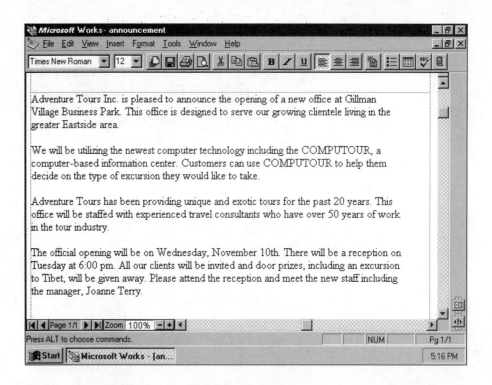

Adventure Tours Inc. is pleased to announce the opening of a new office at Gillman Village Business Park. This office is designed to serve our growing clientele living in the greater Eastside area.

We will be utilizing the newest computer technology including the COMPUTOUR, a computer-based information center. Customers can use COMPUTOUR to help them decide on the type of excursion they would like to take.

Adventure Tours has been providing unique and exotic tours for the past 20 years. This office will be staffed with experienced travel consultants who have over 50 years of work in the tour industry.

The official opening will be on Wednesday, November 10th. There will be a reception on Tuesday at 6:00 pm. All our clients will be invited and door prizes, including an excursion to Tibet, will be given away. Please attend the reception and meet the new staff including the manager, Joanne Terry.

1.13

Positioning the I-beam

Point here and click

Header

Adventure Tours Inc. is pleased to announce the opening of a new office at Gillman Village Business Park. This office is designed to serve our growing clientele living in the greater Eastside area.

The official opening will be on Wednesday, November 10th. There will be a reception on Tuesday at 6:00 pm. All our clients will be invited and door prizes, including an excursion to Tibet, will be given away. Please attend the reception and meet the new staff including the manager, Joanne Terry.

Figure 1.13 shows the I-beam pointer placed between the first and second paragraphs. Complete the following to insert these paragraphs:

1. Place the I-beam pointer between the paragraphs (see Figure 1.13).

2. Click the mouse button to position the insertion point.

3. Press (↵ ENTER).

4. Type the first paragraph to be inserted (refer to Figure 1.12).

5. Press (↵ ENTER) twice.

6. Type the second paragraph to be inserted.

7. Press (↵ ENTER).

When you press (↵ ENTER), Works inserts a symbol called a **paragraph mark**. You can display paragraph marks by using the All Characters command from the View menu. (*Note*: the paragraph marks may already be displayed on your machine. If they currently appear, as shown in Figure 1.14, skip the next two steps.)

8. Click on <u>V</u>iew in the menu bar.

9. Click on <u>A</u>ll Characters.

The paragraph marks appear. A small dot indicating a space also appears wherever the spacebar was pressed. Both the paragraph and the space marks are nonprinting symbols. These marks can be useful when editing a document. For example, if you want to combine paragraphs, you merely delete the paragraph marks that separate them. Combine the first and second paragraphs by deleting the two paragraph marks between them.

10. Position the I-beam pointer on the paragraph mark between the first and second paragraphs (see Figure 1.14).

11. Double-click the mouse button to select the mark.

12. Press (DELETE).

13. Press (← BACKSPACE) to delete the second paragraph mark.

To split a paragraph into two paragraphs, press (↵ ENTER) twice.

14. Press (↵ ENTER) twice.

To remove both the paragraph and space marks from view, choose the All Characters command again.

15. Choose <u>A</u>ll Characters from the <u>V</u>iew menu.

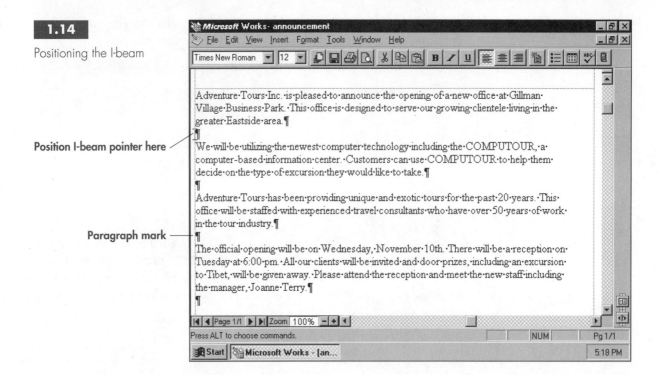

MOVING TEXT

One important feature of a word processing program is the ability to move text within a document. Works provides three methods for moving text within a document:

- *Cut and paste* using the commands from the Edit menu. To use this method, you select the text to move and choose the Cut command from the Edit menu. Then you position the insertion point at the new location and choose the Paste command from the Edit menu.

- *Cut and paste* using the toolbar buttons. This method is the same as the preceding one except that you use the ✄ and 🗐 buttons on the toolbar instead of the menu commands.

- *Drag and drop* using the mouse pointer. To use this method, you point to select the desired text and drag the mouse pointer to the new location. When you release the mouse button, the text stays positioned where the mouse was pointing.

You will practice each of these methods by moving paragraphs within the document. Figure 1.15 shows the second paragraph moved to below the third paragraph.

The first step in moving any text is to select the text. There are two methods for selecting a paragraph: You can drag the I-beam pointer down the paragraph, or you can position the pointer to the left of the paragraph and double-click the mouse button. Figure 1.16 shows the pointer to the left of the paragraph. Notice that the pointer has changed from an I-beam to an arrow. (*Note*: Your screen may look different from the one pictured in Figure 1.16. The document in Figure 1.16 has been scrolled to display the left margin area more fully.)

1.15

The second paragraph moved below the third paragraph

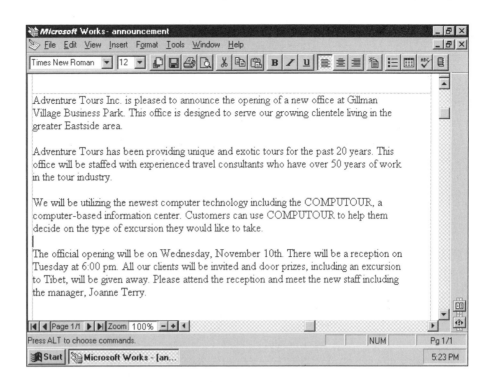

1.16

Pointing to the left of the second paragraph

Point here

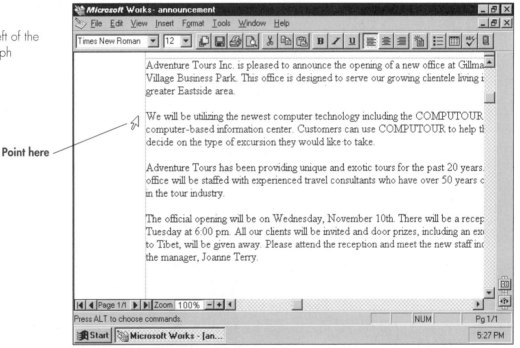

1. **Point to the left of the second paragraph, as shown in Figure 1.16.**

2. **When the pointer changes to an arrow, click the mouse button.**

Only one of the lines in the paragraph is selected.

3. **Double-click the mouse pointer to highlight the entire paragraph.**

remove the highlight, move the pointer to display the I-beam pointer, and then click the mouse button.

4. Move the arrow pointer down and toward the middle of the document until the pointer changes to an I-beam.

5. Click the mouse button to remove the highlight.

Now use the drag method to select the paragraph. An advantage of using the drag method is that you can select a blank line below the paragraph that will move with the paragraph.

6. Point to the left of the second paragraph (see Figure 1.17).

7. Hold down the mouse button and drag the pointer to select the paragraph and the blank line below it (see Figure 1.17).

8. Release the mouse button.

Now move the selected paragraph to below the third paragraph.

9. Click on Edit in the menu bar.

10. Click on Cut.

The paragraph disappears from view. It has been removed from the document and placed in a holding area called the **Clipboard**. Continue by positioning the insertion point where the paragraph will be moved to. In this case, the first line of the selected paragraph will go where the first line of the last paragraph is located.

11. Position the I-beam pointer in front of the *T* in *The* in the third paragraph (see Figure 1.18).

12. Click the mouse button to position the insertion point.

13. Click on Edit in the menu bar.

14. Click on Paste.

The second paragraph is moved to below the third paragraph. Now use the ✂ and 📋 buttons on the toolbar to move the paragraph back to its original location. Start by selecting the third paragraph.

15. Select the third paragraph and the blank line below it.

16. Click on ✂ (see Figure 1.17).

17. Position the I-beam pointer in front of the *A* in *Adventure Tours* in the second paragraph.

18. Click the mouse button to position the insertion point.

19. Click on 📋 (see Figure 1.17).

Finally, use the drag-and-drop method to again move the second paragraph to below the third paragraph (see Figure 1.19). After selecting the paragraph, point to the paragraph and hold down the mouse button. The word "DRAG" appears below the mouse pointer until you actually start to move the pointer by clicking the mouse button. Once you click the mouse button, the word "MOVE" and an insertion point appear below the mouse pointer. Drag the insertion point to the desired location and release the mouse button. Start by selecting the second paragraph.

20. Select the second paragraph and the line below it.

1.17

Dragging the I-beam pointer to select a paragraph and the blank line below it

Point here

Drag to here

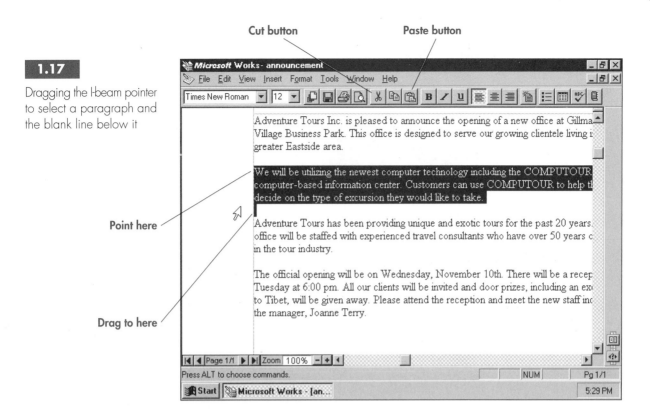

1.18

Positioning the I-beam pointer

Position I-beam pointer here

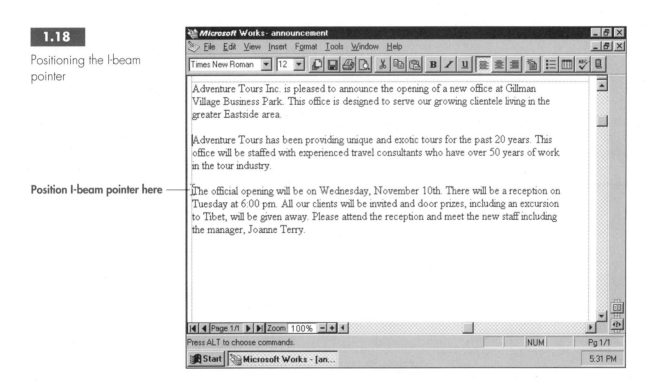

21. Point to the paragraph.

22. Hold down the mouse button.

Notice that the word "MOVE" and the insertion point are displayed.

23. Drag the insertion point to in front of the *T* in *The* in the fourth paragraph (see Figure 1.19).

The drag-and-drop process: Select the text, point to the text, hold down the mouse button, and drag the pointer to the new location

1. Point here —

2. Drag insertion point to here —

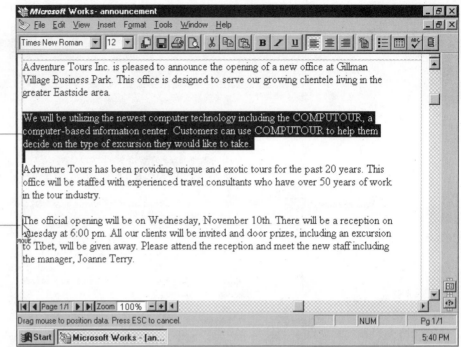

24. **Release the mouse button.**

Although you have been moving entire paragraphs, you can select any amount of text—a word, a sentence, or several paragraphs—to move. It is important to understand that when you select and cut text from a document, the text remains on the Clipboard even after it has been pasted back into the document. Therefore, you could continue pasting the same text in multiple locations.

COPYING TEXT

Text can be copied as well as moved. The methods used to copy text are similar to those used to move text except that the Copy command replaces the Cut command and the paste button 📋 replaces the cut button ✂. Further, CTRL is held down when using the drag-and-drop process to copy text. Figure 1.20 shows the words *PRESS RELEASE* copied across the bottom of the document. Complete the following steps to use each method to copy *PRESS RELEASE*:

1. Press CTRL + END to move to the end of the document.

2. If necessary, press ↵ ENTER twice to add two blank lines.

3. Type PRESS RELEASE

4. Drag the pointer to select the words *PRESS RELEASE*.

5. Choose Copy from the Edit menu.

1.20

The words PRESS RELEASE copied across the bottom of the document

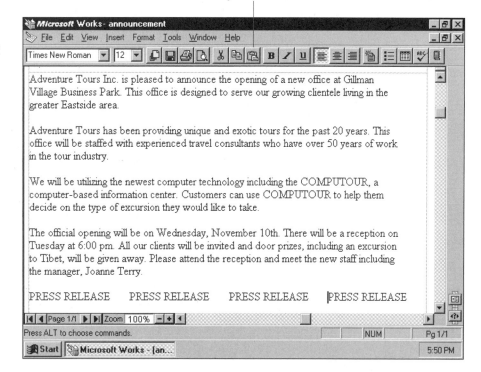

The words *PRESS RELEASE* have been copied to the Clipboard.

6. Press (END) to position the insertion point after *PRESS RELEASE.*

7. Press (TAB ⇥).

8. Choose **P**aste from the **E**dit menu.

9. Press (TAB ⇥).

This time use the paste button 🖺 on the toolbar (see Figure 1.20).

10. Click on 🖺.

Now use the drag-and-drop process. Notice that as you drag the mouse pointer to copy the text, the word "COPY" appears next to the arrow.

11. Press (TAB ⇥).

12. Select the words *PRESS RELEASE.*

13. Hold down (CTRL).

14. Point to the selected text.

15. Hold down the mouse button.

16. Drag the insertion point to the tab position (see Figure 1.21).

17. Release the mouse button.

18. Release (CTRL).

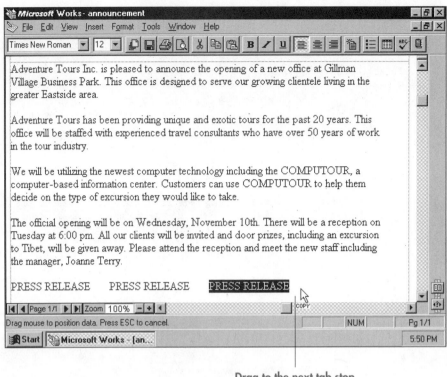

Drag to the next tab stop

ALIGNING TEXT

Microsoft Works provides four ways of aligning text in a document: left, centered, right, and justified. Figure 1.22 shows the same paragraph with these four alignments. **Left-aligned text** gives a flush left side and a ragged right side. This is a common alignment for many types of documents. **Center-aligned text** takes each line and centers it within the margins. This is a common alignment for headings. **Right-aligned text** gives a flush right side and a ragged left side. This alignment is not normally used for paragraphs of text but is used for positioning dates or page numbers at the top or bottom of a page. **Justified alignment** gives a flush edge on both the left and right margins, which Works accomplishes by automatically inserting spaces between words on each line. Justified alignment is often used in documents such as newsletters and magazines. To align text, you select the text, choose the Paragraph command from the Format menu, and set the alignment using the options in the dialog box. You can also click on one of the alignment buttons on the toolbar (see Figure 1.22). Figure 1.23 shows the following changes to the announce document:

- A heading has been inserted and centered.

- All the paragraphs have been justified.

- A date has been entered at the bottom of the document and right aligned.

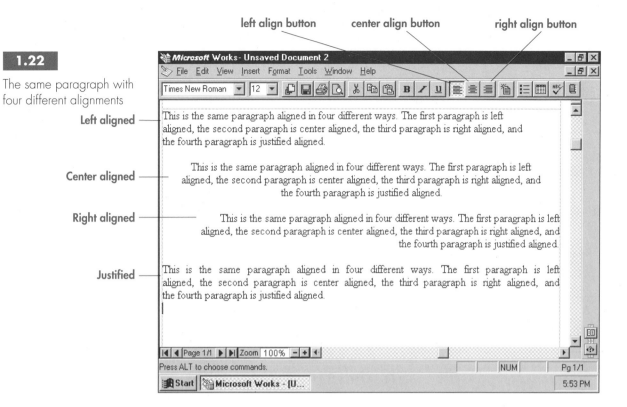

1.22

The same paragraph with four different alignments

Left aligned

Center aligned

Right aligned

Justified

left align button   center align button   right align button

Complete the following steps to duplicate Figure 1.23:

1. Press `CTRL` + `HOME` to move to the beginning of the document.

2. Type ADVENTURE TOURS

3. Press `← ENTER` twice to insert a blank line.

4. Drag the I-beam pointer to select *ADVENTURE TOURS*.

5. Point to ≣ on the toolbar.

Notice that a description of the button appears beneath the button and on the status bar when the pointer rests on the button for a few seconds. This description helps you identify the function or command the toolbar button performs.

6. Click the mouse button to deselect the text.

The heading is centered. Now select the paragraphs and justify them using the Paragraph command in the Format menu.

7. Drag the pointer to select all the paragraphs (but not the *ADVENTURE TOURS* heading or the *PRESS RELEASE* line).

8. Select Paragraph from the Format menu.

The Paragraph dialog box appears with two tabs. This dialog box allows you to change the format of selected paragraphs. In order to change the alignment, you must choose the Indents and Alignment tab.

9. If necessary, click on the Indents and Alignment tab to display these options.

10. Click on Justified in the Alignment section.

Notice the sample shows how selected paragraphs will be aligned.

11. Click on OK.

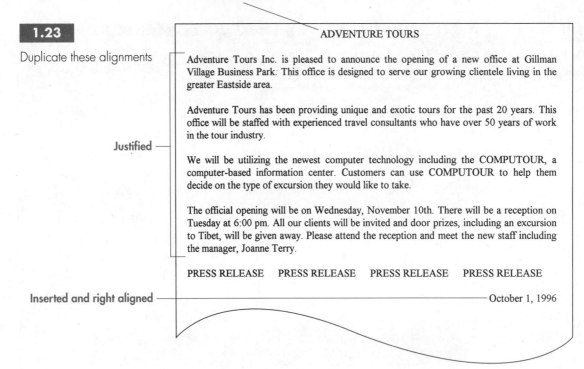

1.23

Duplicate these alignments

Inserted and centered

Justified

Inserted and right aligned

ADVENTURE TOURS

Adventure Tours Inc. is pleased to announce the opening of a new office at Gillman Village Business Park. This office is designed to serve our growing clientele living in the greater Eastside area.

Adventure Tours has been providing unique and exotic tours for the past 20 years. This office will be staffed with experienced travel consultants who have over 50 years of work in the tour industry.

We will be utilizing the newest computer technology including the COMPUTOUR, a computer-based information center. Customers can use COMPUTOUR to help them decide on the type of excursion they would like to take.

The official opening will be on Wednesday, November 10th. There will be a reception on Tuesday at 6:00 pm. All our clients will be invited and door prizes, including an excursion to Tibet, will be given away. Please attend the reception and meet the new staff including the manager, Joanne Terry.

PRESS RELEASE   PRESS RELEASE   PRESS RELEASE   PRESS RELEASE

October 1, 1996

The paragraphs are justified. Look closely, and you can see how additional space has been added between words to make the margins flush on both sides. Complete the document by entering a date and right-aligning it.

12. **Press** `CTRL` + `END` **to move to the end of the document.**

13. **Press** `↵ ENTER` **twice to add a blank line.**

14. **Type** October 1, 1996

15. **Click** ▤ **on the toolbar.**

The date is moved to the right margin of the document. You can return selected text to its original alignment by simply choosing the desired alignment button or, in the case of justified text, using the Paragraph command in the Format menu.

16. **With the insertion point on the date line, click on** ▤ **to left align the date.**

17. **Click on** ▤ **to center align the date.**

18. **Click on** ▤ **to return the date to its right-aligned position.**

This completes the section on aligning text.

SAVING A DOCUMENT UNDER ANOTHER NAME

Earlier you saved the *announcement* document to the data disk. Now you have made changes in the *announcement* document. If you want to save both the original document and the revised document you must use the Save As command and give the revised document a new file name. Complete the following steps to save the revised document as *announcement 2*.

1. Choose Save As from the File menu.

The Save As dialog box appears.

2. Type a:\announcement 2 (**or** b:\announcement 2).

3. Click on Save.

CLOSING A DOCUMENT

After saving a document, you can close it without leaving the Works program. If you attempt to close a document that has not been saved or that has been changed since the last time it was saved, a message will appear, asking if you want to save the changes. After closing a document, you could open another document, create a new document, or exit the Works program. To close a document, you choose the Close command from the File menu.

1. Choose Close from the File menu.

The Works Task Launcher appears onscreen.

OPENING A DOCUMENT

There are two ways you can open a document using the Works Task Launcher. First, if the document was recently opened, you can select it from a list of files under the Existing Documents tab. You would click on the Existing Documents tab to display the list of recently viewed files, click on the file name and choose OK or double-click on the name to open the file. Second, you can click on the button labeled Open a document not listed here. This displays the Open dialog box, which can be used to open the desired file.

1. Click on the Existing Documents tab.

2. Click on the ▦ button labeled "Open a document not listed here".

The Open dialog box appears, which is similar to the Save As dialog box. It allows you to specify the drive and the file name. You could type the drive and file name in the File Name text box, or you could display a list of the files on the data disk and choose from the list. This is done by selecting the drive that contains the data disk. To display a list of the drives, you click on the down arrow in the Look in box. (*Note:* Your screen may already show the correct drive. The following steps show how to change the drive.)

3. Point to ▼ in the Look in box (see Figure 1.24).

4. Click the mouse button.

A list of drive letters appears.

5. Click on the letter of the drive where the data disk is located.

The area beneath the Look in box displays a list of the files on the data disk. To select a file to open, click on the file name and then click on Open. (*Hint:* You can also double-click on a file name to open a file.)

6. Click on *announcement 2.doc.*

7. Click on <u>O</u>pen.

Now close the document.

8. Choose <u>C</u>lose from the <u>F</u>ile menu.

1.24

Pointing to the down arrow in the Look in box

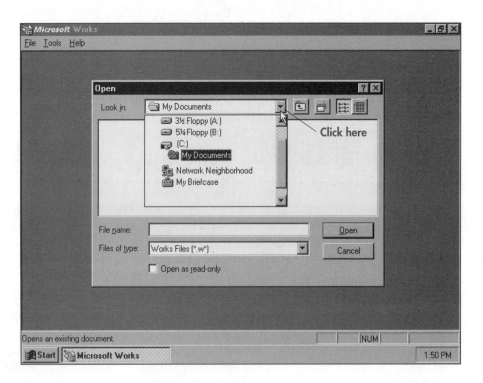

KEY TERMS

aligning text
center-aligned text
Clipboard
close button
command
communications
  application
cut and paste
database application
dialog box
document window
double-click
drag and drop
first page button
Help window
I-beam pointer
insertion point

integrated program
justified alignment
last page button
left-aligned text
maximize button
menu
menu bar
Microsoft Works for
  Windows 95
minimize button
next page button
page buttons
page indicator
paragraph mark
previous page button
restore button
right-aligned text

scroll bars
Shortcut keys
spreadsheet application
Start button
status bar
task bar
Task Wizards
title bar
toolbar
word processor
word processing
  application
word wrap
Works Task Launcher
Zoom
Zoom buttons
zoom indicator

KEY COMMANDS

All Characters
Close
Copy

Cut
Paragraph
Paste

Print
Save
Save As

REVIEW QUESTIONS

1. The title bar displays the name of the _____.

2. **T F** The menu bar displays buttons representing tools that are used as short-cuts in carrying out various functions.

3. **T F** The insertion point is a vertical bar that acts like a cursor.

4. The _____+_____ keys move the insertion point to the beginning of the document.

5. When saving a document, you need to specify the _____ and the _____ .

6. **T F** Dialog boxes are a way for you to provide information to the Works program.

7. List the three methods that can be used to move text.

   a. _____

   b. _____

   c. _____

1.25

Identify the labeled parts

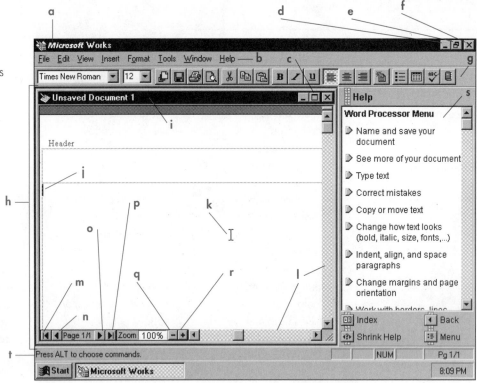

8. To view paragraph marks in a Works document, choose the _____ command from the _____ menu.

9. Identify the labeled parts of Figure 1.25.

a. _____   k. _____

b. _____   l. _____

c. _____   m. _____

d. _____   n. _____

e. _____   o. _____

f. _____   p. _____

g. _____   q. _____

h. _____   r. _____

i. _____   s. _____

j. _____   t. _____

PROJECTS

1. Duplicate the document shown in Figure 1.26. Save the document as *WKS Chapter 1 project 1*. Then edit the document to duplicate Figure 1.27, as follows:

   a. Center the heading.

   b. Justify all paragraphs.

   c. Change *Computour* to *COMPUTOUR*.

   d. Change *very pleased* to *excited*.

   e. Insert *that will fit his or her needs*.

   f. Change *see* to *view*.

   g. Save the document as *WKS Chapter 1 project 1a*.

   h. Print and then close the document.

1.26

Chapter 1 Project 1

Sales Training on Computour

We are very pleased to announce the installation of Computour, a computer-based tour information center. This center consists of a computer and laser video disk player enabling the display, almost instantaneously, of movie clips of the tours we provide.

The computer asks questions to help pinpoint a client's interest. This is how it works. A client sits at the computer and is asked questions about the activities (trekking, kayaking, etc.), the general location, the season, and the price range he or she is interested in. Based on the client's answers, Computour makes suggestions about the type of tour. Then the client can choose from the suggestions and see a video segment of a specific tour or print out information.

In order for you to become familiar with Computour, there will be a training session on Wednesday at 8:00.

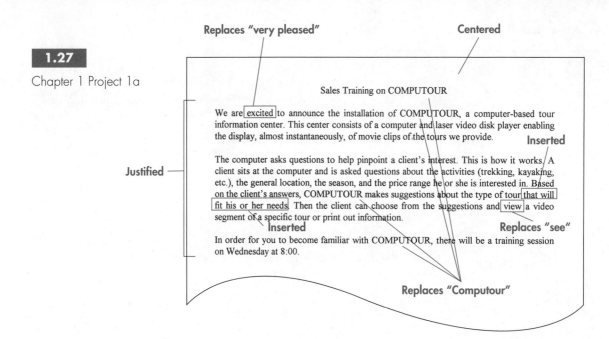

Replaces "very pleased"

Centered

Sales Training on COMPUTOUR

We are excited to announce the installation of COMPUTOUR, a computer-based tour information center. This center consists of a computer and laser video disk player enabling the display, almost instantaneously, of movie clips of the tours we provide.

Inserted

The computer asks questions to help pinpoint a client's interest. This is how it works. A client sits at the computer and is asked questions about the activities (trekking, kayaking, etc.), the general location, the season, and the price range he or she is interested in. Based on the client's answers, COMPUTOUR makes suggestions about the type of tour that will fit his or her needs. Then the client can choose from the suggestions and view a video segment of a specific tour or print out information.

Justified

Inserted

Replaces "see"

In order for you to become familiar with COMPUTOUR, there will be a training session on Wednesday at 8:00.

Replaces "Computour"

2. Choose a help-wanted newspaper advertisement. Use Microsoft Works to write a letter expressing your interest in the job. In the letter mention how your qualifications match the job requirements. Save the letter as *WKS Chapter 1 project 2*, and then print the letter. Close the document.

3. Write a note to a friend indicating that you are taking a class and learning Microsoft Works. In the note, mention five features of the Works program that make it easy to use. Save the document as *ch1_p3*, and then print the document. Close the document.

2

Enhancing a Document

IN THIS CHAPTER YOU WILL LEARN HOW TO:

- Create a memo
- Change type styles
- Change type sizes
- Change fonts
- Use the Help feature
- Work with tabs and leaders
- Work with indents
- Create bulleted lists
- Use the Print Preview feature
- Create hanging indents

In this chapter you will learn how to make changes in a document to enhance its appearance. Although many stylistic changes can be made, this chapter focuses on changes to the type and the paragraph layout. The most common type changes that you can make are:

Type styles	Type sizes	Fonts
bold	size 10 point	**Times New Roman**
italic	size 12 point	Arial
<u>underline</u>	size 14 point	Courier New

Common paragraph enhancements include using tabs and indents, and creating bulleted lists. Figure 2.1 shows the first document that you will develop and enhance. You will design this document in several steps. First, you will create the memo; then you will make changes in the type style, type size, and fonts. The memo is from the manager of the new Adventure Tours office, asking the company president to speak at the Open House ceremony.

CREATING A MEMO

Figure 2.1 shows a typical layout for a memo. Complete the following steps to duplicate this memo:

1. **Start the Works 4.0 program.**

2. **Click on the Works Tools index tab in the Works Task Launcher dialog box.**

3. **Click on**

4. **If necessary, shrink the Help screen and maximize the document window.**

2.1

A memo

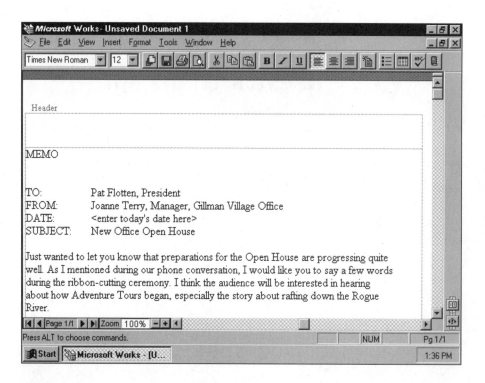

5. **Type** MEMO

6. **Press** (↵ ENTER) **three times.**

7. **Type** TO:

8. **Press** (TAB ⇄) **twice.**

9. **Type** Pat Flotten, President

10. **Press** (↵ ENTER).

11. **Continue to type the remainder of the memo (see Figure 2.1).**

CHANGING TYPE STYLES

Figure 2.2 shows the memo after the following style changes have been made:

- *MEMO* is centered and underlined.

- *TO, FROM, DATE,* and *SUBJECT* are in bold type.

- *Open House* is in italic type.

Begin making these changes by centering *MEMO*.

1. **Double-click on** *MEMO* **to select it.**

2. **Click on** 🔲 **on the toolbar (see Figure 2.2).**

Now you will use the formatting tools to change the **type styles**. Figure 2.2 identifies the bold **B**, italic **I**, and underline **U** buttons. To use these tools, you select the text and click on the desired button. Begin by underlining *MEMO*.

3. **With** *MEMO* **still selected, click on** **U** **(see Figure 2.2.).**

Notice that the Underline button now appears in a lighter shade than the other buttons, giving the impression that it has been pressed. The change in the button's appearance indicates that the selected text has been formatted by underlining it. You can remove the formatting by clicking again on **U**.

4. **Click on** **U** **to remove the underline.**

5. **Underline** *MEMO* **again.**

Next, make the headings bold.

6. **Double-click on the word** *TO* **to select it.**

7. **Click on** **B** **on the toolbar.**

Notice that the Bold button is now a lighter shade than the other buttons.

8. **On your own, make** *FROM, DATE* **and** *SUBJECT* **bold.**

(*Note:* Changing the font to Bold increases the size of the text and may change the alignment of text at the tab stop. If necessary, add or remove tabs to line up the information.)

9. **If necessary, add or remove tab stops to align the data to the right of the bold text.**

2.2

Changes to the memo using the toolbar buttons

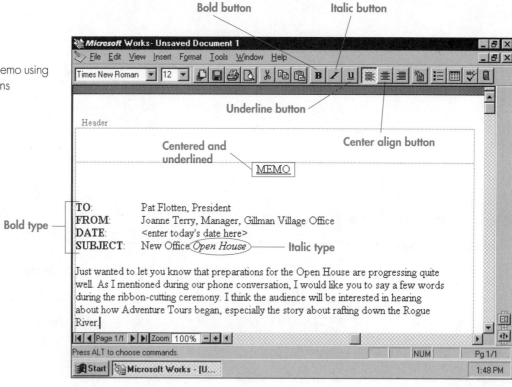

Continue formatting the document by changing *Open House* to italic type.

10. Drag the I-beam pointer across *Open House* to select it.

11. Click on ⬚ (see Figure 2.2).

CHANGING TYPE SIZES

Type sizes are measured in **points**. There are 72 points per inch. A common type size used for text is 12 point, but Works allows you to vary the type size from a few points to more than a hundred points. How large or small the type can be depends on the printer you are using and the font you select. A **font** is a type design. To change the type size, select the text, click on the down arrow next to the Font Size box on the toolbar (see Figure 2.3), and choose the desired size. Figure 2.3 shows the word *MEMO* with a point size of 18.

1. Select *MEMO.*

2. Click on ⬛ next to the Font Size box (see Figure 2.3).

3. If necessary, scroll through the list of font sizes to display 18.

4. Click on 18.

The Font command in the Format menu can also be used to change type size.

WORKS 4 FOR WINDOWS 95

Click here to display list of font sizes

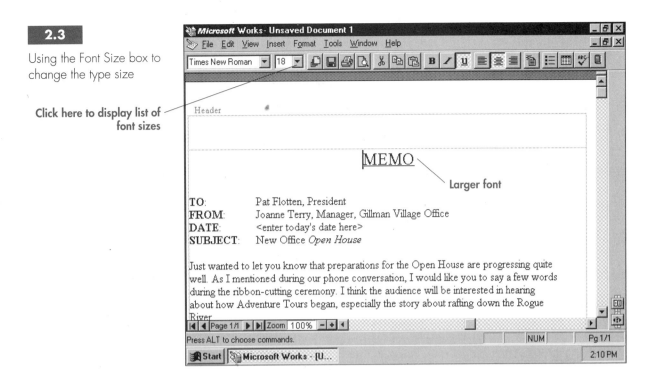

CHANGING FONTS

As we mentioned, a font is a type design. Fonts can be useful in focusing attention on certain text in a document, enhancing readability, and establishing an image. The fonts that are available to you depend on the printer and the program you are using. Works is a Windows program, and several fonts come with Windows. Others can be purchased and installed on your computer.

The font used for the selected text is shown in the Font box on the toolbar. For example, Figure 2.3 shows that the word *MEMO* is displayed in the Times New Roman font. To change a font, you select the text and display the Font box list on the toolbar, or use the Font and Style command from the Format menu. The Font and Style command allows you to change the font, the font size, and the type style all at once. In addition, there is a sample box that displays the results of the changes you have made. Before continuing with this lesson, make sure no text is selected.

1. Point the I-beam to a blank area in the document.

2. Click the mouse button to deselect any selected text.

3. Choose Font and Style from the Format menu.

The Font and Style dialog box appears, displaying the available fonts and text formatting options. The fonts that have a printer symbol next to them can be used with your printer. The fonts that have a TT symbol next to them are Microsoft Windows TrueType fonts. These are **scalable fonts**, meaning the text can be printed in virtually any point size.

Click here to scroll to the top
of the Font list

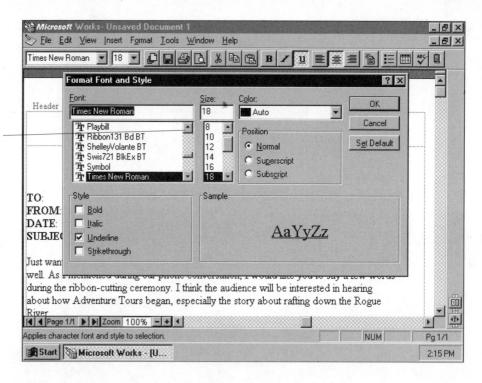

Now scroll the list to display the first font. (This will probably be Arial.) (*Note:* Your list may be different from the one displayed depending on the fonts that have been installed on your computer and are available in Works.)

4. Click on on the scroll bar until the first font in the list is displayed (see Figure 2.4).

5. Click on the first font in the list.

Notice that the Sample box displays the selected font.

6. Continue to preview several fonts.

7. When done, click on Cancel to return to the document.

Figure 2.5 shows the words *Adventure Tours* inserted in the document and changed to a different font, called Arial and enlarged to point size 24. To make these changes, start by inserting the words *Adventure Tours* and then use the Font box on the toolbar to change the font.

8. Press ⌨CTRL⌨+⌨HOME⌨ to move the insertion point to the beginning of the document.

9. Press ⌨↵ ENTER⌨ three times to insert two blank lines.

10. Press ⌨CTRL⌨+⌨HOME⌨.

11. Click on the ⌨U⌨ to deselect it.

12. **Type** Adventure Tours

13. Drag the I-beam across *Adventure Tours* to select the words.

14. Click on ▾ next to the Font box on the toolbar (see Figure 2.5).

Notice that the font names are displayed in the font design that will appear when the font is selected.

Click here to display the list of available fonts

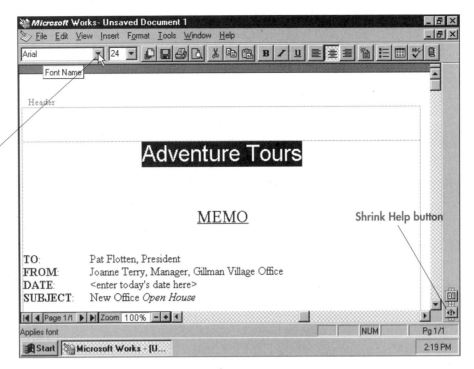

15. If necessary, click on the arrows on the scroll bar until Arial is displayed. (*Note:* If Arial is not available, choose another font.)

16. Click on Arial (or another font of your choice).

17. Enlarge the font size to 24 point.

Adventure Tours is changed to the font and size you specified. Notice that the toolbar shows the font and size for the selected text. This completes the section on changing fonts. Before continuing, save the document with the file name memo and then print it.

18. Choose Save <u>A</u>s from the <u>F</u>ile menu.

19. Type a:\memo (**or** b:\memo).

20. Click on <u>S</u>ave in the Save As dialog box.

21. Choose <u>P</u>rint from the <u>F</u>ile menu.

22. Click on OK in the Print dialog box.

USING THE WORKS HELP WINDOW

If you need help while using the Works program, you can refer to the Help window, which enables you to view instructions on completing tasks. The [?] button on the lower right edge of the Works screen opens the Help window so that you can request information on specific topics, such as typing text or saving a document. You can also display the Help Index, which allows you to search for information using key terms. When using the Index, it is important to remember that information probably will be listed under key terms and command names rather than a related word. For instance, if you want to find information on placing a heading in the middle of the line, you would use specific terms such as formatting, centering, or aligning, not a general word like enhancing. Key terms and command names will help you find information more quickly when using the Help Index. In this section, you will display the Help window and learn the basics of using the Help feature.

1. Click on [?] (see Figure 2.5).

The Help window appears with the Word Processor menu displayed. If you were working with the spreadsheet tool, a different menu would appear in the Help window. To access information from the Word Processor Menu, click on the arrow to the left of the topic you wish to view.

2. Click on [▼] to the left of Name and save your document.

The Word Processor Menu is replaced by a menu for naming and saving a document.

3. Click on the arrow to the left of To name and save your document the first time.

Instructions appear in the window under an index tab labeled Step-by-Step. Notice that another index tab is now available, and this tab is labeled More Info.

4. Click on the index tab labeled More Info.

The More Info index tab lists several options for finding information about saving a document. The Overview button describes the purpose for and process of saving a document.

5. Click on [□] to the left of Overview.

6. Read the information about naming and saving a document in the Overview box.

Notice that, at the bottom of the information in the Overview box, there is a button that can be used to print the Help information. Also note the Done command button on the Overview dialog box that closes the Overview box.

7. Click on Done.

The Help window has another button that is useful when using the Help feature. This button is labeled Back and it takes you through the previous screens that have been displayed in the Help window. Use the Back button to see how this feature works.

8. Click on the Back [◄] button.

Notice that the Help window displays the previous screen, Naming and Saving your document.

9. Click on [◄].

Some topics will not be available using the Word Processor Menu. To find information that is not included on the Help menu, you can use the Index feature. In addition, the Index feature is often a faster way to find the specific information you need.

10. Click on [▦].

The Help Topics: Microsoft Works dialog box appears. This dialog box is divided into two tabs, one labeled Index and one labeled Contents. The Index tab allows you to search for information by typing in a key word. The Contents section of the dialog box allows you to search the Works Help information by selecting a category. You will use the Index feature to practice searching for information based on key words.

11. **If necessary, click in the box under Type a word for the action or item about which you want information.**

12. **Type** font

Notice that as you type, the list box displays topics that relate to what you are typing. The "font size: changing" option should be highlighted. To view the information on this topic, click on the icon to the left of the highlighted text.

13. **Click on the ⊞ next to font size: changing.**

The Help window on the right displays the Step-by-Step and More Info index tabs. To remove the Help Topics dialog box, click on the ⌷Close⌷ button.

14. **Click on ⌷Close⌷ in the Help Topics dialog box.**

15. **Click on ⌷?⌷ to close the Help window.**

In addition to the Help window, Works provides context-specific information when you are working in a dialog box. By pressing ⌷F1⌷ on the keyboard, you can get information about the text or list box that is selected. Try this by choosing the Save As command and then getting help.

16. **Choose Save As from the File menu.**

The Save As dialog box appears. Notice that the File name box is highlighted. When you press ⌷F1⌷, Help information pertaining to the File name text box will appear.

17. **Press ⌷F1⌷.**

A message box appears with information about typing a name in the File name: text box. You can remove the message box by clicking anywhere within the dialog box.

18. **Choose Cancel in the Save As dialog box.**

This completes the section on using the Help feature.

19. **Close the memo document.**

CREATING FURTHER DOCUMENT ENHANCEMENTS

In this section you will learn additional ways to enhance the appearance of a document using tabs, indents, and bulleted lists. Figure 2.6 shows a letter Adventure Tours will send to confirm a client's reservation, and Figure 2.7 shows the same letter with the following changes:

- The first line of the first paragraph has been indented.
- A right-aligned tab and a decimal tab with leaders have been set.
- A bulleted list has been created.

You will create the letter in Figure 2.6 and, as you do, you will add the formatting changes shown in Figure 2.7.

1. Display a new word processor document and maximize the document window.

2. Type the date, address, salutation, and first paragraph of the document shown in Figure 2.6.

Working With Tabs And Leaders

Figure 2.8 shows the **ruler** that can be used to set tab positions. **Tabs** are designated increments across the page, and Works presets **tabs** every half inch. Thus, when you press (TAB ⇆), the insertion point moves to the right one-half inch. If there is text to the right of the insertion point, the text also moves one-half inch to the right. To see how tabs work, complete the following steps to indent the first line of the first paragraph:

1. Choose Ruler from the View menu to display the ruler.

(*Note:* the ruler may already be displayed on your screen.)

2. Position the I-beam in front of the *T* in *This.*

3. Click the mouse button to set the insertion point.

4. Press (TAB ⇆).

The *T* in *This* moves to the first default tab position.

5. Press (TAB ⇆) again.

The *T* in *This* moves to the next tab position. You can move to the left one tab position by pressing (← BACKSPACE).

2.6

A letter

November 25, 1996

Mr. David Gough
9093 Hilltop Drive
Bellevue, WA 98005

Dear Mr. Gough:

This letter is to confirm your reservations for Heli-skiing on the Whistler glacier from June 10th through June 16th. You will be staying at the Whistler View Resort. You may check in after 10:00am on June 10th. Following are the prices you requested for other activities that you might be interested in during your stay. All prices are in Canadian dollars.

Mountain bike rental: $17.45
Golf club rental: 15.00
Bungee jumping: 115.00

For your information, I have listed several restaurants that you might find enjoyable.

Timberline Inn has good steaks.
Ivars specializes in seafood.
Whistler's Mother is best for breakfast.
Black Diamond Run has great pizza.

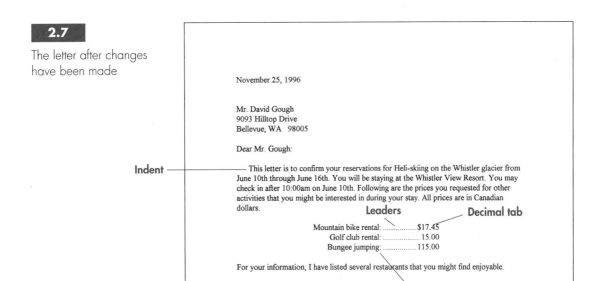

November 25, 1996

Mr. David Gough
9093 Hilltop Drive
Bellevue, WA 98005

Dear Mr. Gough:

Indent — This letter is to confirm your reservations for Heli-skiing on the Whistler glacier from June 10th through June 16th. You will be staying at the Whistler View Resort. You may check in after 10:00am on June 10th. Following are the prices you requested for other activities that you might be interested in during your stay. All prices are in Canadian dollars.

Leaders   Decimal tab

Mountain bike rental: $17.45
Golf club rental: 15.00
Bungee jumping: 115.00

For your information, I have listed several restaurants that you might find enjoyable.

Right-aligned tab

- Timberline Inn has good steaks.
- Ivars specializes in seafood.
- Whistler's Mother is best for breakfast.

Bulleted list

6. Press (← BACKSPACE).

The line moves back one tab position.

7. Press (← BACKSPACE) **again.**

The line returns to the left margin.

There are four types of tabs, each with its own symbol:

- Left (∟) Aligns the text on its left edge at the tab position
- Center (⊥) Centers the text on the tab position
- Right (⌐) Aligns the text on its right edge at the tab position
- Decimal (⊥.) Aligns numbers on their decimal point

To set a tab, you point to the desired location on the ruler and click the mouse button. Figure 2.7 shows the document layout using tab stops and **leaders** (here, made up of periods), which graphically separate the text from the dollar amounts. Leaders often work together with tab settings: you must specify a leader when you create the tab. Then when you press (TAB ⇄), the leader is inserted as the insertion point moves to the next tab setting. Use the ruler to specify a left tab at the 0.25" mark on the ruler.

8. Point to the 0.25" mark on the ruler (see Figure 2.8).

(*Note*: A dialog box may appear asking if you want information regarding indents and tabs. This is part of Works' context-sensitive Help. Choose OK in the dialog box to remove the dialog box from the screen. Then click on the ruler at the 0.25" mark to set the tab stop.)

9. Click the mouse button.

A left-tab symbol appears at the 0.25" mark.

Bullets button

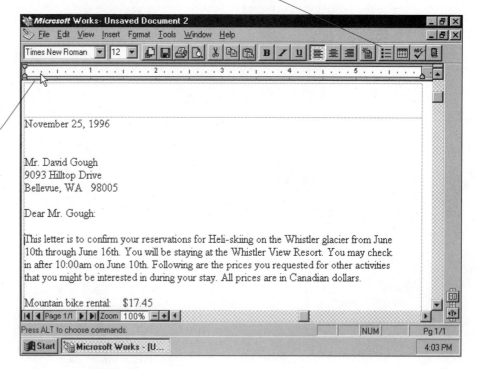

Click here to set a left tab stop

10. Press TAB.

The text moves to the tab position. Now move the insertion point to the end of the document and add a blank line.

11. Press CTRL + END.

12. Press ↵ ENTER **twice.**

Next you will set the tabs used to position the activities and their prices. First erase the tab at the 0.25" mark. To erase a tab stop, you point to the tab symbol on the ruler and drag the symbol down until it disappears from the ruler.

13. Point to the tab stop at the 0.25" mark.

14. Hold down the mouse button and drag the marker down until it disappears from the ruler.

15. Release the mouse button.

Notice that the text in the paragraph above is unchanged by the removal of the tab. This is because you deleted the tab from the blank line where the insertion point is located. Now set a right tab at the 3" mark and a decimal tab with leaders at the 4" mark on the ruler, as shown in Figure 2.9. This time use the Tabs dialog box to set the tabs.

16. Choose Tabs from the Format menu.

The Tabs dialog box appears, allowing you to specify the position and alignment of each tab.

17. Type 3

A right tab set at the 3-inch mark and a decimal tab with leaders set at the 4-inch mark

Decimal tab stop

Right tab stop

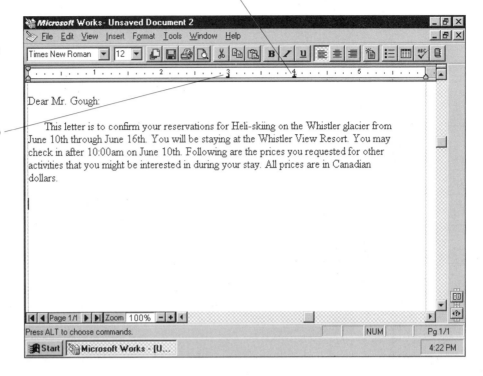

18. Click on <u>R</u>ight in the Alignment section.

19. Click on <u>S</u>et.

The tab stop is added to a list of tab-stop positions in the Format Tabs dialog box. The measurement also appears in the Tab stop position box, and it is highlighted so a new tab stop can be set.

20. **Type** 4

21. Click on <u>D</u>ecimal in the Alignment section.

22. Click on <u>1</u> in the Leader section.

23. Click on <u>S</u>et.

Your dialog box should resemble Figure 2.10.

24. **Click on OK.**

Notice the tab stop indicators on the ruler (see Figure 2.9). Now use these tabs to add the three activity and price lines.

25. **Press** (TAB ⇆).

26. **Type** Mountain bike rental:

27. **Press** (TAB ⇆).

28. **Type** $17.45

29. **Press** (↵ ENTER).

2.10

Using the Format Tabs
dialog box to set a right
tab and a decimal tab
with leaders

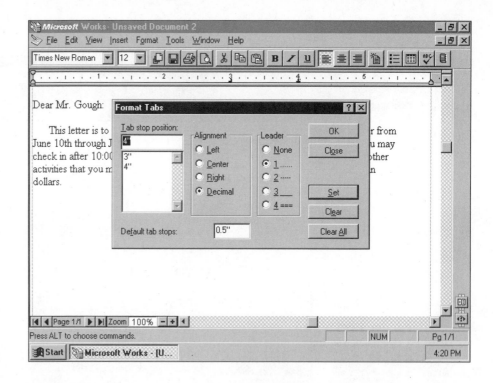

30. Press ⟨TAB ⇄⟩.

31. On your own, complete the activity lines (see Figure 2.7).

Creating Bulleted And Numbered Lists

Figure 2.7 shows the memo with a **bulleted list**. Works allows you to select a list and, use the 🔲 on the toolbar to add bullets to the list. Start by creating a blank line and deleting the tab stops, and then enter the new text.

1. Press ⟨↵ ENTER⟩ twice.

2. Using the mouse, drag the tab markers off the ruler.

3. Type the sentence that starts with *For your information* (see Figure 2.7).

4. Press ⟨↵ ENTER⟩ twice.

Now type the list text.

5. Type Timberline Inn has good steaks.

6. On your own, complete the other two lines (refer to Figure 2.7).

Now add bullets to the list.

7. Drag the pointer to select the three lines of the list.

8. Click on 🔲 on the toolbar (see Figure 2.8).

A bullet appears next to each line. It is important to understand that a bullet is placed at the beginning of each selected *paragraph*. Because you pressed ⟨↵ ENTER⟩ at the end of each line, each line is considered a paragraph. To remove the bullets, you would click on 🔲. You could also choose Paragraph from the Format menu, display the Indents and Alignment tab, and click on the Bulleted check box to remove the check mark. When the check mark is removed, the Bullets will disappear from the selected paragraph(s).

This completes the section on tabs and bulleted lists. Before continuing, deselect the text and save and print the document. Then close the document.

9. Click on a blank area in the document to deselect the text.

10. Choose Save As from the File menu.

11. Type a:\letter (or b:\letter) and click on Save.

12. Print the document.

13. Close the document.

WORKING WITH INDENTS

In this section you will learn how to work with **paragraph indents**, a process used for adjusting margins. Figure 2.11 shows a letter sent by Adventure Tours in response to a request for information about bike excursions in China. Three paragraphs of the letter are indented from both the left and right margins. Paragraph indenting can be used to focus on or emphasize a part of a document, add to the readability of a document by breaking up a standard format, and present a list of items.

To indent a paragraph, you can use either the Paragraph command in the Format menu or the indent markers on the ruler. We will use both methods, starting with the Paragraph command. The letter is a file on the data disk called Bike tours. Use the Open button to open the Bike tours document.

1. Click on the Existing Documents tab in the Works Task Launcher dialog box.

2. Click on the ▦ Open a document not listed here.

3. Click on *Bike tours* in the document list.

4. Click on Open.

The document that appears does not have indented paragraphs. You will format it with indents. Begin by indenting the Great Wall paragraph. When working with indents, you do not need to select (highlight) the entire paragraph. You can simply point to the paragraph and click the mouse button to set the insertion point in the paragraph.

5. If necessary, maximize the document window.

6. Click on the word *Wall* in the second paragraph (see Figure 2.12).

7. Choose Paragraph from the Format menu.

8. If necessary, click on the Indents and Alignment tab to display these options.

Figure 2.13 shows the completed dialog box, which indicates the paragraph will be indented by 0.5 inches from both the left and right margins. Notice the sample box shows an indented paragraph.

9. Type .5 in the Left box under Indentation.

10. Press (TAB ⇆).

11. Type .5 in the Right box in the Indentation section.

12. Click on OK.

October 12, 1996

Brandon Kruse
2010 Yew St.
Olympia, WA 98030

Dear Mr. Kruse:

In response to your request for information about bicycle excursions in China, I have
listed three new tours that we can provide.

The Great Wall - Built nearly 2,000 years ago as protection from northern
invaders, this structure is more than 4,000 miles in length. It is the only
man-made structure that can be seen from the moon. The Great Wall
stretches from Shanghaiguan Pass on the East Coast to Jiayuguán Pass in
the Gobi Desert, crossing five provinces and two autonomous regions. Our
route takes us through the Chinese countryside with stops at palaces,
imperial tombs, and watch towers.

The Silk Road - Take a trip back in time as you travel what was once a
major trade route for caravans carrying silk and spices to the West in
exchange for gold. Travel through the oasis towns located in the
Talimakan desert of northwest China, and visit Moslem mosques. Stay in
yurts inhabited by Turkish-speaking Uygur people.

The Roof of the World - Known as Shangri-La, this autonomous region of
China lies on a plateau at an altitude of more than 12,000 feet. Long
isolated from the rest of the world, Tibet is the home of innumerable
monasteries, including the Potala Palace, home of the spiritual leader of
the Buddhists, the Dalai Lama. Included in the tour will be stops at the
Jokang Temple, Drepung, Sera, and Ganden Monasteries and Lake
Quinghai.

These are new tours, so brochures are not yet available and costs have not been finalized.
The first trips will be in spring of next year. I will provide additional information as it
becomes known. If any of these are of particular interest to you, or if I can help with other
questions, please call me at our new office. I am now located in our new office at the
Gillman Village Business Park. Below are the office hours.

Placing the insertion point

Click here to place the
insertion point

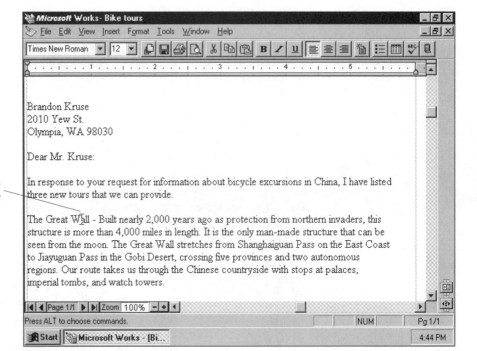

2.13

Indenting a paragraph
using the Format
Paragraph dialog box

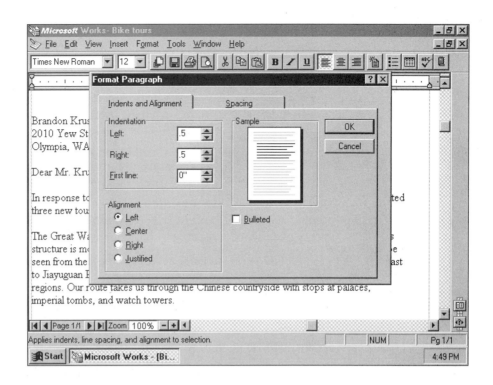

First-line indent marker

2.14

The indent markers
on the ruler

Left indent marker

Indents entire paragraph

Right indent marker

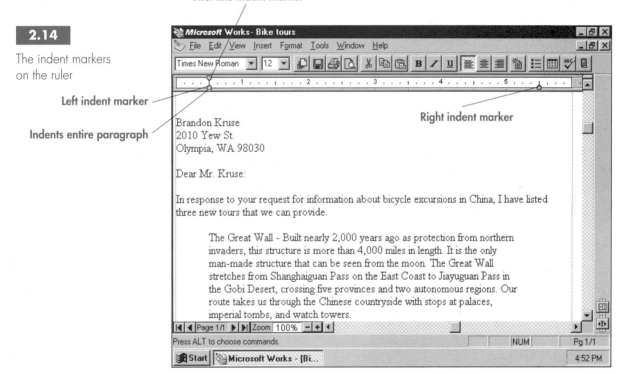

The paragraph is now indented from the left and right margin. Indenting can also be accomplished using the ruler. Figure 2.14 shows the ruler with the indent markers at 0.5" and 5.5". To change the paragraph indent, you place the mouse pointer on the indent marker and drag it to a new location on the ruler. The indent marker on the left end of the ruler is split into three parts, two of which resemble a triangle. The top triangle of the left indent markers changes the position of the first line of the paragraph. Using this part of the marker, you can create a first-line indent or a hanging indent. The bottom triangle of the left indent marker changes the indent of the remaining lines of the paragraph. To indent all lines of a paragraph, you use the box that appears beneath the bottom triangle. The indent marker on the right edge of the ruler changes the entire right edge of the paragraph. Use these indent markers to change the second paragraph of the document.

13. **Place the insertion point anywhere in the second paragraph.**

14. **Use the mouse to drag the box portion of the left indent marker to the 0.5-inch position on the ruler (see Figure 2.15.)**

Notice that when you move the box, both the first line and left indents are changed. Next change the right indent using the ruler.

15. **Using the mouse, drag the right indent marker to the 5.5 inch position on the ruler.**

The first and second paragraphs should be lined up. Now change the third paragraph using either the ruler or the Format Paragraph dialog box.

16. **On your own, indent the left and right margins of the third paragraph.**

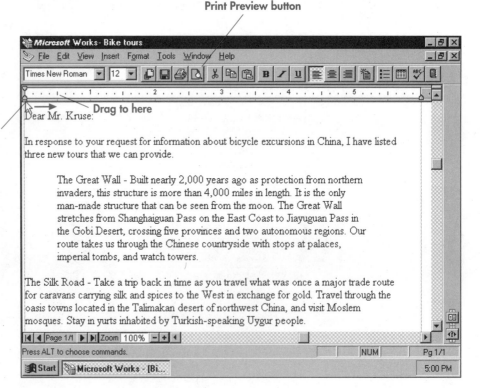

2.15

Creating a left indent using the indent markers on the ruler

WORKS 4 FOR WINDOWS 95

Up to this point you have been viewing only part of the document onscreen. When a document is too large to be fully displayed, as is the Bike tours document, you can use the **Print Preview** feature to see the effects of your formatting changes and judge how an entire document will look when it is printed. To use the preview feature, you can choose Print Preview from the File menu or click on the Print Preview button. Use the Print Preview command to view the entire Bike tours document.

1. Click on on the toolbar (see Figure 2.15).

The screen now displays the entire document, as shown in Figure 2.16. The text has been reduced in size to fit the entire page on the screen, so you are not able to read it clearly. However, you can see the formatting changes made to the document. The three paragraphs are shown indented from the left and right margins.

To further visually distinguish each paragraph, you decide to justify the text under each paragraph heading. To do this, you will use the justified alignment.

2. Click on Cancel to return to viewing the file in the document window.

3. Using the mouse pointer, highlight all three indented paragraphs.

4. Choose Paragraph from the Format menu.

5. If necessary, click on the Indents and Alignment tab in the dialog box.

6. Click on Justified in the Alignment section.

2.16

The Print Preview screen

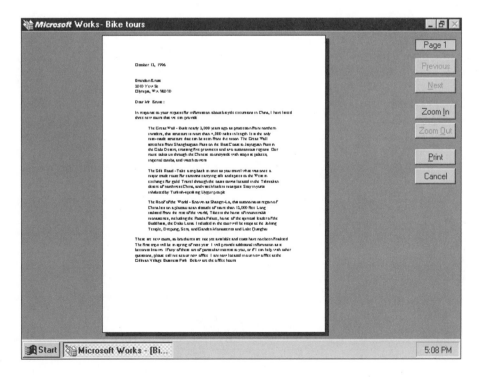

7. Click on OK.

The selected paragraphs are now justified. View the changes in the Print Preview screen.

8. Choose Print Preview from the File menu or click on ▣.

9. Click on Cancel to return to viewing the file in the document window.

CREATING HANGING INDENTS

Figure 2.17 shows the three paragraphs with hanging indents. **Hanging indent** refers to a paragraph in which the first line of text extends beyond the left margin of the other lines of the paragraph. This formatting style can be particularly effective when working with numbered lists. To create a hanging indent with the ruler, you indent the entire paragraph and then drag the first-line indent marker to the location where you want the first line of text to start. Figure 2.18 shows the process for dragging the first-line indent marker to set a hanging indent.

2.17

The three paragraphs with hanging indents

October 12, 1996

Brandon Kruse
2010 Yew St.
Olympia, WA 98030

Dear Mr. Kruse:

In response to your request for information about bicycle excursions in China, I have listed three new tours that we can provide.

The Great Wall - Built nearly 2,000 years ago as protection from northern invaders, this structure is more than 4,000 miles in length. It is the only man-made structure that can be seen from the moon. The Great Wall stretches from Shanghaiguan Pass on the East Coast to Jiayuguan Pass in the Gobi Desert, crossing five provinces and two autonomous regions. Our route takes us through the Chinese countryside with stops at palaces, imperial tombs, and watch towers.

The Silk Road - Take a trip back in time as you travel what was once a major trade route for caravans carrying silk and spices to the West in exchange for gold. Travel through the oasis towns located in the Talimakan desert of northwest China, and visit Moslem mosques. Stay in yurts inhabited by Turkish-speaking Uygur people.

The Roof of the World - Known as Shangri-La, this autonomous region of China lies on a plateau at an altitude of more than 12,000 feet. Long isolated from the rest of the world, Tibet is the home of innumerable monasteries, including the Potala Palace, home of the spiritual leader of the Buddhists, the Dalai Lama. Included in the tour will be stops at the Jokang Temple, Drepung, Sera, and Ganden Monasteries and Lake Quinghai.

These are new tours, so brochures are not yet available and costs have not been finalized. The first trips will be in spring of next year. I will provide additional information as it becomes known. If any of these are of particular interest to you, or if I can help with other questions, please call me at our new office. I am now located in our new office at the Gillman Village Business Park. Below are the office hours.

2.18

Dragging the first-line
indent marker to set a
hanging indent

**Drag the first-line indent
marker to here**

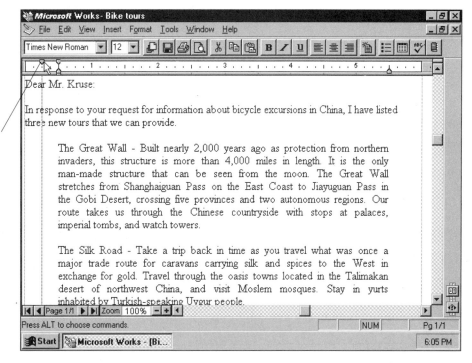

1. Select the Great Wall paragraph.

2. Point to the first-line indent marker.

3. Hold down the mouse button and drag the marker to the 0.25" mark.

4. Release the mouse button.

The first line of the indented paragraph hangs out from the rest of the paragraph. Continue by setting a hanging indent for the other two paragraphs.

5. On your own, create a hanging indent for the other indented paragraphs.

6. Use 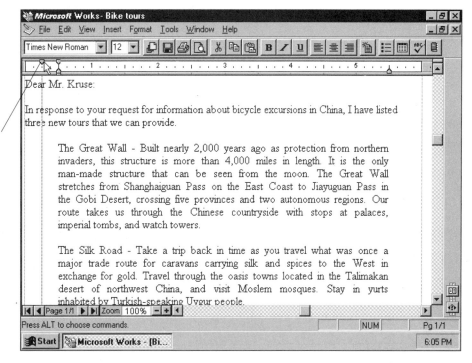 to view the reformatted document.

7. Return to viewing the file in the document window.

8. Save the document as *Bike tours revised*.

9. Close the document.

To remove a hanging indent, you select the paragraph and drag the first-line indent marker towards the right until it is in the same spot as the left-indent marker. In other words, you drag it back to its original position. Hanging (first-line) indents can also be set using the Paragraph command from the Format menu.

KEY TERMS

bulleted list paragraph indent scalable font
font points tabs
hanging indent Print Preview type size
leaders ruler type style

KEY COMMANDS

Font and Style Print Preview Tabs
Paragraph Ruler

REVIEW QUESTIONS

1. Three type styles are bold, _____, and _____.

2. **T F** The Font and Style dialog box can be used to change type styles.

3. **T F** To remove underlining from selected text, you click **B** on the toolbar.

4. **T F** Font refers to the size of a character.

5. Type sizes are measured in _____.

6. **T F** Works Help allows you to search for a topic and display information about the topic, but it does not provide step-by-step instructions.

7. The preset tab positions are at every _____ inch.

8. The _____ key can be used to move the insertion point back one tab position.

9. The four types of tabs are _____, _____, _____, and _____.

10. **T F** To indent a paragraph, you first need to select the entire paragraph.

11. The _____ dialog box is used to create a leader.

1. Open the announcement 2 file that you created in Chapter 1 and edit the document as follows:

   a. Change the heading *ADVENTURE TOURS* to a font of your choice, and change the font size to 24.

   b. Underline the heading *ADVENTURE TOURS*.

   c. Change the words *Wednesday, November 10th* to italic type.

   d. Make bold every occurrence of the words *PRESS RELEASE*.

   e. Save the document as *WKS Chapter 2 project 1*.

   f. Print the document.

   g. Close the document.

2. Open the WKS Chapter 2 project 1 file and edit the document to duplicate Figure 2.19. This involves setting a left tab for the publication titles and a decimal tab with a leader for the prices, then typing the titles and prices. Save the completed document as *WKS Chapter 2 project 2* and then print the document. Close the document.

2.19

The completed WD Chapter 3 project 1a document

TO OUR CLIENTS:

Adventure Tours is proud to announce that we have joined with the Northwest chapter of The Mountaineers to offer you discount prices on their publications. A sample of the books and their prices is listed below. If you would like to receive a catalog, simply contact any of our offices.

The High Sierra	$19.95
A Guide to Rock Climbing	21.95
Himalayan Passage	16.95
Bicycle Touring in Australia	8.95

3. On your data disk is a file called WKS Chapter 2 project 3. Open this file and change the document to duplicate Figure 2.20. This involves indenting each paragraph from both the left and right sides, justifying the text, and changing the list at the bottom of the document to a bulleted list. Save the completed document as *WKS Chapter 2 project 3a* and then print the document. Close the document.

THE MOST COMMONLY ASKED QUESTIONS ABOUT OUR TOURS

Do I need a visa?

The information on what trips require visas is indicated in your trip itinerary. All U.S. citizens traveling to other countries need a valid passport. For your convenience, Adventure Tours provides you with information and the necessary forms to obtain visas through Internet, a professional visa service company.

What gear should I bring?

A detailed list of recommended clothing and personal equipment is made up specifically for each trip. Adventure Tours generally provides all group camping equipment such as tents and cooking gear.

What is the payment schedule?

An initial deposit of $500 is required when you sign up for the trip. Trips costing more than $2500 require a second payment of $500 three months before departure. The final payment is due six weeks before departure.

Is trip cancellation insurance available?

Yes. If you have to cancel your trip due to personal or family illness, this insurance protects all your deposits and payments for both air and land costs. Upon request, we will mail you the necessary forms. Adventure Tours recommends that you purchase this insurance soon after signing up for a trip.

What are my obligations as a trip member?

By participating in an Adventure Tours trip, you assume certain obligations to Adventure Tours and other trip members. It is your responsibility to:

- select a trip appropriate to your interests and abilities
- prepare by reviewing the trip preparation materials sent to you
- bring appropriate gear and clothing
- act in an appropriate and courteous manner

Developing a Multiple-Page Document

- Change margins

- Create page breaks

- Create headers and footers

Figure 3.1 shows a two-page document called History, which relates how Adventure Tours Inc. was created. In this chapter, you will use the History document to learn how to work with multi-page documents by changing margins and page breaks and by inserting page numbers. But before making these changes, you need to know how to change the way the document is displayed onscreen.

VIEWING MULTIPLE-PAGE DOCUMENTS

In Chapter 2 you learned how to use the Print Preview command to view an entire page of a document. Use the History document to review using Print Preview.

1. **Open** *History* **and maximize the document window.**

Using Print Preview you can display each page of a multiple-page document and zoom in and out.

2. **Click on** 🔍.

Page one appears. You can press PAGE DOWN or click on Next to display the second page.

3. **Click on** Next.

The second page of the History document is displayed. Notice that the Next is now gray; this color change indicates that you are viewing the last page of the document. You can use Previous to view the first page.

4. **Click on** ◀.

The Zoom In and Zoom Out in the Print Preview screen allow you to adjust the size of the document display. The Zoom In feature enlarges the document, whereas the Zoom Out reduces the document size. The Zoom Out and Zoom In buttons turn gray when you have achieved the minimum or maximum zoom setting.

5. **Click on** Zoom In.

6. **Click again on** Zoom In.

7. **Click twice on** Zoom Out.

Now close the preview screen and return to the document.

8. **Click on** Cancel **to cancel.**

Now you know how to use the preview screen to view various pages of a long document and to change the size of the display area.

HISTORY OF ADVENTURE TOURS

Adventure Tours was started by two industrious young college students, Brandon James Kruse and Jeremy Jade Gray, who met at Northern Arizona University in Flagstaff. They were members of the college ski team, nicknamed Faceplant. The team practiced at the nearby Snow Bowl ski area in the San Francisco peaks. There is one particularly difficult run, a steep, narrow tree-lined chute, called Terminator, that is avoided by all but the most daring skiers. Informally, the team members decided to have a contest to see who could make it down Terminator the quickest. Brandon and Jeremy tied, and from then on they were great friends.

They realized that they shared a common passion. They loved the outdoors. They got involved in any recreational activity they could, including hiking, camping, biking, and river rafting. It was on a journey down the Colorado River as it ran through the Grand Canyon, that the two hit upon the idea of starting their own tour company. They were both business majors, Brandon in marketing and Jeremy in finance. They felt their business training and experience in working summer jobs would be a good foundation to build on.

However, they were convinced that in order to succeed in the tour industry there were two critical requirements, travel experience and a market niche. As they researched the industry, they realized that most of the tour companies were general-service travel agencies--brokers that booked airlines, hotels, and rental cars. These travel agencies handed out lots of brochures and pushed high markup tours on cruise ships. But often, the travel agents had little travel experience. Brandon tells the story of how his parents booked a hotel in Mexico through a local travel agent, and when they arrived to check in, found the hotel was still being built.

Brandon and Jeremy studied the demographic trends and concluded that the children of the baby boom generation would soon reach the age when they would be interested in traveling and having a travel adventure. Furthermore, this group would have the largest discretionary income of any generation before them. In addition, many previously inaccessible areas of the world were opening up to foreigners, such as China and Russia. Thus, the two decided that their market niche would be active tours to exotic places, like trekking in Tibet.

They were convinced that anyone working for their company, including themselves, needed extensive travel experience. This way the company could build up a reputation as one whose employees had "been there." They knew this

because of its proximity to Asia and because of the outdoor nature of those who lived in the Northwest. Their first booking was a helicopter ski trip to Mt. McKinley in Alaska. The customers were two friends from their old college ski team. The first year Adventure Tours recorded $120,000 in sales. In the following years, the company was to experience dramatic growth. There are now three offices in the greater Seattle area and soon to be a new office in the Gillman Village Business Park on the Eastside. In addition, Adventure Tours is a member of International Excursions, a worldwide network of tour agencies specializing in exotic tours.

Brandon and Jeremy pride themselves in having maintained a small operation that is customer oriented and staffed by those who practice what they provide. To keep current in the field, every year each employee leads at least two tour groups. All the employees are bilingual, and many are fluent in three or more languages.

Adventure Tours has come a long way from the initial idea conceived by two college students as they navigated the white water rapids of the Colorado River deep in the heart of the Grand Canyon.

WORKING WITH MARGINS

Margins provide white space around the text in a document and can aid in the readability of the document. Figure 3.1 shows the History document with Works' preset margins of 1" for the top and bottom and 1" for the left and right. Figure 3.2 shows the first page of the document after changing all the margin settings to 2.0". The Page Setup command from the File menu is used to change margins.

The first page of the History document after changing all the margins to 1.5"

HISTORY OF ADVENTURE TOURS

Adventure Tours was started by two industrious young college students, Brandon James Kruse and Jeremy Jade Gray, who met at Northern Arizona University in Flagstaff. They were members of the college ski team, nicknamed Faceplant. The team practiced at the nearby Snow Bowl ski area in the San Francisco peaks. There is one particularly difficult run, a steep, narrow tree-lined chute, called Terminator, that is avoided by all but the most daring skiers. Informally, the team members decided to have a contest to see who could make it down Terminator the quickest. Brandon and Jeremy tied, and from then on they were great friends.

They realized that they shared a common passion. They loved the outdoors. They got involved in any recreational activity they could, including hiking, camping, biking, and river rafting. It was on a journey down the Colorado River as it ran through the Grand Canyon, that the two hit upon the idea of starting their own tour company. They were both business majors, Brandon in marketing and Jeremy in finance. They felt their business training and experience in working summer jobs would be a good foundation to build on.

However, they were convinced that in order to succeed in the tour industry there were two critical requirements, travel experience and a market niche. As they researched the industry, they realized that most of the tour companies were general-service travel agencies--brokers that booked airlines, hotels, and rental cars. These travel agencies handed out lots of brochures and pushed high markup tours on cruise ships. But often, the travel agents had little travel experience. Brandon tells the story of how his parents booked a hotel in Mexico through a local travel agent, and when they arrived to check in, found the hotel was still being built.

Brandon and Jeremy studied the demographic trends and concluded that the children of the baby boom generation would soon reach the age when they would be interested in traveling and having a travel adventure. Furthermore, this group would have the largest discretionary income of any generation before them. In addition, many previously inaccessible areas of the world were opening up to foreigners, such as China and Russia. Thus, the two decided that their market niche would be active tours to exotic places, like trekking in Tibet.

They were convinced that anyone working for their company, including themselves, needed extensive travel experience. This way the company could build up a reputation as one whose employees had "been there." They knew this would help them with word-of-mouth advertising and referrals. So they set a goal to complete as much travel as they could in the summers and during the breaks between school terms. After graduation, they decided to spend three years traveling around the world and making as many contacts as possible.

In 1990, with a bank loan of $10,000 and what was left of their savings, they opened the first Adventure Tours office in the Pioneer Square district of Seattle. They chose Seattle because of its proximity to Asia and because of the outdoor nature of those who lived in the Northwest. Their first booking was a helicopter ski trip to Mt. McKinley in Alaska. The customers were two friends from their old college ski team. The first year Adventure Tours recorded $120,000 in sales. In the following years, the company was to experience dramatic growth. There are now

1. Choose Page Setup from the **F**ile menu.

The Page Setup dialog box appears. This dialog box has three index tabs: Margins; Source, Size and Orientation; and Other Options. Make sure the Margins index tab is selected. The current margin settings are displayed in the text boxes. A Sample at the top of the dialog box shows the effect of any changes you make to the margin settings. Figure 3.3 shows the changes you will make to the margin settings. The (TAB ⇆) key can be used to move from one margin setting to the next. After changing a margin setting, notice the effect on the sample. The sample will not change until you press (TAB ⇆).

2. Verify that the **T**op margin measurement is highlighted.

3. Type 1.5

4. Press (TAB ⇆).

The sample changes to reflect the new margin value (see Figure 3.3).

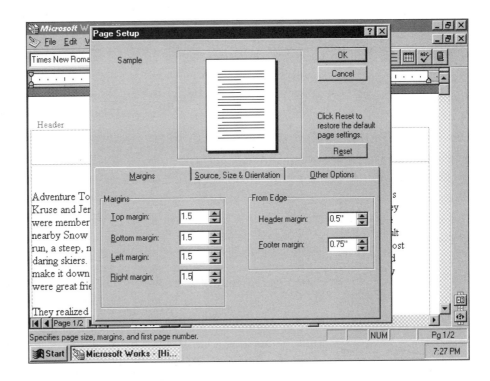

5. On your own, change the bottom, left and right margins to 1.5".

Your dialog box should resemble the one shown in Figure 3.3.

6. When done, click on OK to accept the changes.

7. Click on 🔍.

View both pages of the document to see the effects of the new margin settings.

8. Click on Next.

9. Click on Cancel to close the preview screen.

Now change the margins back to their original settings: top and bottom, 1";
left and right, 1.25".

10. Display the Page Setup dialog box.

11. Change the top margin setting to 1".

12. Change the bottom margin setting to .8".

13. Change the left and right margin settings to 1.25".

14. Choose OK to accept the changes.

This completes the section on working with margins.

Works provides two types of page breaks, automatic and manual. **Automatic page breaks** are those inserted by Works. **Manual page breaks** are those you add to a document at any location. They are useful in preventing an inappropriate automatic page break, such as one that occurs in the middle of a paragraph or between a heading and its corresponding text. The location of each automatic page break is determined by the size of the paper, the size of the font, the margins, and paragraph formatting. Using standard 8.5-inch-by 11-inch paper, a type size of 12 point, and the default margin settings, 46 lines of text will fit on each page. Figure 3.4 shows a printout of the History document. Notice that the automatic page break splits a paragraph at the bottom of the first page. The remainder of the paragraph appears at the top of the second page. To avoid splitting this paragraph, you can insert a manual page break, as shown in Figure 3.5.

There are two ways to insert a manual page break: using the Page Break command from the Insert menu or pressing `CTRL`+`← ENTER`. Both methods require locating the insertion point at the desired line before breaking the page. Complete the following steps to use the Page Break command to insert a page break above the paragraph that is currently split across two pages. Start by displaying the current automatic page break as shown in Figure 3.6.

3.4

The History document showing the automatic page break splitting a paragraph

Automatic page break

The History document after inserting a manual page break to keep the paragraph together

HISTORY OF ADVENTURE TOURS

Adventure Tours was started by two industrious young college students, Brandon James Kruse and Jeremy Jade Gray, who met at Northern Arizona University in Flagstaff. They were members of the college ski team, nicknamed Faceplant. The team practiced at the nearby Snow Bowl ski area in the San Francisco peaks. There is one particularly difficult run, a steep, narrow tree-lined chute, called Terminator, that is avoided by all but the most daring skiers. Informally, the team members decided to have a contest to see who could make it down Terminator the quickest. Brandon and Jeremy tied, and from then on they were great friends.

They realized that they shared a common passion. They loved the outdoors. They got involved in any recreational activity they could, including hiking, camping, biking, and river rafting. It was on a journey down the Colorado River as it ran through the Grand Canyon, that the two hit upon the idea of starting their own tour company. They were both business majors, Brandon in marketing and Jeremy in finance. They felt their business training and experience in working summer jobs would be a good foundation to build on.

However, they were convinced that in order to succeed in the tour industry there were two critical requirements, travel experience and a market niche. As they researched the industry, they realized that most of the tour companies were general-service travel agencies--brokers that booked airlines, hotels, and rental cars. These travel agencies handed out lots of brochures and pushed high markup tours on cruise ships. But often, the travel agents had little travel experience. Brandon tells the story of how his parents booked a hotel in Mexico through a local travel agent, and when they arrived to check in, found the hotel was still being built.

Brandon and Jeremy studied the demographic trends and concluded that the children of the baby boom generation would soon reach the age when they would be interested in traveling and having a travel adventure. Furthermore, this group would have the largest discretionary income of any generation before them. In addition, many previously inaccessible areas of the world were opening up to foreigners, such as China and Russia. Thus, the two decided that their market niche would be active tours to exotic places, like trekking in Tibet.

They were convinced that anyone working for their company, including themselves, needed extensive travel experience. This way the company could build up a reputation as one whose employees had "been there." They knew this would help them with word-of-mouth advertising and referrals. So they set a goal to complete as much travel as they could in the summers and during the breaks between school terms. After graduation, they decided to spend three years traveling around the world and making as many contacts as possible.

In 1990, with a bank loan of $10,000 and what was left of their savings, they opened the first Adventure Tours office in the Pioneer Square district of Seattle. They choose Seattle because of its proximity to Asia and because of the outdoor nature of those who lived in the Northwest. Their first booking was a helicopter ski trip to Mt. McKinley in Alaska. The customers were two friends from their old college ski team. The first year Adventure Tours recorded $120,000 in sales. In the following years, the company was to experience dramatic growth. There are now three offices in the greater Seattle area and soon to be a new office in the Gillman Village Business Park on the Eastside. In addition, Adventure Tours is a member of International Excursions, a worldwide network of tour agencies specializing in exotic tours.

Brandon and Jeremy pride themselves in having maintained a small operation that is customer oriented and staffed by those who practice what they provide. To keep current in the field, every year each employee leads at least two tour groups. All the employees are bilingual, and many are fluent in three or more languages.

Adventure Tours has come a long way from the initial idea conceived by two college students as they navigated the white water rapids of the Colorado River deep in the heart of the Grand Canyon.

manual page break

1. Scroll the document until the automatic page break is displayed.

Now locate the insertion point above the paragraph.

2. Point the I-beam at the beginning of the paragraph above the automatic page break (see Figure 3.6).

3. Click the mouse button to display the insertion point.

4. Choose Page Break from the Insert menu.

A manual page break is inserted at the insertion point location and the paragraph is moved to the top of the next page. The manual page break, which appears on the bottom of the first page, is displayed as a dotted line. To delete a manual page break, click on the dotted line and press (← BACKSPACE). Now use the preview screen to view how the document will print.

5. Click on ▣.

The entire paragraph is now at the top of the second page. Return to the document.

6. Click on [Cancel].

This completes the section on working with page breaks.

Placing the I-beam in front
of the paragraph above
the automatic page break

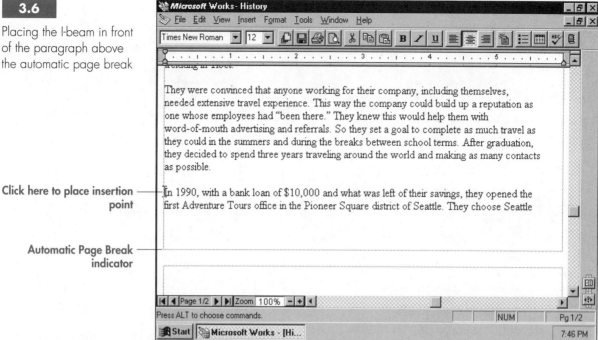

Click here to place insertion
point

Automatic Page Break
indicator

WORKING WITH HEADERS AND FOOTERS

A **header** is text, such as a page number, that is inserted at the top of each page of a document. A **footer** is text inserted at the bottom of each page. Figure 3.7 shows the History document with a header, History, and a footer, Page 1 (or 2), inserted on each page. Headers and footers are displayed in the top and bottom margins of a document. You can create headers or footers by choosing Header or Footer from the View menu or by clicking in the Header or Footer section at the top or bottom of the page. Once the insertion point is in the Header or Footer section, you can add text or special codes, such as a date and time code, document name code, or page number code, that will automatically place the specified information in the header or footer. Also, the header and footer information can be aligned across the page using the alignment buttons or tab stops. Codes can be inserted using the appropriate command from the Insert menu. The Date and Time command allows you to select from several display options, and the result appears at the insertion point. The Page Number and Document Name commands insert a special code that fills in the requested information when the document is printed or displayed in the Print Preview screen.

Complete the following steps to add headers and footers to the History document, as shown in Figure 3.7:

1. Choose <u>H</u>eader from the View menu. *Note:* when you choose Header, a First-time Help dialog box may appear. You will bypass this dialog box by clicking on the OK command button at the bottom.

The insertion point is moved into the Header box at the top of the document. Figure 3.8 shows the header after choosing the Document Name command.

3.7

The History document with the document file name, History.wps, as a header, and Page 1 (on the first page) and Page 2 (on the second page) as footers

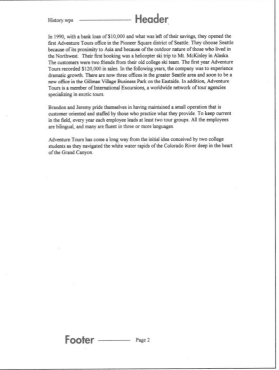

2. Choose Document Name from the Insert menu.

3. Click on [image].

4. Click on [Zoom In].

Notice that the file name, along with the document extension (.wps), is displayed at the left margin in the header.

5. Click on [Cancel].

Now add the word "Page", followed by the page number code to the footer.

6. Choose Footer from the View menu.

7. Type Page and press the spacebar once.

8. Choose Page Number from the Insert menu.

9. Click on [image] to center the footer information.

10. Use [image] to view of the document.

Notice the footer is centered on the page.

11. Return to the document window by clicking on Cancel.

There are instances where you will not want a header or footer to appear on the first page of a document, but only on the remaining pages. Using the Page Setup command, you can choose to have the header or footer begin on the second page of the document, leaving the first page header or footer blank. Now remove the header from the first page of the History document.

The header after choosing the Document Name command from the Insert menu

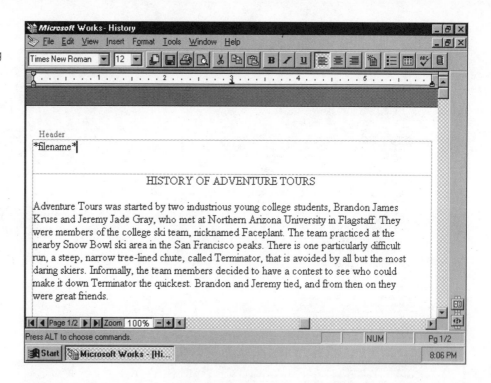

12. Choose Page Setup from the File menu.

13. Click on the Other Options index tab.

Notice the check boxes that allow you to omit the header or footer from page one of the document.

14. Click in the No header on first page check box.

15. Click OK.

16. Preview both pages of the document.

The header now begins on the second page. This completes the section on working with headers and footers.

17. Return to the document.

18. Save the document as *History 2*, print it, then close the document.

KEY TERMS

automatic page break   header   margins

footer   manual page break

KEY COMMANDS

Date and Time   Header   Page Number
Document Name   Page Break   Page Setup
Footer

REVIEW QUESTIONS

1. The default margin settings for a Works' word processing document are top and bottom, _____; left and right, _____.

2. To change margins, use the _____ _____ command.

3. **T   F**   Automatic page breaks are not affected by margin settings.

4. The two methods used to create a manual page break are:

   a. _____

   b. _____

5. **T   F**   Page numbers will only display onscreen when the document is in Print Preview.

6. **T   F**   Headers always display on the top of each page of a document.

PROJECTS

1. Open the History file and complete the following:

   a. Create the following header and right-align it:
      History of Adventure Tours

   b. Create the following footer: Page 1 (date)
      Page 1 will be left aligned at the margin, and the date will be right aligned. (*Hint*: Use the right-aligned tab stop to place the date on the right edge of the footer. Use the commands from the Insert menu for adding the page number and the date.)

   c. Save the document as *WKS Chapter 3 project 1* and then print the document.

2. Open WKS Chapter 3 project 2. Preview the document to see how it will print. This is a two-page document that consists of a memo and information that will eventually be used in a company newsletter. Figure 3.9 shows the document split into three pages, along with several other modifications. Change the document to duplicate Figure 3.9.

   a. Change the left and right margins to 1.5".

   b. Create a page break to separate the memo from the rest of the document.

   c. Create a page break so that the entire last paragraph (Travel Tip of the Month) and its heading are printed on page 3 of the document.

d. Create a left-aligned header, Newsletter, starting on page 2.

e. Create a centered footer, following the style on Page 2, starting on the second page.

f. Make sure the header and footer do not print on page 1 (memo).

g. Save the document as *WKS Chapter 3 project 2a*, then print the document. Close the document.

3. On your own, develop a two- or three-page document. Include a header and footer, change the margins, and create manual page breaks. Save the document as *WKS Chapter 3 project 3* and then print the document. Close the document

3.9

The completed WKS Chapter 3 Project 2a document

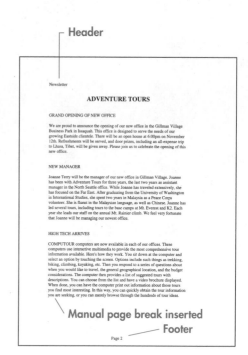

Header

Manual page break inserted

Manual page break inserted

Footer

Proofing a Document, Searching for Text, and Using Graphics

■ Check for spelling errors in a document

■ Use Works' thesaurus to find synonyms and antonyms

■ Search for and replace text in a document

■ Create and insert simple drawings into a document

■ Insert clipart into a document

■ Use WordArt to apply special effects to text

The Microsoft Works program allows you to check for errors in a document using a command called Spelling. In addition, Works has a built-in thesaurus that allows you to insert synonyms and antonyms. Use of the spelling checker and thesaurus are presented in the following sections.

USING THE SPELLING COMMAND

Works contains a list of thousands of words that are found in a standard dictionary. The Spelling command checks each word in a document against this list, and if a word is not found, a dialog box appears with suggested words that have similar spellings. You can then replace the original word with one of the suggestions. To check for spelling, you can use either the Spelling command from the Tools menu or the Spelling Checker button  on the toolbar.

On the data disk is a file called Confirmation letter. Complete the following steps to check this file for spelling errors:

1. **Open *Confirmation letter* and maximize the document window.**

(*Note:* The spelling checker starts at the insertion point and moves to the end of the document. Works allows you to check the entire document starting from any location. However, you may want to press (CTRL)+(HOME) to position the insertion point at the beginning of the document before choosing the Spelling command. In this case, the insertion point is already at the beginning of the document.)

2. **Choose Spelling from the Tools menu.**

The Spelling dialog box appears, as shown in Figure 4.1. The dialog box has, among other features, the following parts:

4.1

The Spelling dialog box

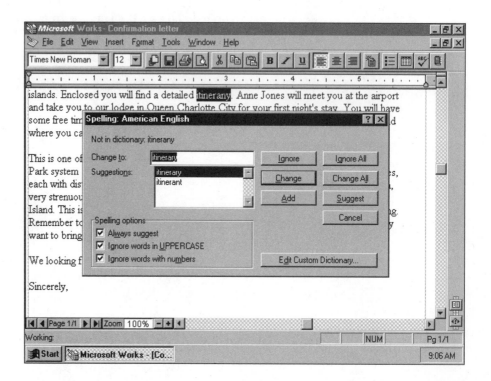

- Not in Dictionary. This text at the top of the dialog box indicates the word that was not found in the dictionary, either because it was misspelled or not included in the Works dictionary. In this case, "itinerany" is not in the dictionary because it is misspelled.

- Change to. This box displays an alternate word, if available, or alternate spelling that can be used to replace the word not found in the dictionary. If the suggestion is not correct or available, you can also type in the correctly spelled word or another word of your choice.

- Suggestions. This list box shows alternate words, if any, that can be selected from and used to replace the word not found in the Works dictionary.

When the spelling checker finds a word that is not in the dictionary, you may do one of the following:

- Change the word by choosing from the Suggestions list or by typing a word of your own into the Change to box and then clicking on the Change button.

- Change all occurrences of the word throughout the document by choosing from the Suggestions list or by typing a word of your own and clicking on the Change All button.

- Not change the word. In many instances, valid words will not appear in the dictionary, for example, a person's or company's name. To avoid changing a word, click on the Ignore button.

- Not change any occurrence of the word. To bypass all occurrences of a word that is spelled correctly but not listed in the dictionary, click on the Ignore All button.

- Add the word to the dictionary. If you are using a word often, such as a company name or a technical term, you can add it to the spelling dictionary by clicking on the Add button.

- Select the Suggest button to display suggestions for replacing the word.

- Cancel the spell checking process.

In this case, the word "itinerany" is misspelled. The Suggestions box lists two suggestions, "itinerary" and "itinerant." "Itinerary" is highlighted and displayed in the Change To box. Thus, to change "itinerany" to "itinerary," you click on the Change button.

3. Click on Change.

The word "itinerany" is replaced by the word "itinerary" and the spelling checker searches for the next word that is misspelled or not included in the Works spelling dictionary. When a word is located, it appears in the Change to box. The next word that appears as not in the spelling dictionary is "Haida." This is the correct spelling, so you can choose Ignore or Ignore All.

4. Click on Ignore All.

The next word identified by the spelling checker is "swilming". Two suggestions are listed, with "swilling" highlighted. You need to select "swimming."

5. Click on swimming in the Suggestions box.

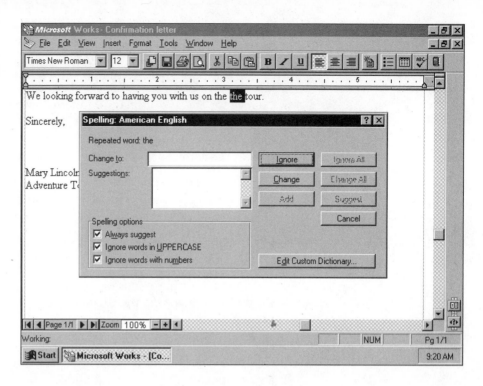

6. **Click on Change.**

The spelling checker now stops at a word that is repeated in a sentence. This is not a misspelled word, but a common typing error. Figure 4.2 shows the dialog box with the message "Repeated word: the" at the top of the box. You can delete the repeated word with the Change button.

7. **Click on the Change button.**

A message appears when the spelling check is finished.

8. **Click on OK.**

It is important to understand that the Spelling command is not a substitute for proofreading a document. You could spell a word correctly, but use it incorrectly, and the spelling checker would not catch the error. For example, you might type "form" instead of "from" or "their" instead of "there." Therefore, you should always proofread your document to check for such errors.

USING THE THESAURUS

Works provides a **thesaurus** that can be used to replace words in a document with their synonyms (words with similar meanings) and antonyms (words with opposite meanings). To replace a word with its synonym or antonym, you click on a word in the document and choose the Thesaurus command from the Tools menu. A dialog box appears with a list of synonyms and antonyms. You can then choose a word from the list and have it replace the word in the document. One use of the thesaurus is to find a word that is more appropriate than a word currently used in the document. At Adventure Tours, Mary Lincoln, who is writing the confirmation letter, decides that the word "challenging" is not a strong enough word to describe the kayaking trip, so she decides to use the Works thesaurus to find an alternative. Start by selecting the word challenging in the second paragraph.

1. **Double-click on the word** *challenging* **to select it.**

2. **Choose** **T**hesaurus from the **T**ools menu.

The Thesaurus dialog box appears, as shown in Figure 4.3. The highlighted word, challenging, is displayed in the Looked up: box. The Meanings: box displays the word "ambitious" (an adjective), and the Replace with **s**ynonym: list box displays the word "ambitious" along with several other synonyms.

3. **Click on** *rigorous* **in the list of synonyms.**

4. **Click on the** **R**eplace button.

The word "challenging" is replaced with the word "rigorous." Another use of the thesaurus is to find a synonym for a word that is used too often. In the Confirmation letter document, the word "bring" appears more than once in the last three sentences of the second paragraph, so it makes sense to replace a few instances of this word with a synonym. This time, instead of selecting the entire word, just point and click on the word.

5. **Click on** *bring* **in the last sentence of the second paragraph.**

6. **Choose** **T**hesaurus from the **T**ools menu.

Several words are displayed in the Replace with **s**ynonym: list box.

7. **Click on** *carry* **in the synonyms list.**

8. **Click on the** **R**eplace button.

9. **Save the document as** *Confirmation letter 2.*

10. **Print and close the document.**

This completes the section on using the thesaurus.

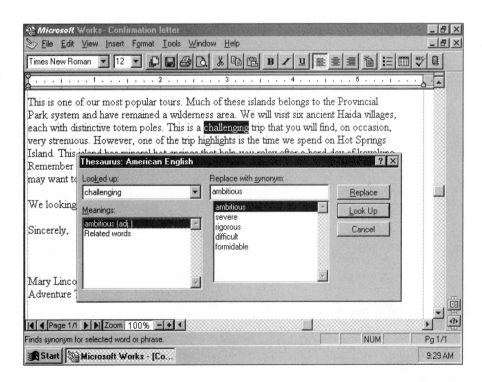

4.3

The word "ambitious" displayed in the Thesaurus dialog box

Using the Find command in the Edit menu, you can search for text within a document. The text can be a single character, a word, or a phrase. You can also search for formatted text, such as any instances of the word "Tours" that are in bold type. In this section you will use the Find command to search for text in a document called Fort Worden bike tour. This document is an announcement concerning a new biking excursion offered by Adventure Tours. Start by opening the document.

1. **Open** *Fort Worden bike tour.*

The search process starts at the insertion point, just like with the Spelling Checker, and usually you will want the search to start at the beginning of the document. Because you have just opened this file, the insertion point is already at the beginning of the document.

2. **Choose** **F**ind **from the** **E**dit **menu.**

The Find dialog box appears, containing the following features:

- Fi**n**d What. In this box you type the text you want to find.

- Find **w**hole words only. Normally Works searches for any string of characters that matches the text you have specified. For example, if you search for "out," Works would find "out," "outline," "outside," "without," and so on. If you choose the Find whole words only option, however, only the specific word (that is, "out") would be found.

- Match **c**ase. If this checkbox is selected, only text that matches the case you have specified would be found. For example, if you search for "MEMO," you would not find "Memo" or "memo."

Now continue by searching for the word "Port." The insertion point is in the Find What box, so you can begin typing.

3. **Type** Port

4. **Make sure the Match** **c**ase **and Find** **w**hole **word only check boxes are not selected.**

Your dialog box should resemble Figure 4.4.

5. **Click on** **F**ind **Next.**

Works begins the search, stops at the word "Port," and highlights it. At this point you could cancel or continue the search process.

6. **Click on** **F**ind **Next.**

The word "ports" is found; however, the "s" is not highlighted.

7. **Click on** **F**ind **Next.**

The word "Port" is found.

8. **Click on** **F**ind **Next.**

The word "Port" is found.

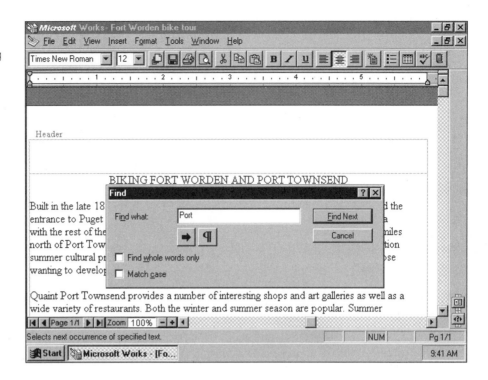

9. Click on **Find Next**.

The word "opportunity" is found; however, only the letters "port" are highlighted in this word.

10. Click on **Find Next**.

11. Click on **Find Next** again.

A message appears, indicating that Works has finished searching the document. It asks if you want to continue searching from the beginning of the document. Choose No and press (CTRL) + (HOME) to return the insertion point to the top of the page.

12. Click on **No**.

13. Press (CTRL) + (HOME) **to return the insertion point to the top of the page.**

Now perform a search using the Find whole words only option and see how the results of the search differ.

14. Click in the Find **w**hole words only check box to select this option.

15. Click on **Find Next**.

"Port" is found and highlighted. Continue to use the Find Next button until you reach the end of the document. Notice how only the words that match the whole word, that is, Port, are found. Neither "ports" nor "opportunity" is found this time.

16. On your own, continue to click on **Find Next** until you reach the end of the document.

17. When the message indicating the end of the search appears, click on No.

18. Press (CTRL) + (HOME).

Now perform another search for the word "Port," but this time use the Match Case option so that only "Port" and not "PORT" or "port" is found.

19. Click in the Match case check box to turn on this option.

20. Click on Find Next.

21. On your own, complete the search process; notice how only exact matches to the word "Port" are found.

22. When the end-of-search message appears, click on No.

23. Click on Cancel to close the dialog box.

REPLACING TEXT IN A DOCUMENT

Works provides a way for you to search for and replace text in a document. This is useful if you want to change a word that appears several times in a document. For example, you might want to replace the word "Port" with "PORT." Another use of the Replace command is to change the format of a word or words. For instance, you could replace all occurrences of a word in normal type with the same word in bold type. The replace process is similar to the find process. You use a dialog box to specify the text you want to find. Then you specify the text you want to use as a replacement. The Replace command is in the Edit menu. Complete the following steps to replace "Fort Worden" with "FORT WORDEN":

1. Press (CTRL) + (HOME).

2. Choose Replace from the Edit menu.

The Replace dialog box appears. Notice that "Port" is still in the Find what: box. Figure 4.5 shows the changes you will make.

3. Type Fort Worden

4. Press (TAB ⇆) to move the insertion point to the Replace with: box.

5. Type FORT WORDEN

Your dialog box should resemble Figure 4.5.

6. Click on Find Next.

The words "Fort Worden" in the first sentence are highlighted.

7. Click on Replace.

"Fort Worden" is replaced with "FORT WORDEN," and the next occurrence of "Fort Worden" is highlighted.

8. Click on Replace.

9. Click on Replace.

10. Click on No in the message box.

4.5

The completed Replace dialog box that will replace Fort Worden with FORT WORDEN

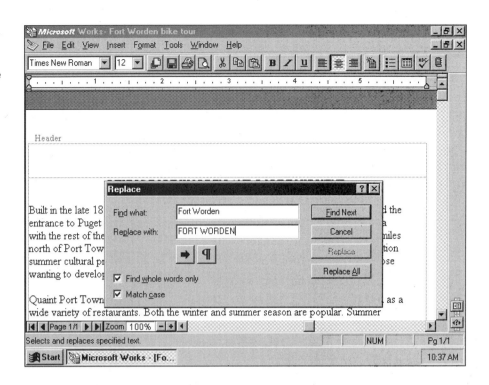

In the steps you just completed, you changed each occurrence of Fort Worden one at a time. You could have changed them all at once using the Replace All button. It is a good idea to save a document before using the Replace All command, so if you make a mistake you can return to the original document.

11. **Close the Replace dialog box and save the document as *Fort Worden bike tour 2*.**

Now change all occurrences of "FORT WORDEN," except the heading, back to "Fort Worden."

12. **Choose Replace from the Edit menu.**

13. **Type FORT WORDEN**

14. **Press [TAB].**

15. **Type Fort Worden**

16. **Click in the Find whole words only check box to turn off this option.**

17. **Click in the Match case check box to turn off this option.**

18. **Click on Find Next.**

The words "FORT WORDEN" in the heading are highlighted. You do not want to replace "FORT WORDEN" in the title, so choose the Find Next button.

19. **Click on Find Next.**

Now you can use the Replace All button to change all occurrences of "FORT WORDEN" to "Fort Worden."

20. **Click on Replace All.**

21. **Close the Replace dialog box and save the document as *Fort Worden bike tour 3*.**

22. **Print and close the document.**

Works allows you to enhance a document by inserting drawings, clip art, and text with special effects. Figure 4.6 shows a document that includes all of these enhancements. You can use commands from the Insert menu to duplicate Figure 4.6. Start by using Microsoft Draw to create the logo.

Using Microsoft Draw

Works provides a drawing tool, Microsoft Draw, that can be used to create simple drawings. Once a drawing has been created, it can be inserted into a Works word processing document. To start the Draw program, you open a document, position the insertion point, and choose Drawing from the Insert menu.

1. Open the word processing file called Graphics.

2. Position the insertion point below the sentence that starts "This is an example of a new logo. . . ."

3. Choose Drawing from the Insert menu.

4. If necessary, maximize the Drawing window.

The Draw program appears, as shown in Figure 4.7. This Figure labels the drawing tools and the pointer (selection) tool. To create a drawing, you select the desired tool and draw on the palette. If you make a mistake, you can use the pointer tool to select a part of the drawing and then choose Clear from the Edit menu. Or you can use the Select All command from the Edit menu and then choose Clear to delete the entire drawing. Complete the following steps to create the logo show in Figure 4.6.

5. Click on ▢.

6. Draw a rectangle like the one shown in Figure 4.8 by dragging the mouse pointer.

7. Click on A.

8. Point to the upper-left corner of the rectangle (see Figure 4.8).

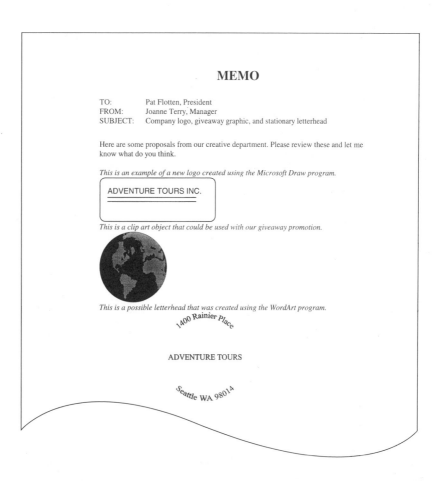

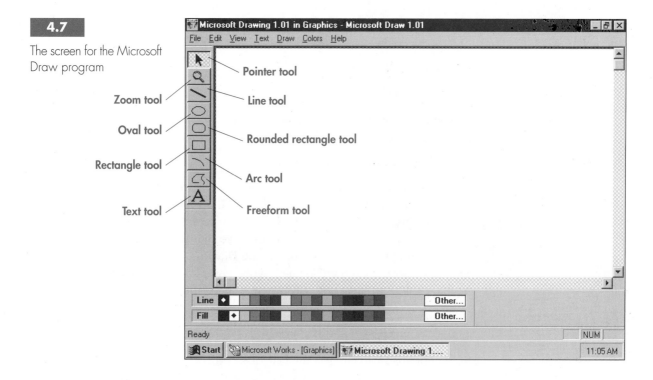

Click here to place insertion point

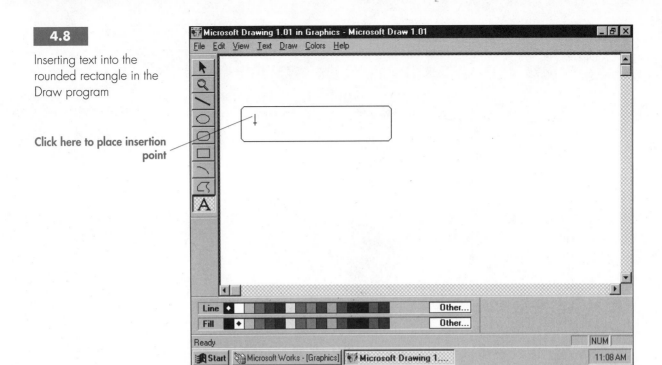

9. Click the mouse button to display an insertion point.

10. **Type** ADVENTURE TOURS INC.

11. **Press** ⌐← ENTER⌐ .

12. **Click on the** ◥.

13. **Draw the two lines beneath the words** *ADVENTURE TOURS INC.*

14. **Click on File in the menu bar.**

15. **Choose Exit and Return.**

A message appears asking if you want to save the changes to the Microsoft Drawing in the Graphics document.

16. **Choose Yes to save the drawing.**

The drawing is inserted into the document and is treated as an **object**, which is a document or portion of a document that has been pasted into another document. In this, the object is a Microsoft Draw object. Any object can be selected by clicking on it. Furthermore, you can make changes to the drawing by double-clicking on the object, which opens the Drawing window, and then choosing Exit and Return from the File menu when you're finished changing the picture. You can delete an object by selecting it and pressing the ⌐DELETE⌐ key.

Using ClipArt

Several premade drawings, called clip art, come with the Works program. These drawings can be inserted into a word processing document as shown in Figure 4.6. Complete the following steps to insert the globe graphic into the memo.

1. Position the insertion point below the sentence that starts with the words "This is a clip art object. . . ."

2. Choose ClipArt from the Insert menu.

The Add New Pictures dialog box may appear. Make sure there is a check mark in the Microsoft Works Clipart check box. (*Note:* clip art is included with many software applications, but the list in your Add New Pictures dialog box may include other programs (that have been installed on your computer).

3. Verify that Microsoft Works ClipArt is selected, then click on OK.

The Microsoft ClipArt Gallery 2.0 dialog box appears, allowing you to select a drawing. Take a moment to review the drawings that are available.

4. Use the scroll bar in the Pictures list to view drawings from the current category.

5. Click on the Maps-International category in the Categories: list on the left.

6. Click on the middle globe to select it.

7. Click on Insert.

The clip art image is inserted into the document.

Using WordArt

Microsoft Works provides a feature called **WordArt** that allows you to create text objects with special effects. Figure 4.9 shows a design created using the WordArt program. To create such designs, you choose Object from the Insert menu and choose Microsoft WordArt 2.0; then you complete the dialog box to create the desired object. You cannot create drawings using WordArt; rather, you type the desired text and then apply the special effects to the text. Complete the following steps to create the circular text effect shown in Figure 4.9.

1. Place the insertion point below the sentence that starts "this is a possible letterhead."

2. Choose WordArt from the Insert menu.

4.9

A text object created using WordArt

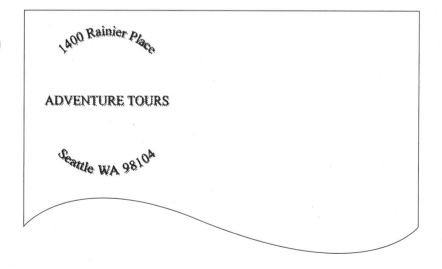

The Enter Your Text Here dialog box appears. The document also shows the words "Your Text Here" surrounded by a slashed-line border. The toolbar is replaced with a new set of buttons used to customize the WordArt object. Begin by typing the text.

3. **Type** 1400 Rainier Place

4. **Press** (↵ ENTER).

5. **Type** ADVENTURE TOURS

6. **Press** (↵ ENTER).

7. **Type** Seattle WA 98104

8. **Click on** ☒ **to remove the dialog box (see Figure 4.10).**

The words "Adventure Tours" replace the words "Your Text Here," and the dialog box disappears. Notice that the box displaying the text is too small. You can resize this text box by moving the **sizing handles** to the desired location. To enlarge the box, click in a blank area outside of the box, place the mouse pointer on one of the handles that appears on the edge, and drag to the desired size.

9. **Click in a blank area outside of the box.**

10. **Place the mouse pointer on the sizing handle at the bottom middle of the box (see Figure 4.11).**

Notice that the mouse pointer turns into a box with two arrows and the word "RESIZE" is displayed. This pointer allows you to change the size of the box.

11. **Drag the sizing handle to enlarge the box, as shown in Figure 4.11.**

To change the arrangement of the text and the type style, you must use the WordArt commands that are displayed when you double-click on the object.

12. **Double-click on the WordArt object.**

4.10

Closing the dialog box used to create WordArt

Click here to close the box

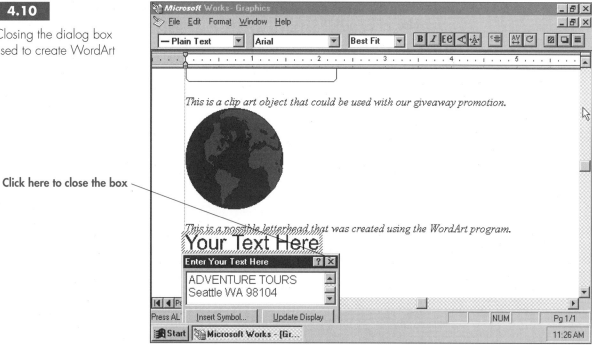

4.11

Resizing the WordArt object

Point here and drag to resize

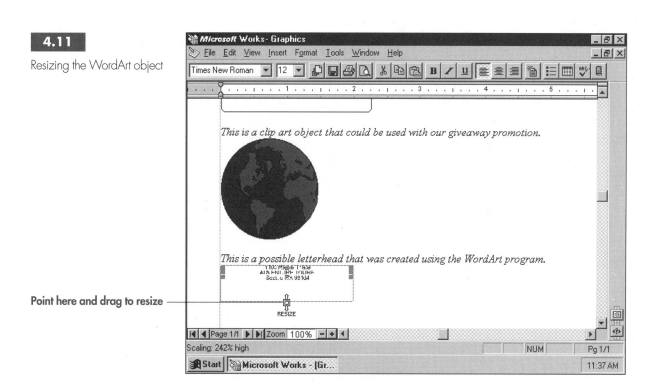

The slashed-line border is displayed, and the toolbar changes to the WordArt options.

13. Click on ☒ to remove the Enter Your Text Here dialog box.

14. Click on ▾ next to the box that says "Plain Text" (see Figure 4.12).

15. Click on the Button (Pour) option ⊖ from the options displayed (see Figure 4.12).

Before continuing to customize the WordArt picture, take a moment to display some of the other available designs.

16. On your own, change the WordArt design from Button (Pour) to other design options and view the results.

17. Choose ⊖ again.

Next, you will add a shadow to the text and change the font.

18. Choose Shadow from the Format menu.

19. Choose the third shadow option from the left (see Figure 4.13).

20. Click on OK.

21. Select the Times New Roman font from the list on the toolbar (or another font if Times New Roman is not available).

22. Click outside of the WordArt box to see the results.

4.12

Selecting a WordArt design

Click on the Button
(Pour) option

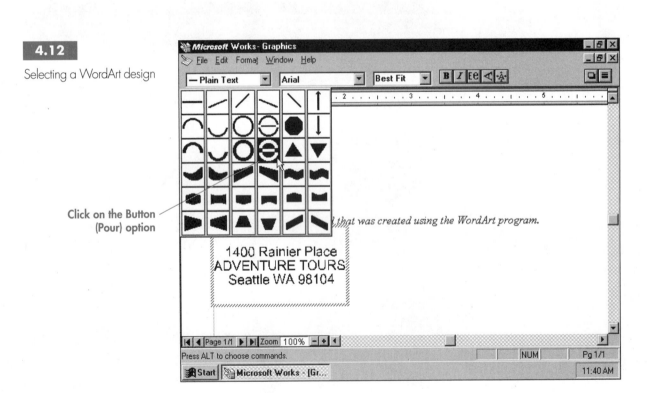

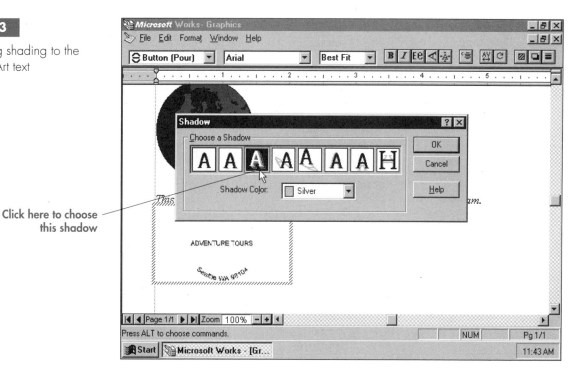

Click here to choose
this shadow

The WordArt toolbar disappears and the normal Works word processing
screen is displayed. Notice that a box and sizing handles now appear around
the WordArt. You can click outside of the WordArt box to remove the border
and sizing handles, and to view the object.

23. **Resize the object, if necessary.**

24. **Click in a blank area on the document to remove the box and sizing handles.**

Your document should resemble Figure 4.6.

To change the text of the WordArt, double-click on the object. The Enter Your
Text Here dialog box will appear, allowing you to make changes to the text.
To delete a WordArt object, select it and press (DELETE). Now save the docu-
ment that contains this WordArt object.

25. **Save the document as *Adventure Tours Graphics*.**

26. **Close the document.**

This completes the section on using WordArt.

KEY TERMS

antonyms	Microsoft Draw	synonyms
ClipArt	Replace command	Thesaurus command
Find command	Spelling command	WordArt

KEY COMMANDS

ClipArt

Drawing

Exit and Return

Find

Replace

Shadow

Spelling

Thesaurus

WordArt

REVIEW QUESTIONS

1. **T F** During a spelling check, when a word is not found in the dictionary you are given the opportunity to change the word.

2. **T F** The Spell Checker is a substitute for proofreading.

3. The Thesaurus command can be used to display both _____ and antonyms.

4. **T F** When using the Find command, you can search for a word but not a phrase.

5. To create a drawing, you choose Drawing from the _____ menu.

6. To create a WordArt object, you choose _____ from the _____ menu.

PROJECTS

1. Open WKS Chapter 4 project 1 and complete the following:
   a. Use the Spelling command to check for and correct spelling errors.
   b. Save the document as *WKS Chapter 4 project 1a* and then print the document. Close the document.

2. (*Note:* This project requires that you first complete Project 1.) Open WKS Chapter 4 project 1a and complete the following:
   a. Use the Find command to locate the word "handy."
   b. Use the Thesaurus command to display a list of synonyms for "handy."
   c. Choose a word from the list to replace "handy."
   d. Use the Find command to search for each occurrence of the word "sickness," and count the number of times the word appears in the document.
   e. Use the Replace command to replace all occurrences of "form" with "Form."
   f. Save the document as *WKS Chapter 4 project 2*, then print the document. Close the document.

3. Use WordArt to create the various textual objects shown in Figure 4.14. Save the document as *WKS Chapter 4 project 3*, then print the document. Close the document.

4.14

Objects created using WordArt

1400 Rainier Place
ADVENTURE TOURS
Seattle WA 98104
1400 Rainier Place
ADVENTURE TOURS
Seattle WA 98104
ADVENTURE TOURS
ADVENTURE TOURS
1400 Rainier Place
ADVENTURE TOURS
Seattle WA 98104
ADVENTURE TOURS

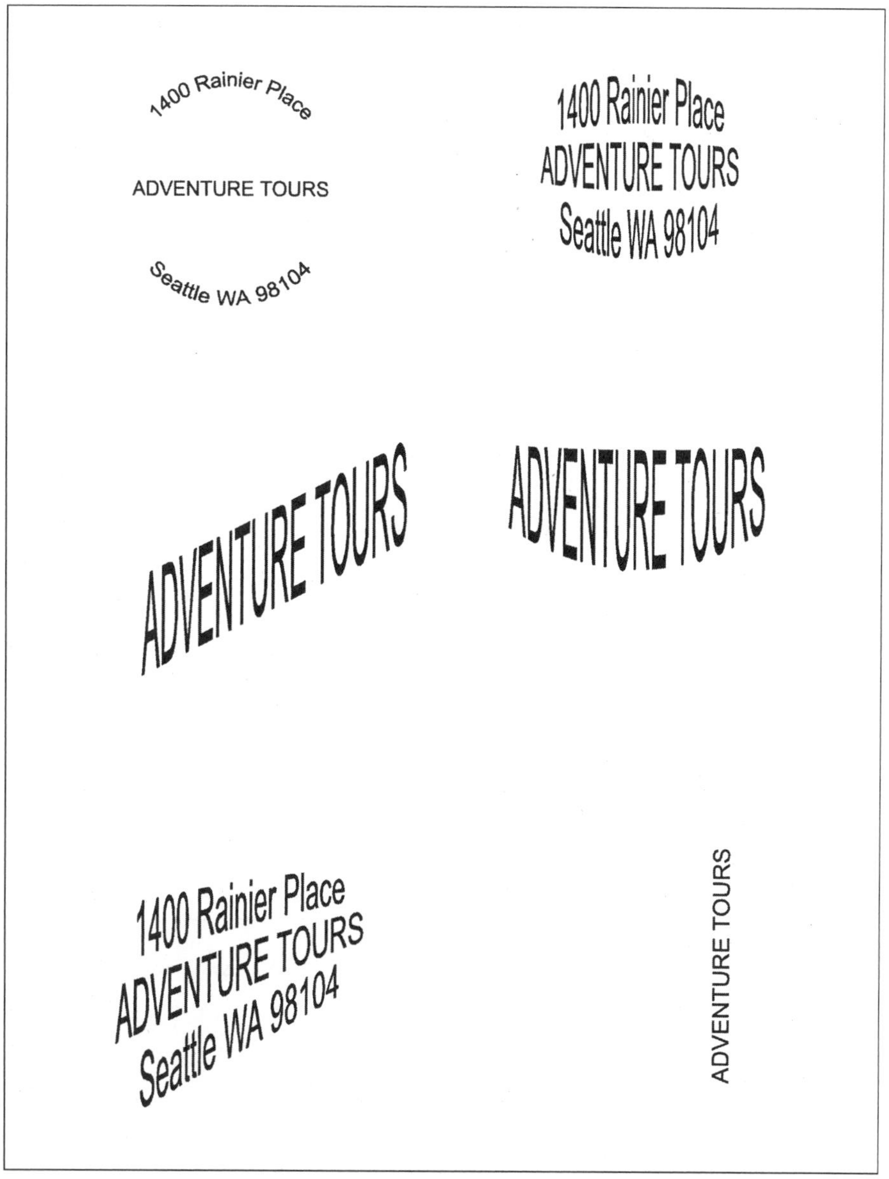

5

Introduction to Spreadsheets

- Describe the parts of a spreadsheet

- Use Works to develop spreadsheet documents

- Distinguish between text, numbers, formulas, and functions

- Use the SUM function and the AutoSum tool

- Save, print, open, and close spreadsheet documents

- Format cells and change column widths

A **spreadsheet application** is useful when you are developing documents that include numbers and calculations. Figure 5.1 shows three documents developed by Adventure Tours using the Works spreadsheet application: a monthly budget, an income forecast, and a survey form. These documents have three important features in common:

- They use numbers.

- They include calculations (such as totals).

- They are laid out in rows and columns.

The spreadsheet application is specifically designed to be used in developing these types of documents. Figure 5.2 shows the proposed budget for Adventure Tours' new Eastside office as it was developed in Works. Notice that the spreadsheet application is also laid out in rows and columns. Notice, too, that each number has a precise location in a particular row and column and that some of the numbers are the result of calculations. A spreadsheet makes it easy for you to enter numbers and perform calculations as you develop these types of documents. In addition, once you have developed a document, you can easily make changes in the numbers, and Works will quickly update the calculations. This allows you to perform **what-if analysis**, which involves trying different alternatives to see the results. For example, by changing one or two values in a Works spreadsheet, you can see what happens to profit if income increases by 10 percent or if advertising expenses decreases by 5 percent. Another important feature of the Works spreadsheet application is that you can create a chart using the numbers in the spreadsheet document. Figure 5.3 shows a chart using the income forecast numbers.

5.1

Three spreadsheet documents

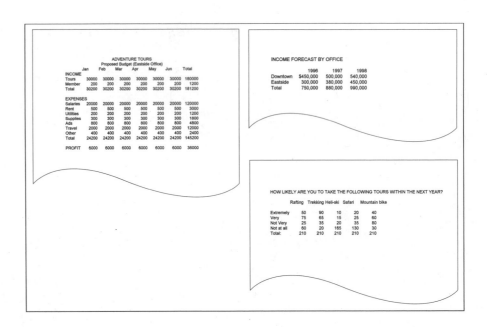

The proposed Adventure Tours budget as developed in Works

	A	B	C	D	E	F	G	H
1				ADVENTURE TOURS				
2				Proposed Budget (Eastside Office)				
3		Jan	Feb	Mar	Apr	May	Jun	Total
4	INCOME							
5	Tours	30000	30000	30000	30000	30000	30000	180000
6	Member	200	200	200	200	200	200	1200
7	Total	30200	30200	30200	30200	30200	30200	181200
8								
9	EXPENSES							
10	Salaries	20000	20000	20000	20000	20000	20000	120000
11	Rent	500	500	500	500	500	500	3000
12	Utilities	200	200	200	200	200	200	1200
13	Supplies	300	300	300	300	300	300	1800
14	Ads	800	800	800	800	800	800	4800
15	Travel	2000	2000	2000	2000	2000	2000	12000
16	Other	400	400	400	400	400	400	2400
17	Total	24200	24200	24200	24200	24200	24200	145200
18								
19	PROFIT	6000	6000	6000	6000	6000	6000	36000

A chart created using the numbers in the spreadsheet

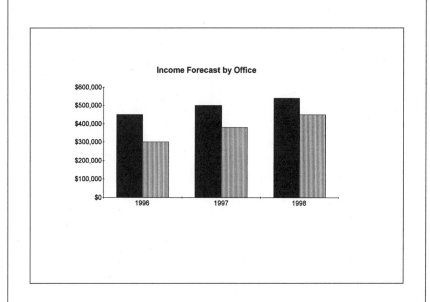

INCOME FORECAST BY OFFICE

	1996	1997	1998
Downtown	$450,000	500,000	540,000
Eastside	300,000	380,000	450,000
Total	750,000	880,000	990,000

Income Forecast by Office

5.4

The Works spreadsheet window

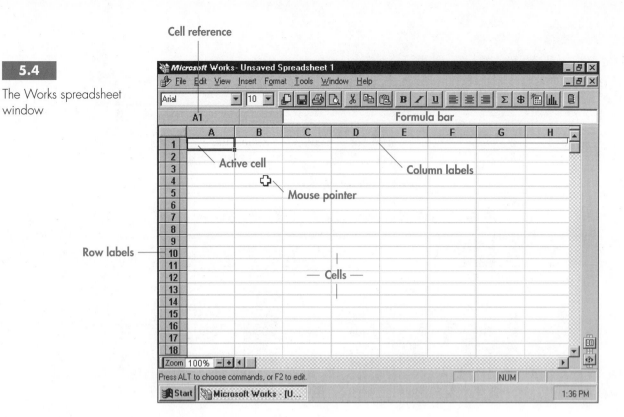

GETTING STARTED WITH THE WORKS SPREADSHEET APPLICATION

The spreadsheet application can be started by choosing the Works Tools index tab in the Works Task Launcher.

1. **Start the Works program and click on the Works Tools index tab.**

2. **Click on [icon].**

The Works spreadsheet window appears. Because Microsoft Works is an integrated program, many of the parts of the spreadsheet window are the same as those of the word processor window, including the title bar; minimize, maximize, restore, and close buttons; the menu bar; toolbar; status bar; and scroll bars. Before studying the parts of the screen that are unique to the spreadsheet window, use the maximize button to enlarge the document window.

3. **Click on [icon] to enlarge the document window.**

Refer to Figure 5.4 as you review the parts of the Works spreadsheet window:

- **Cell reference**. The cell reference displays the name of the cell (A1) that is currently selected on the spreadsheet.

- **Formula bar**. The formula bar displays the entry, if any, for the selected location. Currently, no entry is in cell A1.

- **Column labels** (A, B, . . ., H). Column labels identify the columns.

- **Row labels** (1, 2, . . ., 18). Row labels identify the rows.

- **Cells** (A1, A2, A3, . . .). A **cell** is the intersection of a row and column. Any data you type is entered into a cell.
- **Active cell**. The active cell is the cell that is currently selected (surrounded by a darkened border).
- **Mouse pointer**. The mouse pointer is used to select a cell or cells.

MOVING AROUND THE SPREADSHEET

The Works spreadsheet is 256 columns wide and 16,384 rows deep. Because it is so large, you can see only a small part of the entire spreadsheet at any one time. The columns are identified by letters: A, B, C, and so on. After column Z comes column AA, AB, AC, et cetera. The rows are identified by numbers: 1, 2, 3, and so on. The intersection of a row and column defines a cell. Therefore, each cell has a unique name determined by its column and row. For example, where column A and row 1 intersect is cell A1; where column D and row 17 intersect is cell D17. To select a cell prior to entering data, you point to the cell with the mouse pointer, which is shaped like a cross, and click the mouse button. Or you can use the cell selector keys as listed below:

Press	To move
↑ ↓	Up or down one row
← →	Left or right one column
HOME	To column A of the current row
CTRL + HOME	To cell A1
PAGE DOWN	Down one screen
PAGE UP	Up one screen
CTRL + PAGE DOWN	Right one screen
CTRL + PAGE UP	Left one screen

(*Note:* When two keys are to be used together, such as CTRL + PAGE DOWN, you hold down the first key and press the second key. Then release the first key.)

Take a few moments to practice using the cell selector keys to select various cells. Cell A1 should already be selected. As the selected cell, A1 has a darkened border around it and is displayed in the cell reference.

1. Press ↓ to move to cell A2.

Now the cell reference displays A2.

2. Press → to move to cell B2.

3. Press PAGE DOWN to move to cell B20 (down one screen).

4. Press PAGE UP to move back to cell B2 (up one screen).

5. Hold down CTRL and press PAGE DOWN to move one screen to the right (cell H2).

6. Press HOME to move to column A (cell A2).

7. On your own, use the cell selector keys to move around the spreadsheet.

8. When done, press CTRL + HOME to move to cell A1.

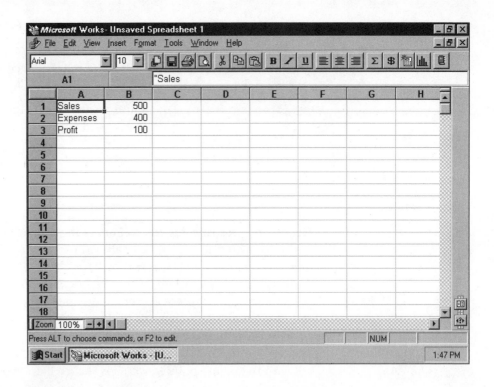

ENTERING DATA INTO THE SPREADSHEET

As already explained, data (text, numbers, formulas) are entered into cells. To enter data into a spreadsheet, you select the desired cell and type the data into the cell. Then you press (↵ ENTER) or an arrow key to move to another cell. Practice entering data into cells by duplicating the simple spreadsheet in Figure 5.5.

1. **With cell A1 selected, type** Sales

Notice that as you type, the word *Sales* is displayed in the cell and on the Formula bar.

2. **Press** (→).

The cell selector moves to cell B1.

3. **Type** 500

4. **Press** (↵ ENTER).

Notice that the active cell is still B1. Pressing (↵ ENTER) signals that you are finished entering data into the cell. You must press (↵ ENTER) or choose a new cell before using the menu commands.

5. **Select cell A2.**

6. **Type** Expenses

This time instead of pressing (↵ ENTER), press the (→) key. This action will complete the entry and select B2, the next cell to the right.

7. **Press** (→) **to select cell B2.**

8. **Type** 400

9. **Select cell A3.**

10. **Type** Profit

11. **Select cell B3.**

ENTERING FORMULAS

Now that you've entered all the data, you need to enter a formula to calculate the profit. A **formula** is used to perform calculations in a spreadsheet. Works allows you to use cell references and numbers in formulas so that the calculation provides a new value based on existing values in the spreadsheet. Formulas begin with an equal sign and must include at least one arithmetic operator. Examples of formulas are:

=B1+B2   Adds the numbers in cells B1 and B2 together

=A5+20   Adds 20 to the number in cell A5

=D12–D13   Subtracts the number in cell D13 from the number in cell D12

=A3*10–B4   Multiplies the number in cell A3 by 10 and then subtracts the number in cell B4

=F20/3   Divides the number in cell F20 by 3

=C15*10%   Multiplies the number in cell C15 by 10%

The arithmetic operators are:

+   Addition

–   Subtraction

*   Multiplication

/   Division

^   Exponentiation (for example, 5^2 would be 5^2)

If you are using more than one operator in a formula, Works assigns a preference to the order in which the operations are carried out. Therefore, you need to understand the order in which the operations occur. The order of preference for arithmetic operators is:

- Exponentiation

- Multiplication and division (left to right)

- Addition and subtraction (left to right)

For example, in the formula =10+4/2, the result would be 7 if you performed the operations starting from the left and moving to the right (10+4=14; 14/2=7). However, because Works assigns an order of preference for operations, the correct answer is 12. Remember, division is given preference over addition, so the operation is 4/2=2; 2+10=12. You can use parentheses to change the order of operation. Operations within parentheses are calculated first, then any other operations are carried out according to Works' order of preference. Thus, =(10+4)/2 would be evaluated as 10+4=14; 14/2=7.

When working with a spreadsheet, you want to construct formulas using cell references instead of the numbers within the cells whenever possible. That way, when you change data in a cell, you do not have to also change the formula. The formula makes its calculation using whatever data is in the cell. In our example from Figure 5.5, the formula to calculate the profit is =B1–B2. Insert this formula into your spreadsheet now.

1. **Select cell B3, if it is not already active.**

2. **Type** =B1–B2

Notice that as you enter the formula, the formula bar changes to display three buttons. The ☒ is called the cancel box and can be used to leave the editing mode without saving changes to the cell. The ☑ is called the enter box and is used to accept the entry. The ? activates the context-sensitive help feature in Works. All cell entries must be completed either by selecting a new cell, pressing (↵ ENTER), or clicking on ☒ or the ☑. When an entry is completed, the boxes disappear from the formula bar.

3. **Point to ☑ on the formula bar.**

4. **Click the mouse button.**

The profit, 100, is displayed in cell B3. However, notice that the formula bar displays the actual entry, =B1–B2. Because this formula contains cell references, not data, any change in the data in cells B1 or B2 will be recalculated automatically and reflected in B3. To see how this works, change Sales to 600.

5. **Select cell B1.**

6. **Type** 600 **and press** (↵ ENTER).

Profit is recalculated to 200. Now, change Expenses to 450.

7. **On your own, select cell B2 and change the expenses figure to 450, using ☑ on the formula bar to complete the entry. Note that Profit is again automatically recalculated.**

Because the formula contains cell references, you have created a relationship between cells B1, B2, and B3. Thus, any changes you make in B1 or B2 are reflected in B3.

Now try creating a different relationship among these cells. Assume you anticipate that your expenses will be 80 percent of your sales. You can enter a formula in B2 to calculate the expenses no matter what the sales.

8. **Select cell B2. Type** =B1*80%

9. **Press** (↵ ENTER).

With this formula, if you change the sales data, both the expenses and the profit figures will change accordingly.

EDITING DATA IN A SPREADSHEET

Works provides several ways for you to make changes in, or edit, the spreadsheet data. To replace data in a cell, you select the cell and type the new entry. Practice editing data by changing the word *Sales* to the word *Income*.

1. **Click on cell A1 to select it.**

2. **Type** Income **and press** (↵ ENTER).

You can edit the contents of a cell without retyping the entire entry. For example, if you want to change *Profit* to *Our Profit*, you can insert the word *Our* into the cell using the formula bar.

3. **Select cell A3.**

4. **Point the I-beam between the *P* in *Profit* and the double quotes in the formula bar (see Figure 5.6).**

5. **Click the mouse button to set an insertion point.**

6. **Type** Our

7. **Press the spacebar.**

8. **Click on** ☑ **to complete the entry.**

To delete an entry, you select the cell and press (DELETE). Delete the words *Our Profit*.

9. **Press** (DELETE).

5.6

Positioning the insertion point on the formula bar

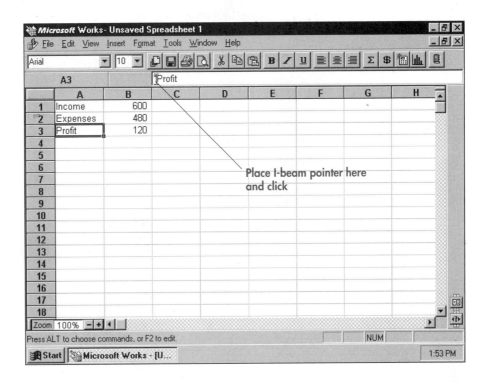

The words *Our Profit* are deleted from the cell. You can undo several actions, including clearing the contents of a cell, by using the Undo command in the Edit menu.

10. Click on Edit in the menu bar.

11. Click on Undo Clear.

The words *Our Profit* reappear.

You can delete several entries at a time by highlighting the cells and pressing DELETE . Continue by deleting all the entries. To highlight the cells, point to the upper-left corner of the cell range (cell A1), hold down the mouse button, and drag the mouse pointer to the lower-right corner of the cell range (cell B3). Figure 5.7 shows this process.

12. Point to cell A1.

13. Hold down the mouse button.

14. Drag the mouse pointer to cell B3.

15. Release the mouse button.

16. Press DELETE .

17. Click on cell A1 to remove the highlight.

5.7

Selecting a range of cells

Point here

Drag to here

In the spreadsheet application, Works makes a distinction between text entries and number entries. In this section, you will work with both types of spreadsheet data entries. Following are important differences in working with text and numbers:

- Text entries can display across several cells.

- Number entries must fit within the cell.

- Text entries are left aligned in a cell (but can be changed to right or center aligned).

- Numbers are right aligned in a cell (but can be changed to left or center aligned).

Figure 5.8 shows a proposed budget for Adventure Tours that includes several text and number entries. Notice that the heading, "Adventure Tours," appears to be in cells A1 and B1. However, as the formula bar shows, the entire entry is in cell A1 only. Although the heading appears in cell B1, this cell is actually empty. If you were to enter data in cell B1, the heading would be truncated. Figure 5.9 shows the heading after *1996* is entered into B1. Now, because there is data in B1, only the part of the heading that fits into A1 is displayed. Make this entry now.

1. **Select cell A1, if it is not already the active cell.**

2. **Type** Adventure Tours **and press** (↵ ENTER).

AutoSum button

5.8

A spreadsheet with several text and number entries

5.9

The heading, Adventure Tours, is truncated after entering 1996 into cell B1

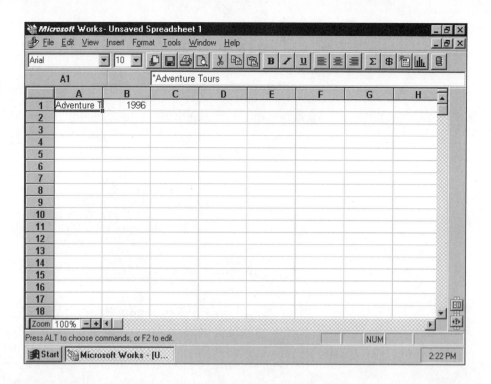

5.10

Three number entries

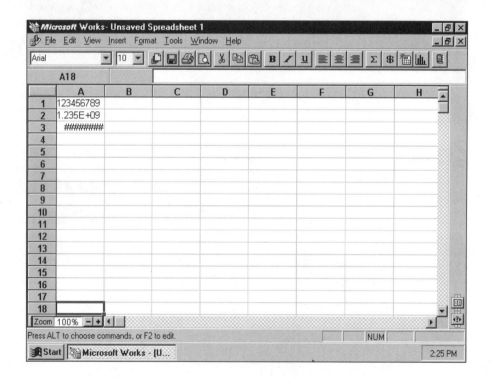

WORKS 4 FOR WINDOWS 95

Now make an entry into cell B1.

3. **Select cell B1.**

4. **Type** 1996

5. **Press** (↵ ENTER).

With an entry in B1, the heading in A1 is truncated. The word *Tours* has not been erased; it simply cannot display in cell B1. To see that the entire heading is still intact, select cell A1.

6. **Select cell A1.**

Notice that the formula bar displays the entire heading, *Adventure Tours*. Now delete the entry in cell B1 so that the entire heading displays again.

7. **Delete the entry in cell B1.**

As with text, numbers that are larger than the cell width are not displayed in adjacent cells. Instead, they are displayed in scientific notation or as a series of pound signs (#). Figure 5.10 shows three number entries. The entry in cell A1 fits within the cell. The entry in cell A2 is displayed in scientific notation because it is too large to fit within the cell. (*Note:* Scientific notation is used to denote very large numbers or very small numbers.) Cell A3 is filled with pound signs, indicating that the number is too large to fit in the cell width. The pound sign provides additional information about a numerical entry: it indicates that the number has been formatted to display symbols such as a dollar sign, comma, or decimal point. Formatted numbers do not display in scientific notation; otherwise, the number in cell A3 would appear in scientific notation like the number in cell A2 above. Later in this chapter you will learn how to change the column width to accommodate large numbers.

The alignment of the entry in the cell is another distinction between text and numbers. As shown in Figure 5.8, the text entries are left aligned and the number entries are right aligned within the cells. This makes the spreadsheet easier to read by lining up the numbers and helping prevent text and numbers from running together.

Begin constructing the Adventure Tours budget spreadsheet, as shown in Figure 5.8.

1. **Select cell A2.**

2. **Type** Proposed Budget (Eastside Office)

3. **Select cell A4.**

4. **Type** INCOME

5. **Select cell A5.**

6. **On your own, complete the entries for cells A5, A6, B5, and B6 (see Figure 5.8).**

7. **Select cell A7.**

8. **Type** Total

9. **Select cell C7.**

10. **Type** =B5+B6

11. Press (← ENTER).

12. Type EXPENSES into cell A9.

13. On your own, complete the entries for cells A10 through A15 and B10 through B15.

14. Type Total into cell A16.

15. Select cell C16.

At this point you could add the expenses using the formula =B10+B11+B12+B13+B14+B15. However, Works provides an easier way to add a group of cells—the SUM function.

USING FUNCTIONS

Along with formulas, Works provides an array of **functions**, which are preset formulas that perform arithmetic, statistical, and financial operations on the values in a spreadsheet. As noted above, functions also provide shortcuts to long or complex formulas. The formula =B10+B11+B12+B13+B14+B15, for example, can be replaced with the function =SUM(B10:B15). This SUM function adds, or sums, the range of cells specified in the parentheses. The format for a function is =*function name(cell range)*, where

■ = indicates, along with the function name, that this is a function.

■ *function name* indicates the function.

■ *(cell range)* indicates the group of cells on which the function will be performed.

A cell range is enclosed in parentheses and includes the first cell in the range, a colon, and the last cell in the range.

Examples of functions are:

=AVERAGE(C12:C17) Calculates the average of the numbers in cells C12, C13, C14, C15, C16, and C17.

=MAX(D2:H2) Determines the highest number from the numbers in cells D2, E2, F2, G2, and H2.

=MIN(D2:H2) Determines the lowest number from the numbers in cells D2, E2, F2, G2, and H2.

Now use the SUM function to total the expenses.

1. Select cell C16, if it is not already active.

2. Type =SUM(B10:B15)

3. Press (← ENTER).

The result of the SUM function, 294000, is displayed in cell C16, as shown in Figure 5.8.

Works provides a shortcut, the **AutoSum tool**, for summing a row or column of numbers. When you click on the AutoSum button Σ on the toolbar as shown in Figure 5.8, Works automatically inserts the SUM function in the active cell. If you select a cell at the bottom of a column of numbers, Works assumes that you want to add the column. If you select a cell to the right of a row of numbers, Works assumes that you want to add the row. Try using the AutoSum button to total Adventure Tours' expenses, and then place that total in cell B16.

1. Select cell B16.

2. Click on Σ on the toolbar (see Figure 5.8).

The numbers in cells B10 through B15 are highlighted, and the formula bar displays =SUM(B10:B15).

3. Click on ✔.

The total, 294000, appears in cell B16. In this case, you selected a cell at the bottom of a column of numbers, so Works assumed you wanted to add the column and display the result in the selected cell. Before continuing, delete the entry in cell B16.

4. Press (DELETE).

Now complete the remainder of the budget spreadsheet.

5. Type PROFIT into A18.

6. Select cell C18.

To calculate the profit, you subtract the expenses from the income. The formula is =C7–C16. Instead of typing this formula, you can select the cells to build the formula as follows:

7. Type =

8. Press (↑) eleven times to select cell C7.

9. Type –

10. Press (↑) two times to select cell C16.

11. Press (↵ ENTER).

The formula is entered, and the result (10000) is displayed. Using the (↑) button may seem more time-consuming than typing a formula. However, this technique is useful for long or complicated formulas because it can help prevent typing errors.

The spreadsheet is complete, and you can now save it.

SAVING A SPREADSHEET

The process for saving a spreadsheet document is similar to the process for saving a word processing document. Save the budget spreadsheet with the file name *Adventure Tours budget*.

1. **Insert the data disk in the appropriate drive.**
2. **Choose Save As from the File menu.**

The most important information you need to specify in the Save As dialog box are the disk drive and the file name. In this book we assume you are working with drive A. If you are working with drive B, you need to specify B whenever the instruction is given to specify A. Now save the file to drive A (or B) with the file name Adventure Tours budget. Works allows you to specify the drive along with the file name in the File name text box. Thus, the entry is a:\Adventure Tours budget (or b:\Adventure Tours budget). You can type the entry in uppercase or lowercase letters. With the file in the File name box highlighted:

3. **Type** a:\Adventure Tours budget (**or** b:\Adventure Tours budget)
4. **Click on Save.**

You are returned to the spreadsheet. Notice that the file name is now displayed on the title bar.

PRINTING A SPREADSHEET

To print a document, you display the spreadsheet onscreen and choose the Print command from the File menu. Then you complete the dialog box that appears onscreen. You can preview a spreadsheet just as you did a word processing document. Make sure the printer is ready; then preview how the document will print, and print it.

1. **Click on** [icon].

The Print Preview screen is displayed, showing how the document will print on a page. You can use the pointer to select an area of the page, and click the mouse button to enlarge it. Notice that the pointer appears as a magnifying glass with the words *ZOOM* printed along the bottom of the handle.

2. **Point to the top of the page and click the mouse button.**

The selected area is enlarged to make it easier to read. You can enlarge the page one more time.

3. **Point to the word *EXPENSES* and click the mouse button.**

You click the mouse button once again to return to the full-page view.

4. **Click the mouse button.**

The Print Preview screen has a button that allows you to print the document. Selecting this button is the same as choosing the Print command from the File menu.

5. **Click on** [Print].

The document is printed. If you want to specify which pages of a multiple-page document you want to print or how many copies of the document you want to print, you must use the Print command from the File menu.

The printout you just made uses Works' default settings. For example, Works will not print gridlines, as shown in Figure 5.11, unless you specify them. Figure 5.12 shows the document printed with gridlines and with row and column headings. These changes can be made using the Page Setup dialog box. Complete the following steps to duplicate the printout shown in Figure 5.12:

1. Choose Page Setup from the File menu.

The Page Setup dialog box appears. This dialog box is identical to the one you used with the word processing tool. It has three index tabs that display different setup options. The gridlines and row and column headings options are found in the section labeled Other Options.

2. Click on the Other Options index tab.

The gridlines and row and column headers options are located at the left side of the dialog box. These options can be turned on and off by clicking on them. A check mark appears in the box next to them when they are activated. Figure 5.13 shows that the Print gridlines option is turned on.

3. Click in the Print gridlines check box.
4. Click in the Print row and column headers check box.
5. Click on OK to return to the spreadsheet.
6. Click on ⬛.

The document now appears with the gridlines and row and column headers.

7. On your own, print the document.

5.11

The document printed without gridlines

```
Adventure Tours
Proposed Budget (Eastside Office)

INCOME
Tours            300000
Members            4000
Total                       304000

EXPENSES
Salaries         250000
Rent               6000
Utilities          3000
Ads                8000
Travel            24000
Other              3000
Total                       294000

PROFIT                       10000
```

5.12

The document printed with row and column headers and gridlines

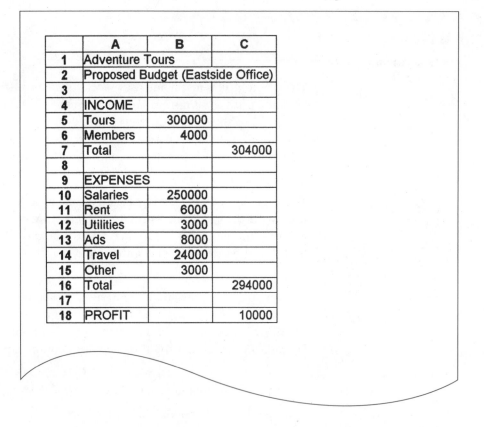

	A	B	C
1	Adventure Tours		
2	Proposed Budget (Eastside Office)		
3			
4	INCOME		
5	Tours	300000	
6	Members	4000	
7	Total		304000
8			
9	EXPENSES		
10	Salaries	250000	
11	Rent	6000	
12	Utilities	3000	
13	Ads	8000	
14	Travel	24000	
15	Other	3000	
16	Total		294000
17			
18	PROFIT		10000

5.13

The Print gridlines option turned on

Click here to choose the Print gridlines option

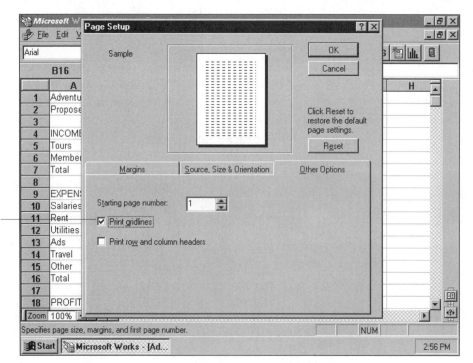

CLOSING A SPREADSHEET

When you have finished working with a spreadsheet, you can use the Close command from the File menu to close it. If you have not saved the document, or if you have changed the document and not saved the changes, a message will appear when you try to close the document window. To illustrate this, you will make a change to the Adventure Tours budget document and then try to close it.

1. Type 220000 in cell B10 as the salaries expense.
2. Press (↵ ENTER).
3. Choose Close from the File menu.

A box appears with the message "Save changes to Adventure Tours budget?"

4. Click on Yes.

The edited document replaces the previously saved document, and the spreadsheet window is removed from the screen. If there are no more open documents, the Works Task Launcher appears.

OPENING A SPREADSHEET

To open a spreadsheet document, you can click on the Existing Documents index tab, and then choose a spreadsheet from the recently viewed documents list, or you can click on the Open a document not listed here button. Figure 5.14 shows Adventure Tours budget displayed in the recently viewed documents list. To choose from this list, double-click on the file name. Practice opening a spreadsheet now.

1. Click on the Existing Documents index tab to display the list of recently viewed files.
2. Click on Adventure Tours budget.
3. Click on OK.

The Adventure Tours budget document is opened.

4. Click on ▣ in the document window.

5.14

Selecting a recently viewed
document from Existing
Documents index tab

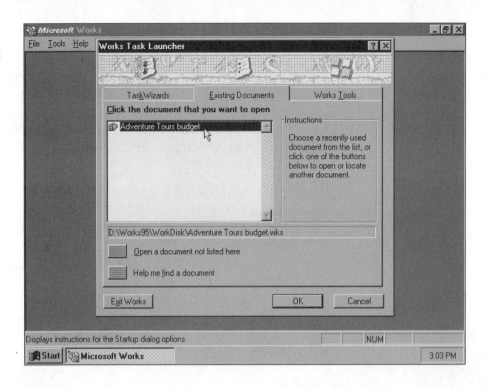

USING THE WORKS TOOLBAR

Works provides several tools that can be used as shortcuts when carrying out various Works commands. Initially, one toolbar is displayed near the top of the spreadsheet screen. Other toolbars, such as the Chart and Drawing toolbars, can be displayed as needed. Figure 5.15 labels the following three commonly used tools on the toolbar:

5.15

Commonly used buttons on
the toolbar

Task Launcher button

Save button

Print button

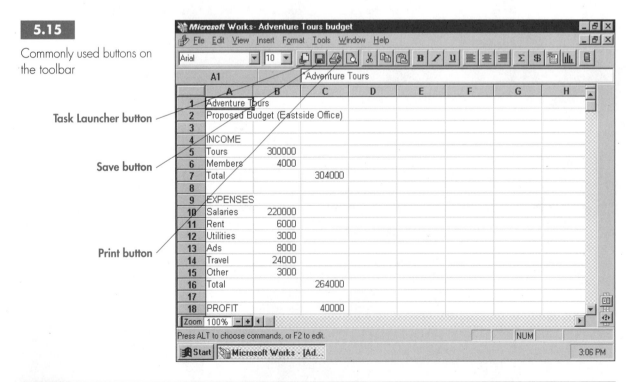

- The Task Launcher button ⬚. Click on the Task Launcher button to display the Works Task Launcher dialog box.

- The Save button ⬚. Click on the Save button to save the displayed spreadsheet. If the document was previously saved, it is saved again, and any changes will overwrite the previous version, with the same file name. If the document has not been previously saved, the Save As dialog box appears, allowing you to specify a drive and file name. Be careful with this tool. Often, you will create a document and save it. Then you will make changes in the document and decide to save both versions. As indicated, if you use the Save button to save the revised version, the *same* file name is used and the old document is overwritten or *replaced* by the new version. To save both documents, you would use the Save As command and assign a different file name to the newly revised document.

- The Print button ⬚. Click on the Print button to print the displayed document. As with the Save button, be careful with the Print button. When you click on this button, neither the Print dialog box nor the Print Preview screen appear. It is advisable to preview any document before printing it to make sure it will print the way you desire.

When you point to a button, its name appears below the arrow pointer. Also, a description of the tool's function is displayed on the status line. To see how this works, point to the Print button now.

1. Point to ⬚.

2. Read the description at the bottom of the screen.

3. On your own, point to the other buttons and read their descriptions.

(*Note:* You may not yet understand the function of every tool. Many of them will be explained in later chapters.)

FORMATTING CELLS

Works allows you to use special characters, including dollar signs, commas, and decimal places, when entering numbers in a spreadsheet. However, there are two default formatting constraints you need to consider. First, when you enter a number with decimal places, any zeros at the end of the number may not be displayed. For example, when you enter the number 4.50, it may appear in the cell as 4.5. Because the zero has no significance in the value of the number, it is deleted. However, you can format the cell so that it will display a zero in the second decimal place. Second, when you use special characters, you may find that the number is too large to fit within the cell width. In this section you learn how to enter these special characters and format cells.

In the Works spreadsheet application, you can display numbers in a variety of ways. For example, you could display the number 1000 with decimal places (1000.00), with commas (1,000), or with both (1,000.00). You can even display negative numbers. The number format you choose depends on your needs and preferences. However, you need to remember that the value of a number that you enter in a cell may differ from the number as it appears in the spreadsheet. For instance, you might enter the number 555.75 in a cell. If you later format that cell to display no decimal places, the number will appear in the spreadsheet as 556 (rounding up occurs for digits 5 and above). However, the *value* of the number remains 555.75, and this value is used in any calculations.

Figure 5.16 shows the budget spreadsheet with the numbers formatted to display commas. You will use the Number command to format the numbers.

1. **Drag the mouse to select cells B5 through C18.**

2. **Choose Number from the Format menu.**

The Format Cells dialog box appears, with the Number index tab displayed. Under the Format options, the general option is active, so the Sample box shows how numbers will appear with no other formatting.

Below is a description of the common number formats available in Works and an example of each.

Format	Displays numbers	Example
General	As precisely as possible	300000
Fixed	With a specified number of decimal places (0 to 7)	300000.00
Currency	With a $, comma, and specified number of decimal places	$300,000.00
Comma	With a comma and the specified number of decimal places	300,000.00

5.16

All numbers formatted with commas

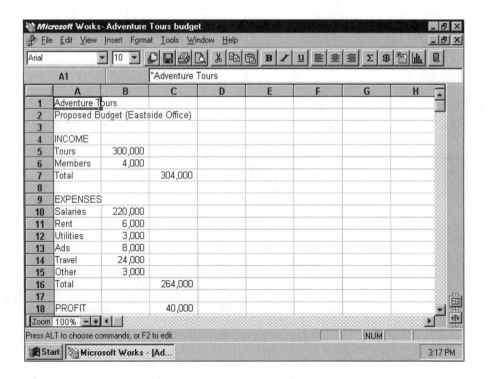

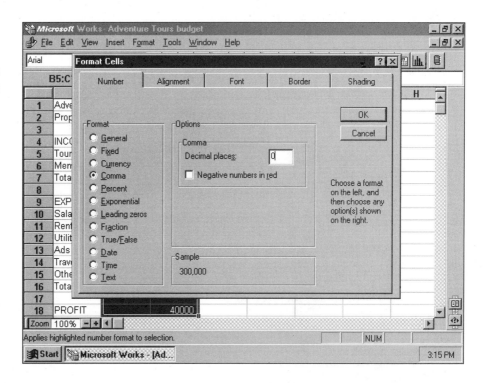

Select several of the formats and see how the sample in the dialog box changes.

3. **Click on Fixed.**

Notice that the sample changes to 300000.00.

4. **Click on Currency.**

The sample changes to $300,000.00.

5. **Click on Comma.**

The sample changes to 300,000.00. Now change the number of decimal places to 0.

6. **Type 0 in the Decimal places box.**

Your dialog box should resemble the one in Figure 5.17.

7. **Click on OK.**

All the numbers now display commas. Continue by formatting the profit value in the currency format with no decimal places.

8. **Select C18.**

9. **Choose Number from the Format menu.**

10. **Click on Currency in the Format list.**

11. **Change the decimal places to zero.**

12. **Click on OK.**

The total profit number is displayed with a dollar sign and commas, but with no decimal places.

At times a formatted number will be displayed as a series of pound signs. The pound sign indicates that the number is too large to be displayed within the current cell width. To remove the pound signs so that the number will appear, you must increase the column width. This can be done by choosing the Column Width command in the Format menu or by using the mouse pointer to drag the column lines. You will use both methods to change the size of the columns. First, reduce the size of columns B and C so that the numbers are too large for the cells they are displayed in.

1. **Select cells B5 through C18.**

2. **Choose Column Width from the Format menu.**

The Column Width dialog box appears. You can type in a new column width or click on the Best Fit option. You will reduce the width of the column by entering a new number.

3. **Type** 7

4. **Click on OK.**

(*Note*: If the first time Help dialog box appears, click on OK to close it.)

Notice that some numbers are displayed as # signs. The # symbols indicate that the number has been formatted and it is too large to be displayed in the current cell width. With these columns still highlighted, select the Best Fit option from the Column Width dialog box.

5. **Choose Column Width from the Format menu.**

6. **Click on Best Fit.**

7. **Click on cell A1 to remove the highlighting.**

The dialog box closes, the column widens, and the # signs are replaced with the numbers. Now use the drag method to increase the width for column A.

8. **Point to the line between the A and B column headings (see Figure 5.18).**

5.18

Pointing to the line between the A and B column headings

Point here

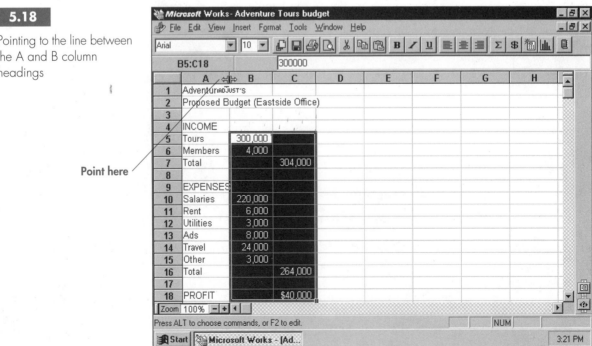

Notice that the pointer changes to a double arrow and the word ADJUST appears.

9. **Hold down the mouse button, and drag the line to the right of the word** *Tours* **in row 1.**

10. **Release the mouse button.**

Now save the document using a different name and print it.

11. **Choose Save** **As** **from the** **File** **menu.**

12. **Type** a:\Adventure Tours budget 2 **(or** b:\Adventure Tours budget 2**).**

13. **Click on** **Save.**

14. **Print the document.**

EXITING THE SPREADSHEET APPLICATION

To exit the spreadsheet application, simply close all open documents.

1. **Choose** **Close** **from the** **File** **menu to close the** *Adventure Tours budget 2* **document.**

After closing all documents, the Works Task Launcher is displayed.

2. **Click on** E**xit Works in the Works Task Launcher.**

When you are done using the computer, be sure to remove your data disk from the disk drive.

KEY TERMS

active cell	column labels	row labels
AutoSum	formula bar	spreadsheet application
cell	formulas	SUM function
cell reference	functions	what-if analysis

KEY COMMANDS

Column Width	Number	Undo Clear
Exit Works	Page Setup	

REVIEW QUESTIONS

1. **T F** A Works spreadsheet is also called a document.

2. Where a row and a column intersect is called a _____.

3. The (HOME) key selects column _____.

4. Formulas begin with an _____ _____.

5. **T F** Text entries must fit within the cell width to be displayed properly.

6. Numbers that are too large to fit in a cell will display in scientific notation or as a series of _____.

7. The _____ tool can be used as a shortcut for summing a group of numbers.

PROJECTS

1. Complete the spreadsheet, Income Forecast by Office, shown in Figure 5.1. Use formulas for all calculations. Format the first number to display a dollar sign and all the other numbers to display commas. Include your name at the bottom of the document. Save the spreadsheet as *WKS Chapter 5 project 1*, then print the document. Close the document.

2. Complete the spreadsheet, Survey Results, shown in Figure 5.1. Use the sum function or the AutoSum tool for all calculations. Include your name at the bottom of the document. Save the spreadsheet as *WKS Chapter 5 project 2*, then print the document. Close the document.

3. Adventure Tours will be having a grand opening of their new Eastside office. A breakdown of the costs for the event follows. Create a spreadsheet showing these costs and include a total. Format the numbers to display commas and two decimal places. Format the total to display a dollar sign. Include your name at the bottom of the document. Save the spreadsheet as *WKS Chapter 5 project 3*, then print the document. Close the document.

Publicity	100
Food	500
Drinks	300
Banner	75
Invitations	150
Mailing	300
Door Prize	1,000
Misc.	200

4. Develop a college or household budget of your own. Use formulas and functions for all calculations. Include your name at the bottom of the document. Save the spreadsheet as *WKS Chapter 5 project 4*, then print the document. Close the document.

Developing and Analyzing a Worksheet

- ◼ Enter a series of dates

- ◼ Copy data and formulas

- ◼ Move data

- ◼ Perform what-if analyses

- ◼ Insert rows and columns

Point here and click to
change the Zoom percentage

Works provides several shortcuts for entering data in a spreadsheet. These
include copying and moving data as well as filling in a group of cells with
series data such as a series of months. Figure 6.1 shows Adventure Tours' six-
month proposed budget for the Eastside office. You will develop this spreadsheet using several shortcuts for entering the numbers and headings.
However, before you begin work on the spreadsheet, you need to understand
the function of the Zoom percentage feature.

CHANGING THE ZOOM

The spreadsheet you will create in this chapter is larger than the one you
worked with in Chapter 5. Depending on the monitor you are using, the
entire spreadsheet may not appear onscreen at one time. To adjust the
onscreen appearance of the spreadsheet, you can use Works' **Zoom percentage** tool. The Zoom percentage, which is displayed at the bottom of the
spreadsheet window, is typically set at 100%. By adjusting this percentage,
you control the display of information onscreen. To change the zoom for a
spreadsheet, point to the percentage indicator and click the mouse button. A
menu appears giving standard percentages and an option called Custom. The
Custom command displays the Zoom dialog box and places your insertion
point in the Custom text box so a number can be entered. The Custom option
is ideal if you want to choose a percentage not included in the list, such as
95%. Change the zoom on this spreadsheet to 95% so your screen matches
the figures in this chapter.

1. Start the Works program and click on the Works <u>T</u>ools index tab.

2. Click on [icon].

3. Click on [icon].

4. Point to the percentage box next to the word *Zoom* on the bottom of the spreadsheet window (see Figure 6.1).

5. Click the mouse button.

6. Choose <u>C</u>ustom from the menu that appears.

The Zoom dialog box appears. Change the Custom option to 95%.

7. Verify that the insertion point is in the Custom text box.

8. Type 95 and click on OK.

The Zoom percentage should reflect the changes you made in the dialog box, and your screen should match the figures in this chapter.

ENTERING A SERIES OF DATES

Works enables you to quickly enter a series of dates (January, February, March, and so on) into a spreadsheet by typing the first date and then using the mouse pointer to select and complete the cells that will contain the other dates. The Edit menu contains the command that is used to perform this operation—Fill Series. Complete the following steps to enter the dates using the fill process. You will start by typing the heading into cell A1.

1. With cell A1 selected, type ADVENTURE TOURS

2. Select cell D1.

3. Type Proposed Budget (Eastside Office)

4. Select cell B3.

5. Type January and press (↵ ENTER).

Notice the box that appears on the bottom-right corner of the selected cell (B3). The box is used to copy the contents of the selected cell into adjacent cells. Figure 6.2 illustrates the process of automatically adding the months to a spreadsheet. Place the mouse pointer on the box in the bottom-right corner of cell B3. The mouse pointer becomes a plus sign and the word "FILL" appears beneath the plus sign. When you see the word "FILL," hold the mouse and drag the pointer to select the other cells (C3 through G3). Finally, you release the mouse button. This procedure can also be accomplished by highlighting the cell range (B3 through G3), choosing Fill Series from the Edit menu, and then selecting Month from the dialog box. Use the mouse to perform the fill operation now.

6. Place the mouse pointer on the bottom-right corner of cell B3 (see Figure 6.2).

7. Hold down the mouse button and drag the pointer to select cells B3 through G3.

8. Release the mouse button.

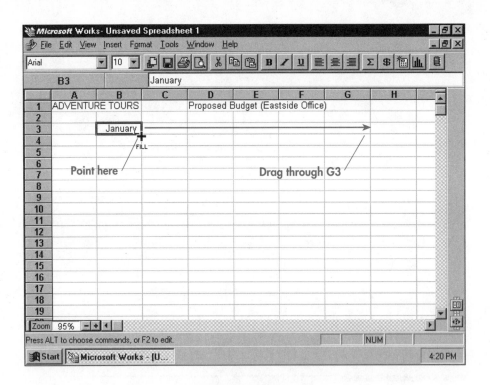

6.3

The headings in column A
and the numbers in
column B

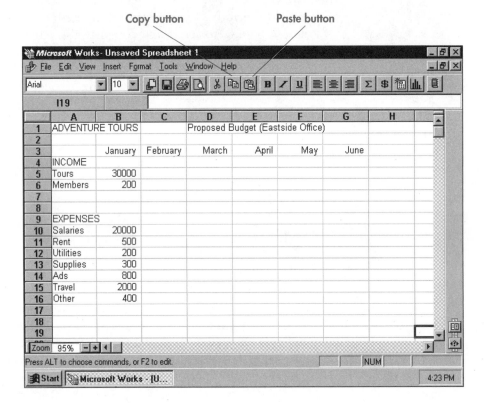

The months appear in the selected cells. This same process can be used to enter
a series of years (1996, 1997, 1998, . . .) and numbers (100, 200, 300, . . .).
The Fill Series dialog box also allows you to specify a value. For example, you can
start with the number 500 and set the value to increase by 100. The resulting

series will be 500, 600, 700, and so on. Continue creating the budget spreadsheet by entering the headings in column A and the numbers in column B, as shown in Figure 6.3.

9. **On your own, enter the headings in column A and the numbers in column B.**

Your spreadsheet should resemble Figure 6.3.

COPYING SPREADSHEET DATA

Notice in Figure 6.1 that the numbers in this budget are the same for each month. But you don't have to enter them one by one. Instead, you can enter the numbers for January and then use Works' copy feature to quickly enter the numbers for the other months. There are three methods used to copy data within a spreadsheet: the **Copy** and **Paste commands** from the Edit menu or the Copy ▤ and Paste ▤ buttons on the toolbar, the Fill command from the Edit menu, and the **drag-and-drop** process using the mouse. You will practice using each of these methods to copy the budget numbers from January to the other months. Start by using the copy-and-paste method to copy the tour income from cell B5 to cells C5 through G5.

1. **Select cell B5.**

2. **Choose Copy from the Edit menu.**

The entry (30000) in cell B5 is placed into a holding area called the **Clipboard**.

3. **Select cell C5.**

4. **Choose Paste from the Edit menu.**

A copy of the number (30000) is pasted into the selected cell. The original number remains on the Clipboard and can be copied or pasted into other cells. Next, use the ▤ to paste copies of the number into additional cells.

5. **Point to D5.**

6. **Hold down the mouse button and drag the pointer to select cells D5 through G5 (see Figure 6.4).**

7. **Release the mouse button.**

8. **Click on ▤ (see Figure 6.3).**

The number (30000) is copied from the Clipboard to the selected cells. Now use the copy-and-paste method to copy the members' income (200) from cell B6 to cells C6 through G6.

9. **On your own, copy the members' income into cells C6 through G6.**

Next you will use the Fill Right command to copy the salaries (20000) from cell B10 to cells C10 through G10. The process is to select the cell to be copied and the cells to be copied to, and then choose Fill Right from the Edit menu. You can perform the Fill operation using the mouse by pointing to the box in the bottom-right corner of the selected cell and dragging the pointer through the other cells. Use the Fill Right command to add these numbers to the spreadsheet.

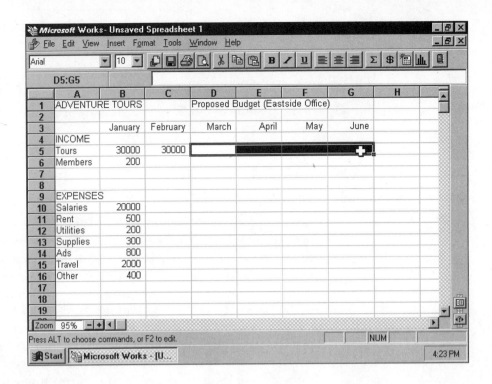

10. **Select cells B10 through G10.**

11. **Choose Fill Right from the Edit menu.**

The number (20000) is copied to the selected cells. Now use the Fill Right command to copy the rent expense (500).

12. **On your own, copy the rent expense in row 11.**

Until now you have been copying one cell at a time. You can copy more than one cell using either the copy/paste or fill process. Use the fill process with the mouse to copy the remaining entries.

13. **Select cell B12 through B16.**

14. **Place the mouse pointer on the box in the bottom-right corner of cell B16 and drag the pointer through cell G16.**

The numeric entries are completed. The copying method you should use is dependent upon where you are copying the data. The Fill commands are used to copy data from a cell(s) to an adjacent cell(s). The copy/paste method can be used when you are not copying to adjacent cells.

A quick way to copy one or more cells is the drag-and drop process. Practice the drag-and-drop method by copying the word *Total* from cell A7 to A17. You will need to use the CTRL key and the mouse to perform this operation.

15. **Select cell A7.**

16. **Type** Total **and press** ↵ ENTER .

17. **Point to the bottom border of cell A7.**

Notice the pointer changes to an arrow with the word "DRAG" below it.

18. **Hold down the mouse button.**

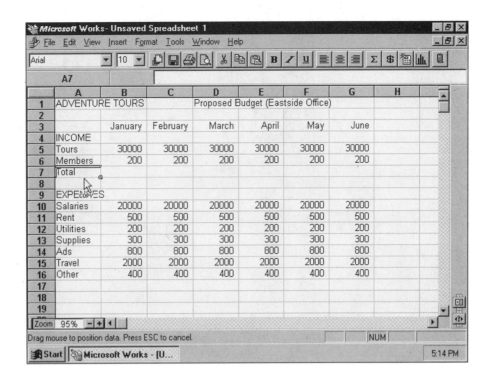

The word "DRAG" beneath the pointer arrow changes to "MOVE".

19. While holding down the mouse button, hold down the CTRL key.

The word "MOVE" beneath the pointer arrow changes to "COPY" (see Figure 6.5).

20. Drag the pointer to cell A17.

21. Release the mouse button.

22. Release CTRL.

The word *Total* is copied to cell A17.

23. On your own, use the drag-and-drop method to copy the word *Total* to cell H3.

COPYING FORMULAS AND FUNCTIONS

Any of the three copying methods discussed above also can be used to copy formulas and functions. Figure 6.6 shows the formulas that are to be entered in the spreadsheet to calculate the income totals for each month. Notice that the formulas are the same except that the cell references change relative to the column. That is, =B5+B6 for column B and =C5+C6 for column C. When you copy a formula, Works will automatically change cell references relative to the new location. To practice copying formulas, you will enter the formula for column B and then copy it to the other columns.

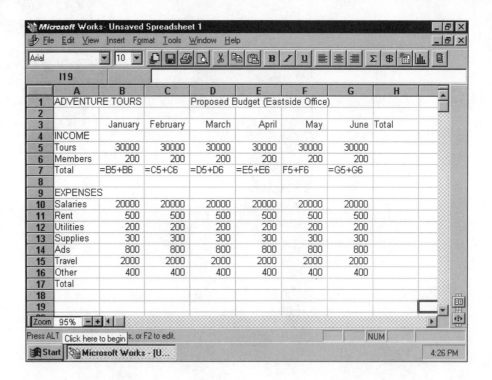

1. Select cell B7.

2. Type =B5+B6 and press (↵ ENTER).

3. Use the mouse and choose the Fill Right command and the mouse to copy the formula in cell B7 to cells C7 through G7 (see Figure 6.6).

4. Select cell C7.

Notice that the formula bar displays =C5+C6. Now complete the Total rows for the EXPENSES and PROFIT sections of the spreadsheet.

5. Select cell B17.

6. Click on Σ.

7. Click on the ✓ on the formula bar.

8. On your own, copy the function across the row.

9. Type PROFIT into cell A19.

10. Select cell B19.

11. Type =B7–B17 and press (↵ ENTER).

12. On your own, copy the formula across the row.

Now complete the Total column (column H).

13. Select cell H5.

14. Click on Σ to enter the SUM function.

15. Click on ✓ on the formula bar.

Copying information down a column of cells is the same as copying to cells across a row, except that you choose the Fill Down command from the Edit menu or, if using the mouse for the fill process, drag the pointer down the column.

16. Use the Fill Down command or the mouse to copy the function in cell H5 to cells H6 and H7.

17. On your own, total the Salaries row.

18. On your own, copy the formula to total the other expense categories.

19. On your own, total the PROFIT row.

The values in your spreadsheet should resemble those in Figure 6.1.

WORKING WITH ABSOLUTE CELL REFERENCES

As was mentioned earlier, when you copy a formula the cell references change relative to the formula's new location. Sometimes, however, you might not want the cell references to change, and this link may not be desirable. Consider, for example, column I in Figure 6.7, which shows the percentage that each expense category is of the total expenses. Salaries are budgeted at 82.64 percent of total expenses and ads at 3.31 percent. Figure 6.8 shows the formulas used to calculate these percentages. Notice that one cell reference in each formula, H17 remains the same for all the formulas. This is because H17 represents total expenses, which must be divided into each expense category to determine the budget percentage for each category. Therefore, when copying the formula, you do not want Works to change the H17 cell reference. Instead, you want cell H17 to be fixed in the formula as an **absolute cell reference**, that is, one that does not change when the formula is copied. To designate an absolute cell reference, you precede the column letter and row number by dollar signs ($) in the formula.

6.7

The percentage each expense category is of the total expenses

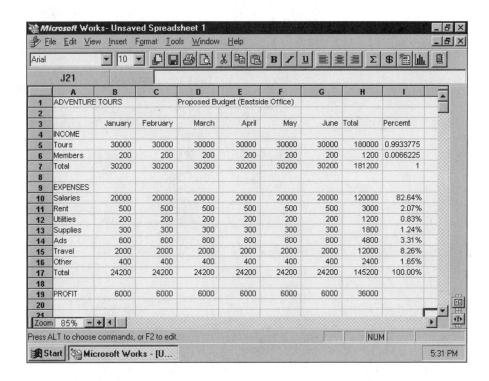

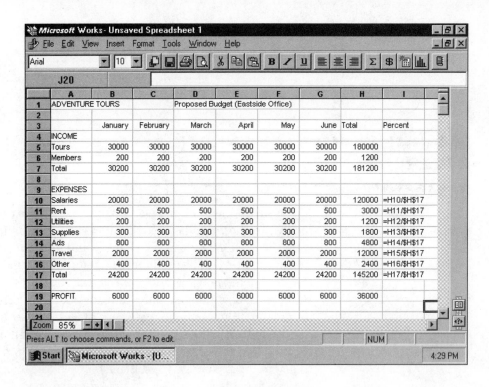

Before working with the formulas in column I, change the Zoom command to display more of the spreadsheet.

1. Click on the Zoom indicator on the bottom of the spreadsheet window.

2. Click on **C**ustom.

3. Type 85 in the **C**ustom text box.

4. Click on OK.

Now Column I is fully displayed.

5. Type Percent into cell I3.

6. Select cell I10.

7. Type =H10/$H$17 and press (↵ ENTER).

Notice that the result is displayed as a decimal, 0.8264463. Later you will learn how to change the display to a percentage.

8. Copy the formula through cell I17.

Now follow the same sequence of steps to calculate income percentages.

9. Select cell I5.

10. Type =H5/$H$7 and press (↵ ENTER).

11. Copy the formula through cell I7.

Again, notice that the formula is copied with relative cell references and an absolute cell reference.

FORMATTING ENTRIES AS PERCENTS

The formulas you have just entered display the results as decimals rather than percentages. If nothing else was done to the spreadsheet, the Percent column could be misleading or at least confusing. For example, the Salaries value in this column would be read as .8264463 percent. That is, less than 1 percent. The number should actually read 82.6446 percent. There are two ways to correct the display. First, you could change the formula by multiplying it by 100 (=H10/$H$17*100). Second, you could format the entry to display in percentage format. When you format an entry to display as a percentage, Works multiplies the entry by 100 and enters a percent sign (%) after the number. Figure 6.7 shows the results of formatting data in the Percent column as actual percentages. To do this, you select the cells to be formatted and use the Number command from the Format menu.

1. Select cells I10 through I17.

2. Choose Number from the Format menu.

3. Click on Percent.

4. Click on OK.

The numbers are displayed as percentages with two decimal places. It is important to understand that the value of the number has not changed: what has changed is how the number is displayed in the spreadsheet. Now format the other numbers.

5. Select cells I5 through I7.

6. On your own, format the cells to display percentages with two decimal places.

MOVING SPREADSHEET DATA

Works provides two methods to move spreadsheet data: cut-and-paste and drag-and-drop. The cut-and-paste process is similar to the copy-and-paste process. You select the desired data to move and choose the Cut command from the Edit menu or click on the Cut button ✄. The data is removed from the spreadsheet and placed on the Clipboard. Then you select the location to which you are moving the data and choose Paste from the Edit menu or click on 📋. The drag-and-drop process involves pointing to the border of the selected cell or cell range and dragging the pointer to the desired location. Try the drag-and-drop method by moving the words *Proposed Budget (Eastside Office)* to cell A2. (*Note:* To select the words, you do not need to select all the cells that the words appear in, only the cell the words are entered in.)

1. Click on cell D1.

2. Point to the bottom border of cell D1.

3. When the word "DRAG" appears, click and hold down the mouse button.

4. When the word "MOVE" appears beneath the pointer, drag the pointer to cell A2. Notice the box that moves along with the pointer.

5. Release the mouse button.

The selected text is moved to cell A2. Now save and print the spreadsheet.

6. Save the spreadsheet as *6 month budget.*

7. Print the spreadsheet.

PERFORMING A WHAT-IF ANALYSIS

The budget you have just developed forecasts Adventure Tours' profit for the next six months. If their income and expenditure projections are accurate, they will generate $36,000 in profits. However, the budget is based on the assumption that income and expenses will remain constant throughout the six months. This may be true for some items such as rent, but it is reasonable to assume that most items will vary. For example, income in June may be higher than the other months because more people travel during the summer. Therefore, the budget is best used as a model to perform a **what-if analysis**, a type of analysis that forecasts different outcomes according to different initial assumptions. For example, a what-if analysis can reveal how profits would be affected if income doubled in June or if advertising expenses increased by 10 percent in May. Because formulas have been used to establish relationships among cells, the results of any data changes you make are immediately displayed. Complete the following what-if scenarios, and note the effect of data changes on overall profits. Let's begin by asking "What would happen to profits if the income from tours doubled in June?"

1. Type 60000 **into cell G5.**

Notice how each of the two Totals and the Profit values changed. Now ask "What would happen if advertising expenses increased by 10 percent in May?" and examine the results.

2. Type 880 **into cell F14.**

What if salaries increased by 10 percent in June? This time use a formula to calculate the new number. Take the value in F10 (May salaries) and multiply it by 110 percent.

3. Select cell G10.

4. Type =F10*110% **and press** (↵ ENTER).

Each individual change you have made recalculates the profit.

In a what-if analysis you can make individual changes in the spreadsheet or you can make multiple changes at one time. For example, say Adventure Tours wants to know the result of increasing sales by 5 percent each month. One process for calculating this increase is to enter a formula for February and copy the formula for the other months. The formula for February would be the January value multiplied by 105 percent, the formula for March would be the February value multiplied by 105 percent, and so on. Practice this method now.

5. Select cell C5.

6. Type =B5*105% and press (↵ ENTER).

7. Copy the formula to March through June.

8. Click on D5.

Notice that the entry in the formula bar is =C5*105%. Each month there is a five percent increase in tours income over the previous month. Now any change in one month will be reflected in the subsequent months. Change January tours income to 40000.

9. Type 40000 into cell B5.

All the months are increased accordingly. Now suppose that, instead of a percentage increase each month, Adventure Tours decides that it would like to know the result of increasing the income from tours by a fixed amount ($1000) each month. Again, a formula could be entered and then copied. The formula for February would be the January amount plus 1000.

10. Select cell C5.

11. Type =B5+1000 and press (↵ ENTER).

12. Copy the formula to the other months (cells D5 through G5).

Now assume that Adventure Tours wants to see the results of increasing the members' income by 10 percent each month.

13. On your own, enter and copy the formula to calculate the members income based on a 10-percent increase each month.

Next assume that Adventure Tours wants to see the results of increasing the members' income by $50 each month.

14. On your own, enter and copy the formula to calculate the members income based on a $50 increase each month.

INSERTING ROWS AND COLUMNS

Works allows you to insert blank rows and columns to make room for additional data. Figure 6.9 shows a new expense category inserted at row 16 and a new month inserted at column H. To insert a row or column, you select the row or column and use the Insert Row or Insert Column command from the Insert menu. Complete the following steps to duplicate Figure 6.9:

1. Click on row heading 16 to select (highlight) the row.

2. Click on Insert in the menu bar.

3. Click on Insert Row.

A blank row is inserted at row 16. The data in the original row 16 has been moved to row 17, the data in row 17 moved to row 18, and so on.

6.9

The spreadsheet after
inserting a new row at 16
and a new column at H

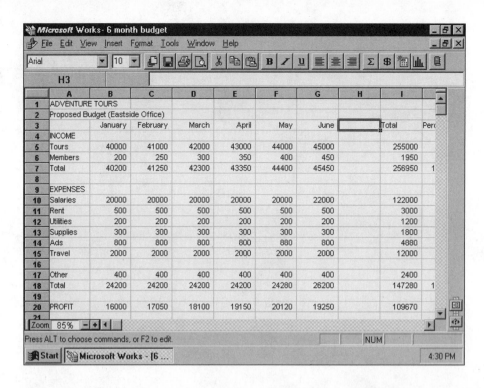

6.10

The 7 month
budget document

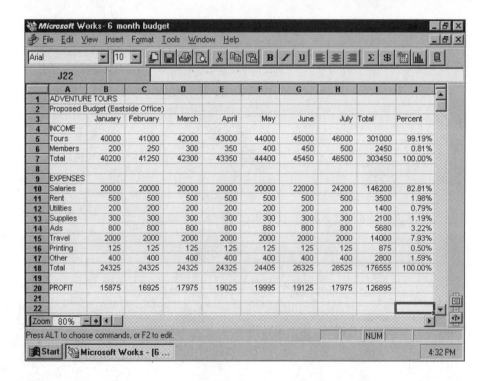

4. Click on column heading H to select the column.

5. Choose Insert Column from the Insert menu.

A blank column is inserted at column H. Your screen should resemble Figure 6.9. Now complete the column and row data entries.

6. Type July into cell H3.

7. Select cells G5 through G20.

8. Use the mouse to copy the information into cells H5 through H20.

9. Type Printing into cell A16.

10. Type 125 into cell B16.

11. Copy the value in cell B16 (125) to the other months (cells C16 through H16).

Because you have inserted a column (H) outside the range used to calculate the totals (B–G), you will need to reenter the function for the total column. First, change the Zoom to 80% to display the total and percent columns.

12. Click on the Zoom percentage and choose Custom from the menu that appears.

13. Type 80 and choose OK.

14. Select cell I5.

15. Click on Σ to recalculate the total income from tours.

16. Copy the function to total the other rows (cells I6 and I7; I10 through I18).

17. On your own, complete the percentage for the Printing expense category.

Your document should resemble Figure 6.10.

18. Save the document as *7 month budget*.

19. Close the document window.

This completes the section on inserting rows and columns.

KEY TERMS

absolute cell reference
Clipboard
copy and paste

cut and paste
drag and drop
fill

what-if analysis
zoom percentage

KEY COMMANDS

Copy
Custom
Fill Down

Fill Right
Fill Series
Insert Column

Insert Row
Number
Paste

REVIEW QUESTIONS

1. **T F** The Copy and Paste commands and the Fill commands are two methods used to copy data in a spreadsheet.

2. When using the drag-and-drop method to copy data, you use the _____ key.

3. A cell reference that does not change when a formula is copied is called a(n) _____ cell reference.

4. **T F** Formatting a number to display a percent sign automatically multiplies the number by 100.

5. **T F** Inserting rows and columns is done with the Insert Row and Insert Columns commands from the Insert menu.

PROJECTS

1. Adventure Tours wants to log the number of phone calls per hour it receives during one week. This information will help them decide whether they need to purchase a new phone system. Use the Works spreadsheet application to develop the following form. Use the Fill Series command to create the row and column labels. Use the SUM function or the AutoSum button to enter the total once, and then copy the formulas to the other cells. Include your name at the bottom of the document. Save the spreadsheet as *WKS Chapter 6 project 1*. Print the document with gridlines and with row and with column headings. Close the document.

PHONE CALLS RECEIVED:

	Mon	Tue	Wed	Thu	Fri	Sat	Total
9:00							0
10:00							0
11:00							0
12:00							0
1:00							0
2:00							0
3:00							0
4:00							0
Total	0	0	0	0	0	0	0

2. Adventure Tours will be installing a computerized tour information system called Computour. This system will use compact disks to provide electronic brochures of various tours. The monthly fee for updating the CDs is $100. Using the 6 month budget spreadsheet, insert a row above the Travel expense category and enter a new category, Computour. Enter the value 100 for January, and copy this value for the other months. Calculate the Total column and the Percent column. If needed, increase the column width for column A so that the heading, Computour, fits. Use the drag-and-drop method to move the heading, ADVENTURE TOURS, to column C and to move the subheading, Proposed Budget (Eastside Office), to column F. Include your name at the bottom of the document. Save the spreadsheet as *WKS Chapter 6 project 2*. Print the document with gridlines and with row and column headings. Close the document.

3. Below is the proposed budget for Adventure Tours' downtown office. Develop a spreadsheet using this information. Use the Fill Series process for entering the month headings, and use the various copy processes for entering the numerical data. Complete the total and profit rows and the total and percent columns on your own. Use formulas and functions for all calculations. Include your name at the bottom of the document. Save the spreadsheet as *WKS Chapter 6 project 3*. Print the document with gridlines and with row and column headings. Close the document.

ADVENTURE TOURS

Proposed Budget (Downtown Office)

	Jan	Feb	Mar	Apr	May	Jun	Total	Percent
INCOME								
Tours	40000		40000		40000		40000	40000
Members		250	250	250	250	250	250	
Total								
EXPENSES								
Salaries			30000	30000		30000	30000	30000
Rent	600	600	600	600	600	600		
Utilities	220	220	220	220	220	220		
Supplies		400	400	400	400	400	400	
Ads	1000	1000	1000	1000	1000	1000		
Travel	2500	2500	2500	2500	2500	2500		
Other	400	400	400	400	400	400		
Total								
PROFIT								

4. Below is an analysis of Adventure Tours' actual and forecasted income, expenses, and profit for 1997. Duplicate this spreadsheet. The % Difference column is calculated by dividing the Difference amount by the Actual amount. Format the percents to display two decimal places. Use formulas and functions for all calculations. Include your name at the bottom of the document. Save the spreadsheet as *WKS Chapter 6 project 4*. Print the document with gridlines and with row and column headings. Close the document.

COMPARISON OF ACTUAL AND FORECASTED NUMBERS FOR 1997

	1997 (Actual)	Difference	1997 (Forecast)	% Difference (Act-For)
Income	450,000	400,000	50,000	11.11%
Expenses	420,000	375,000	45,000	10.71%
Profit	30,000	25,000	5,000	16.67%

7

Viewing, Enhancing, and Linking Spreadsheets

IN THIS CHAPTER YOU WILL LEARN HOW TO:

- Center a heading across several columns
- Align data within cells
- Create borders and patterns
- Change fonts, font sizes, and type styles
- Use AutoFormat
- View different parts of a large worksheet
- Change margins
- Select an area of a worksheet to print
- Hide cells from view
- Link spreadsheet data and a chart with a word processing document

In this chapter, you will learn how to make changes in a spreadsheet to enhance its appearance. Works allows you to make several types of changes to make a document easier to read and more interesting to view, as well as to draw the reader's attention to specific parts of the document. Figure 7.1 shows the Adventure Tours budget document after the following changes have been made:

- The heading, ADVENTURE TOURS, has been centered across the spreadsheet and changed to a different font and size.

- The subheading, *Proposed Budget (Eastside Office),* has been centered across the spreadsheet and formatted in italic type.

- The column headings have been right aligned within the cells.

- The words *Total* are centered in the cells.

- The spreadsheet has a single-line border around it.

- The column headings have a double-line border around them.

- The overall profit has a thick-line border around it.

- The Total rows have a single line above them.

- The PROFIT row has a double line above it.

- The column headings have a dotted pattern within the border.

- The words *INCOME, EXPENSES*, and *PROFIT* are in bold type.

- The numbers are formatted to display commas.

- The gridlines have been removed from the spreadsheet.

In this chapter, you will practice making these and other formatting changes to an Adventure Tours budget document.

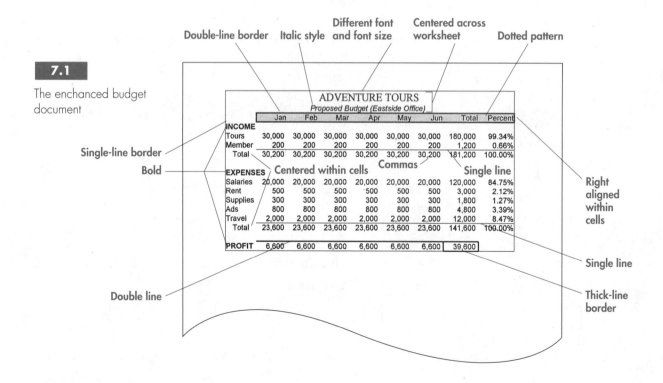

7.1

The enchanced budget document

ALIGNING DATA IN THE SPREADSHEET

Start by opening the new budget spreadsheet called Budget 6 month. This spreadsheet is similar to the 7 month budget spreadsheet you created in Chapter 6.

1. **Start Works.**

2. **Open** *Budget 6 month.*

3. **Click on** 🔲.

To view the entire document onscreen, change the Zoom to 85%.

4. **Click on the Zoom percentage box.**

5. **Choose C̲ustom.**

6. **Type** 85 **and click on OK.**

The entire spreadsheet should be displayed onscreen. Works allows you to align data within cells and across cells. Data can be right, left, or center aligned within a cell and center aligned across cells. The default setting for text entries is left aligned, and the default setting for numeric entries is right aligned. You can change the alignment by selecting the desired cells and choosing one of the alignment buttons on the toolbar (see Figure 7.2) or by choosing the Alignment command from the Format menu.

Figure 7.2 shows the heading and subheading centered across the spreadsheet. To center an entry across cells, you must use the Alignment command. In this case you will center the words ADVENTURE TOURS across cells A1 through I1.

7. **Select cells A1 through I1.**

8. **Choose A̲lignment from the Fo̲rmat menu.**

7.2

The alignment buttons

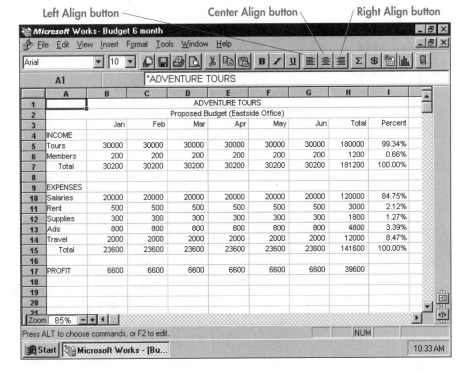

The Format Cells dialog box appears with the Alignment index tab displayed. The Alignment options apply to horizontal alignment of text and vertical alignment. The **Center across selection** option is part of the horizontal alignment options.

9. Click on Center across selection.

10. Click on OK.

It is important to understand that the heading, ADVENTURE TOURS, is still located only in cell A1, although it displays in other cells as well. To check this, select cell D1.

11. Click on D1.

Notice that the formula bar is empty, indicating there is no entry in this cell.

12. Click on A1.

Notice that the formula bar displays "ADVENTURE TOURS."

13. On your own, center *Proposed Budget (Eastside Office)* across the spreadsheet.

Next you will right-align the column headings using the Right Align button.

14. Select B3 through I3.

15. Click on ▤.

Now center (within the cell, not across cells) the word *Total*.

16. Select A7.

17. Click on ▤.

18. On your own, center-align the word *Total* in cell A15.

This completes the section on aligning data. Remember, you can center-align data across several cells, and you can center, right-align, and left-align data within a cell. You can align numbers as well as text.

WORKING WITH BORDERS AND LINES

Works allows you to format any cell or cells to display borders or lines. Figure 7.3 shows the use of several types of borders, which we outline here:

- Single-line border completely surrounding the spreadsheet
- Double-line border around the column headings
- Thick-line border around the overall profit
- Single lines above the Total rows
- Double line above the PROFIT row

These **borders** (or outlines) and **lines** are created using the Border command from the Format menu. Before duplicating Figure 7.3, you need to turn off the display of the gridlines. This will make it easier for you to see the borders you create.

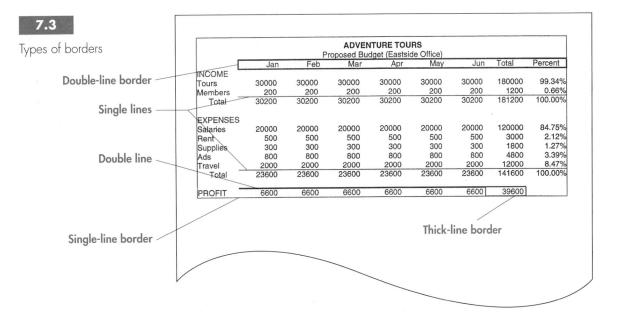

Double-line border

Single lines

Double line

Single-line border

Thick-line border

1. Choose <u>G</u>ridlines from the <u>V</u>iew menu.

The gridlines are removed from the display. It is important to understand that this change affects only the display on the monitor and not the printout. To specify not to print gridlines, you use the Page Setup command in the File menu.

2. Choose Page Setup from the <u>F</u>ile menu.

3. Click on the <u>O</u>ther Options index tab.

4. Click in the Print <u>g</u>ridlines check box to turn off this option.

5. Choose OK.

Now insert the borders and lines. Start with the border around the entire spreadsheet. The first step is to select the cells.

6. Select cells A1 through I17.

7. Choose <u>B</u>order from the Fo<u>r</u>mat menu.

The Format Cells dialog box appears with the Border index tab displayed. The Outline option under Border places a border around the entire selected cell or cell range. The other options place a line at the top, bottom, left, or right of the selected cell or cell range. In the Line Style box you can choose from dotted, dashed, thin, thick, single, and double lines. Currently, the single thin line is selected as indicated by the darkened border around that style. You need to select Outline so a border will appear around the entire cell range (A1 through I17).

8. Click inside the box next to the word <u>O</u>utline.

Your screen should resemble Figure 7.4.

9. Click on OK.

The border is inserted in the spreadsheet. It is difficult to see the border because the cells are still highlighted.

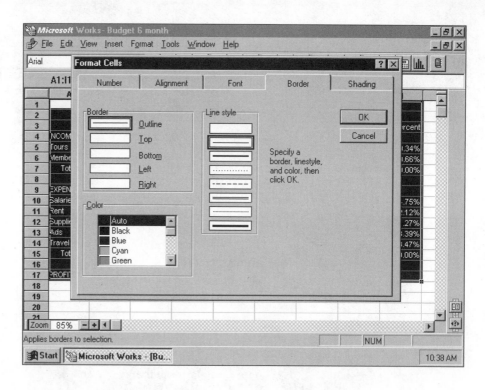

10. Click on cell A1 to remove the highlighting from the other cells.

Now preview the document to see how it will print.

11. Click on 🔍.

The document appears with the border. (*Note*: The entire border may not display.) Next, insert a double-line border around the column headings.

12. Click on Cancel to return to the spreadsheet.

13. Select cells B3 through I3.

14. Choose Border from the Format menu.

15. Click on the double-line style to select it.

16. Verify that the double line is displayed in the Outline box.

17. Click on OK.

18. Preview the document.

19. Return to the spreadsheet.

Next insert a thick-line border around the overall profit number in cell H17.

20. On your own, insert a thick-line border around the overall profit total. (*Hint*: Choose the thick line in the Border dialog box.)

21. Preview the document.

Use the Zoom feature to view the profit number.

22. **Point to the profit total and click the mouse button.**

The area surrounding the pointer is enlarged, and you can see the thick border.

23. **Return to the spreadsheet.**

The last border lines you will insert are those above the total and profit rows. Notice (in Figure 7.3) that these are not outline borders but rather single or double lines that appear above the selected rows. Start with the income Total row.

24. **Select cells B7 through I7.**

25. **Choose Border from the Format menu.**

26. **Click inside the box labeled Top box (indicating that the line will go on top of the selected cells).**

27. **Click on OK.**

Now complete the expenses Total row border.

28. **On your own, insert the line on top of the expenses Total row.**

Next, add a line above the PROFIT row. The line will extend only to G17, because H17 already has a border.

29. **Select cells B17 through G17.**

30. **On your own, display the Border tab in the Format Cells dialog box.**

Notice that there is a bottom line indicated for the selected cells. This is because row 17 is the bottom row of the spreadsheet, and the spreadsheet has a border around the outside. Continue by specifying a line above the selected row.

31. **Click in the Top box.**

32. **Click on OK.**

If you change your mind about a border, you can remove the border by clearing the border line options in the dialog box. For example, if you want to remove the line on top of the PROFIT row, you highlight the row, click on the blank line style, then click on the Top option in the dialog box. Do this now.

33. **With cells B17 through G17 highlighted, choose Border from the Format menu.**

34. **Click in the blank box under Line style.**

35. **Click twice inside the Top box and choose OK. (*Note*: the Top box should be clear before choosing OK.)**

36. **Preview the document and return to the spreadsheet.**

Continue by reinserting the top line for the PROFIT row. But this time make it a double line.

37. **On your own, insert a double line on top of the PROFIT row.**

38. **Preview the document.**

39. **View the changes and return to the spreadsheet.**

Chapter 7   *Viewing, Enhancing, and Linking Spreadsheets*   WK**139**

WORKING WITH PATTERNS

Works allows you to insert a **pattern** that gives a shading effect to parts of the spreadsheet. You might add a pattern to a portion of a spreadsheet to call attention to an important area or to make column headings stand out. Patterns can make your document more readable, but you should use them judiciously. Figure 7.5 shows the column headings formatted with a pattern. The pattern helps draw the reader's eyes to the headings, which provide context for the columns of data. To insert a pattern, select the cell or cell range and choose the Shading command from the Format menu.

1. Select cells B3 through I3.

2. Choose Shading from the Format menu.

The Format Cells dialog box appears with the Shading index tab displayed.

3. Use the scroll bar arrows to scroll through the Pattern list box and view the options.

4. Click on the pattern with the fewest dots.

Notice that the Sample box displays the selected pattern.

5. Click on OK.

The pattern is inserted in the selected cells.

6. On your own, insert a pattern in cell H17, the overall profit total.

To remove a pattern, you choose None in the Pattern list box.

7. On your own, remove the pattern from cell H17.

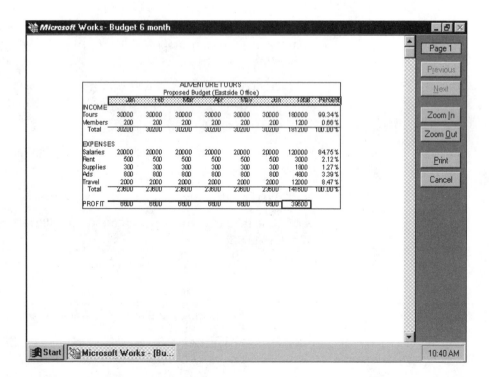

7.5

The print preview screen displaying the cells formatted with a pattern

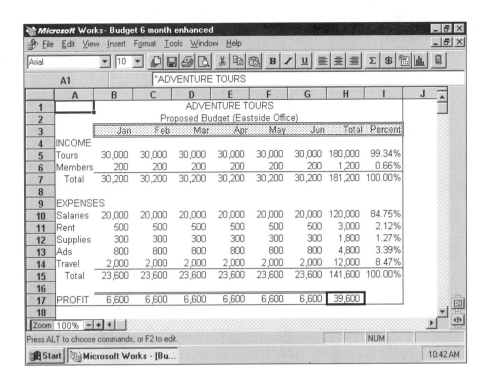

In Chapter 6 you learned how to format numbers to display commas, dollar signs, decimal places, and so on. Now change the number formatting to include commas as shown in Figure 7.6.

8. Select cells B5 through H17.

9. Choose **Number** from the **Format** menu.

10. Click on **Comma**.

11. Change the number of decimal places to 0.

12. Click on **OK**.

Before continuing, save the document.

13. Save the document as *Budget 6 month enhanced*.

CHANGING FONTS AND FONT SIZES

A **font** is a type design. Fonts vary from plain to fancy, and they are selected according to their use in a document. For instance, a heading may be formatted in a larger and more eye-catching font than the document's body text. Fonts generally add variety to the appearance of a document and can even give it character. For example, Figure 7.7 shows the effect of changing the heading ADVENTURE TOURS to a more distinctive font and font size. However, use restraint when selecting fonts—too many different fonts in one document can be distracting for the reader. You change the font using the Font and Style command. First select the heading.

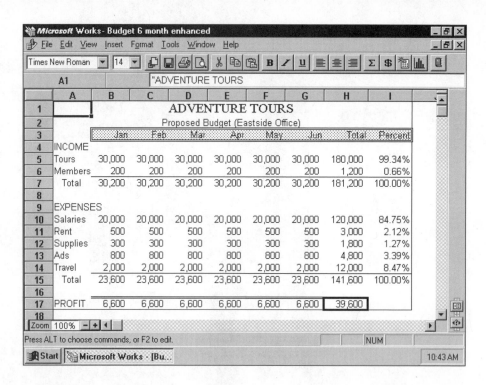

1. **Select cell A1.**
2. **Choose Font and Style from the Format menu.**

The Font tab of the Format Cells dialog box appears. You will use the dialog box to change the font to Times New Roman and the font size to 14. Figure 7.8 shows the completed dialog box. Start by scrolling the Font list to display Times New Roman.

3. **Point to ▼ in the Font list scroll bar (see Figure 7.8).**

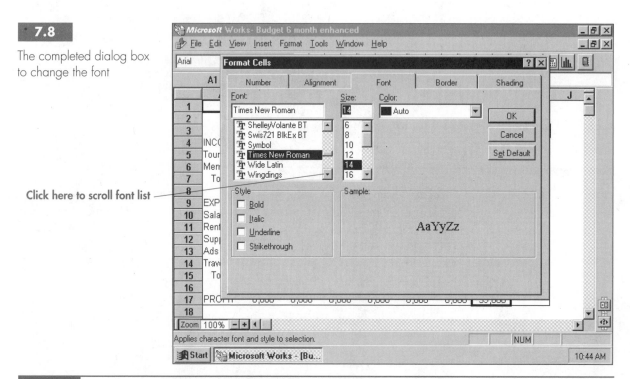

4. Hold down the mouse button to scroll the list until Times New Roman appears. (*Note:* If Times New Roman is not available, choose another font.)

5. Click on Times New Roman to select it.

6. Type 14 in the <u>S</u>ize box to change the font size to 14.

Your screen should resemble Figure 7.8. Notice that the Sample box shows how the text will appear using the selected font and font size.

7. Click on OK to leave the dialog box.

The heading is changed to the new font and font size.

CHANGING TYPE STYLES

Type styles, such as **bold** and *italic,* affect the way characters appear and are printed. They are useful for adding emphasis and drawing the reader's attention to a particular part of the document. Figure 7.9 shows the document with the following type style changes:

The subheading, *Proposed Budget (Eastside Office),* is in italic type.

The section labels INCOME, EXPENSES, and PROFIT are in bold type.

The Bold **B** and Italic *I* buttons on the Formatting toolbar are used to change type styles.

1. Click on cell A2 to select the subheading.

2. Click on *I* (see Figure 7.9).

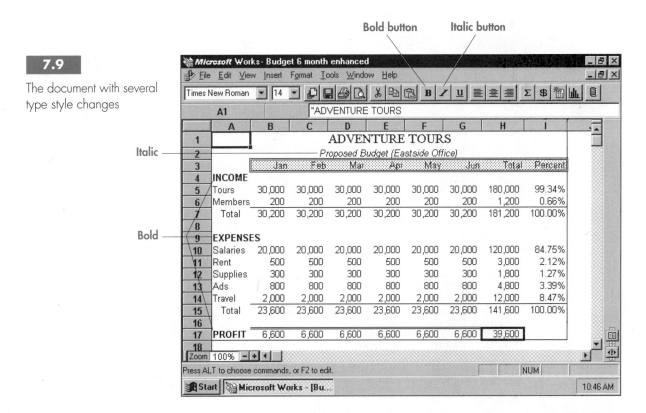

7.9

The document with several type style changes

3. Click on cell A4 to select *INCOME*.

4. Click on 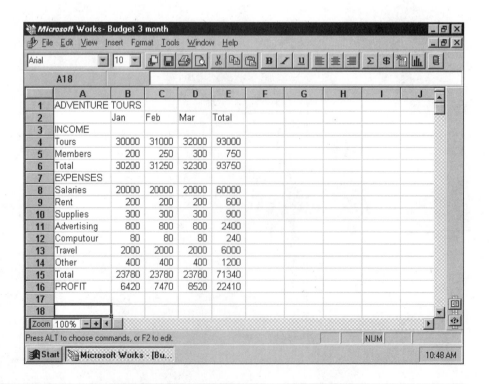 (see Figure 7.9).

5. On your own, change EXPENSES and PROFIT to bold type.

(*Note:* To turn off bold or italic, you select the cell with the formatted text and click on the button again.)

This completes the section on changing type styles.

6. Save the spreadsheet as *Budget 6 month completed*.

7. Close the document.

USING AUTOFORMAT

The features you have learned thus far give you many ways to change the appearance of a spreadsheet. If you are in a hurry to format a spreadsheet, you may want to take advantage of the AutoFormat feature in Works. With **AutoFormat** you can quickly enhance the appearance of a spreadsheet document by choosing from a list of formats. To use AutoFormat, simply select the block of cells to which you want to apply the format and then choose the AutoFormat command from the Format menu. A dialog box appears with a list of formats. You can choose a format and view an example before applying the format to your spreadsheet.

To practice using the AutoFormat feature, you will use a spreadsheet called Budget 3 month. Figure 7.10 shows the spreadsheet without any formatting; that is, all of the default settings for font, font size, type style, and alignment were used. Figure 7.11 shows the same spreadsheet after applying an AutoFormat option.

7.10

The Budget 3 month spreadsheet using default format settings

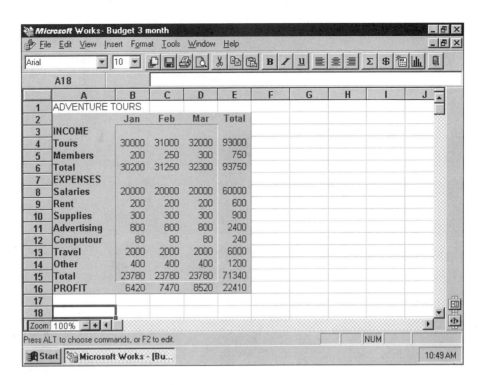

1. Open *Budget 3 month* and maximize the document window.

2. Use the View menu to turn off the view of the gridlines.

3. Select cells A2 through E16 (do not select row 1).

4. Choose AutoFormat from the Format menu.

Figure 7.12 shows the AutoFormat dialog box that appears. A list of formats is displayed in the upper-left corner of the dialog box. An example of the high-lighted format, Plain, is also displayed. To choose a different format for the spreadsheet you click on the desired format.

5. Click on Classic Rule.

6. Click on OK.

7. Click on cell G1 to remove the highlight from the block.

The spreadsheet appears with the formatting changes. It is important to understand that even if you use AutoFormat to make changes to part of your document, you can still make changes to other parts using the processes you have learned in this book. For example, if you wanted to add dollar signs, you could highlight the desired cells and change the numeric format. In addition, you can use the Undo command to undo this format and then select another. Try using the Undo command now.

8. Choose Undo Format from the Edit menu.

9. Highlight cells A2 through E16.

10. Choose AutoFormat from the Format menu.

Now take a moment to view the other formats.

11. Click on each format to select it and view the sample.

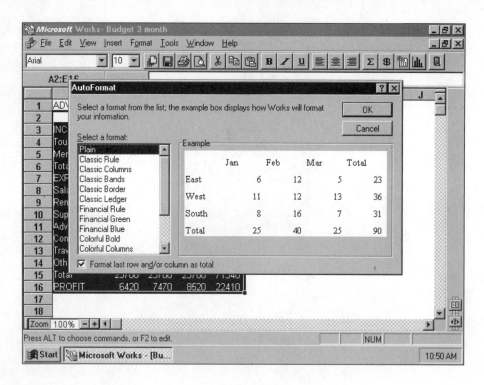

12. When done viewing each format, click on the 3D Effects 1 format.

13. Click on OK.

14. Click on cell G1 to remove the highlight.

15. Save the spreadsheet as *Budget 3 month formatted.*

16. Print the spreadsheet.

17. Close the spreadsheet.

This completes the section on formatting your spreadsheet.

WORKING WITH LARGE SPREADSHEETS

Until now you have been working primarily with relatively small spreadsheets, that is, those that will fit on the screen and that print on a single sheet of paper. When you work with large spreadsheets, you need to know how to change the view so that more of the spreadsheet appears onscreen. You also need to know how to manipulate the spreadsheet to print more of the spreadsheet on one page of paper.

Viewing Different Parts of a Spreadsheet

Figure 7.13 shows the screen view of a large spreadsheet, Budget 12 month. This document is a twelve-month budget for Adventure Tours. Notice that only columns A through H and rows 1 through 17 are fully displayed. You have been using the Zoom percentage box to change the screen display. You will now use the Zoom command to view more rows and columns of a spreadsheet.

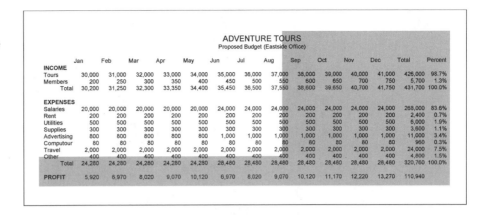

ADVENTURE TOURS
Proposed Budget (Eastside Office)

	Jan	Feb	Mar	Apr	May	Jun	Jul	Aug	Sep	Oct	Nov	Dec	Total	Percent
INCOME														
Tours	30,000	31,000	32,000	33,000	34,000	35,000	36,000	37,000	38,000	39,000	40,000	41,000	426,000	98.7%
Members	200	250	300	350	400	450	500	550	600	650	700	750	5,700	1.3%
Total	30,200	31,250	32,300	33,350	34,400	35,450	36,500	37,550	38,600	39,650	40,700	41,750	431,700	100.0%
EXPENSES														
Salaries	20,000	20,000	20,000	20,000	20,000	24,000	24,000	24,000	24,000	24,000	24,000	24,000	268,000	83.6%
Rent	200	200	200	200	200	200	200	200	200	200	200	200	2,400	0.7%
Utilities	500	500	500	500	500	500	500	500	500	500	500	500	6,000	1.9%
Supplies	300	300	300	300	300	300	300	300	300	300	300	300	3,600	1.1%
Advertising	800	800	800	800	800	1,000	1,000	1,000	1,000	1,000	1,000	1,000	11,000	3.4%
Computour	80	80	80	80	80	80	80	80	80	80	80	80	960	0.3%
Travel	2,000	2,000	2,000	2,000	2,000	2,000	2,000	2,000	2,000	2,000	2,000	2,000	24,000	7.5%
Other	400	400	400	400	400	400	400	400	400	400	400	400	4,800	1.5%
Total	24,280	24,280	24,280	24,280	24,280	28,480	28,480	28,480	28,480	28,480	28,480	28,480	320,760	100.0%
PROFIT	5,920	6,970	8,020	9,070	10,120	6,970	8,020	9,070	10,120	11,170	12,220	13,270	110,940	

1. **Open** *Budget 12.*

The Zoom command from the View menu works like the Zoom percentage on the horizontal scroll bar. Using the Zoom command, you can specify how much to reduce the size of the entries. Figure 7.14 shows the zoom reduced so the entire spreadsheet is in view.

2. **If necessary, maximize the document window.**

3. **Choose** **Zoom** **from the View menu.**

The Zoom dialog box appears, allowing you to select from several different magnifications. The 100% option is the current view and can be selected if you want to return to this view. The 200% option doubles the size of the spreadsheet, the 75% option reduces the spreadsheet to three-quarters of its original size, and so on. The Custom option allows you to specify any percentage.

4. **Click on** **75.**

5. **Click on OK.**

Almost the entire spreadsheet is displayed using this view.

6. Choose <u>Z</u>oom from the <u>V</u>iew menu.

7. Double-click on <u>5</u>0.

Now the entire spreadsheet is displayed. However, the numbers are somewhat difficult to read. The blank columns at the right of the spreadsheet indicate that there is room to increase the spreadsheet size and still fit it on the screen. Therefore, adjust the magnification to 59%.

8. Choose <u>Z</u>oom from the <u>V</u>iew menu.

9. Type 59

10. Click on OK.

Again, all the data is displayed, filling the entire width of the screen. Remember, you have changed only how the spreadsheet displays, not how it will print. It will print in the size shown in the 100% view. Now return the view to 100%.

11. On your own, use the Zoom dialog box to return the view to 100%.

As you have just seen, changing the magnification is a way to view different parts of a large spreadsheet. However, as you reduce the magnification, the size of the entries are reduced, and the document becomes harder to read. Another way to view a large spreadsheet, which doesn't affect the on-screen size of its entries, is to split it.

Splitting a Spreadsheet

Suppose you want to see the effect on total expenses of increasing the travel expense in March to $4,500. The total expenses are located in column N, and the March expenses are in column D. Using the 100% view (with the standard character size and column width), you cannot view both of these columns at one time. However, by splitting the spreadsheet you can view two different parts of the spreadsheet at the same time. It is like having two monitors viewing the same spreadsheet. Figure 7.15 shows the spreadsheet after splitting it at column D. Notice that columns A through D are displayed at the left of the split, and columns D through I at the right of the split. The column where the split occurs appears in *both* views. You can scroll each side independently of the other. Figure 7.16 shows the right side scrolled to display columns N and O. With this view you could make a change in the March numbers and see the effect on the totals. To split a spreadsheet, you choose the **Split command** from the Window menu. Complete the following steps to split the Budget 12 month spreadsheet.

1. Change the zoom to 90% so the Total expenses row (Row 19) is displayed.

2. Choose Split from the <u>W</u>indow menu.

A horizontal and vertical line appear. The horizontal line allows you to split the spreadsheet by rows whereas the vertical line allows you to split the spreadsheet by columns. In this case you want to split the spreadsheet at row D.

7.15

The spreadsheet after splitting it at column D

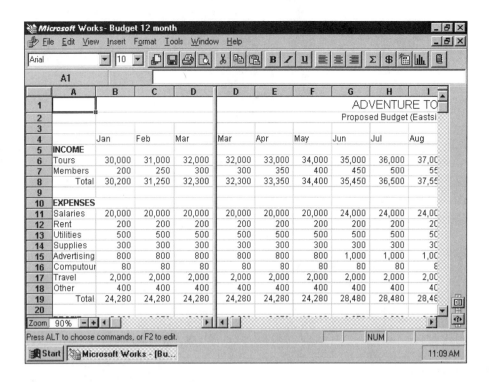

7.16

The right side scrolled to display columns N and O

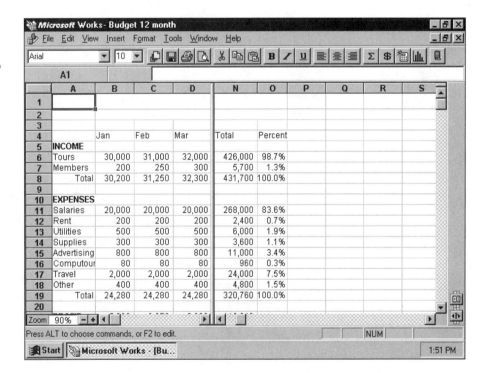

3. Drag the lines to the top of the spreadsheet by positioning the mouse pointer at the top of the spreadsheet between columns D and E, as shown in Figure 7.17.

4. Click the mouse button to split the spreadsheet.

The spreadsheet is split into two parts. You can move between the two parts by selecting cells in each one, and you can scroll each part separately from the other. Currently, the left side is selected. Click on a cell in the right side and use the →̇ key to scroll this side of the split.

Horizontal line

Place pointer here

Vertical line

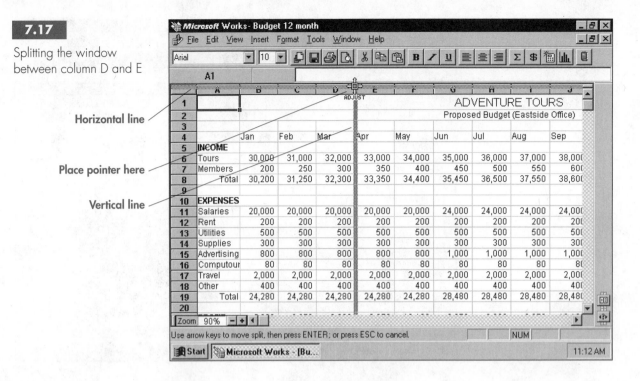

5. Click on cell E1.

6. Press ⟶ ten times to bring the Total and Percent columns into view.

Notice that the right side of the split spreadsheet scrolls while the left side remains unchanged. Now scroll the right side until the Total column (N) is next to the March column (D).

7. Press ⟶ until column N is next to Column D.

Your screen should resemble Figure 7.16. With this view you can make a change in the travel expense for March and see the effect on the total expenses. Note the current total expenses in cell N19, 320,760.

8. Click on cell D17 (March travel expense).

9. Type 4500 and press ⟵ ENTER.

The total expenses change to 323,260.

10. On your own, change the advertising expense for February to 1200. Notice the change in the total expenses.

To remove the split, you drag the line to the row headings at the left side of the spreadsheet.

11. Point to the line.

12. Hold the mouse button down and drag the line to the row headings (see Figure 7.18.)

13. Release the mouse button.

14. Press HOME.

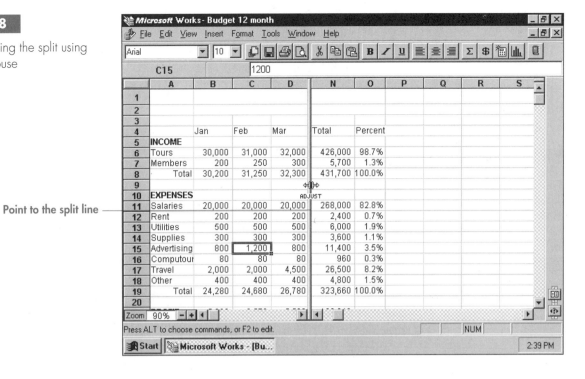

Point to the split line ———

Printing a Part of the Spreadsheet

There are many reasons why you might want to print only portions of a large spreadsheet. For instance, you might want to review only one quarter's income, or only the last six month's expenses. Figure 7.19 shows a printout of Adventure Tours' income data for the first seven months of the current year. To print only a portion of a spreadsheet, you highlight the desired cells and choose the Set Print Area command from the Format menu. First you need to select the desired area.

1. Select cells A4 through H8.

2. Choose Set Print Area from the Format menu.

A Print Area message appears, stating that Works will only print the high-lighted cells.

3. Read the message that appears.

4. Click on OK.

5. Click on to see how the selected area will print.

6. When done viewing, return to the spreadsheet.

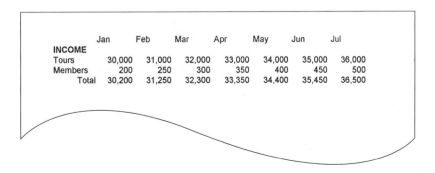

Now set the print area to include the entire spreadsheet.

7. **Select cells A1 through O21.**

8. **Choose Set Print Area from the Format menu.**

9. **Click on OK when the Print Area message appears.**

PRINTING NONADJACENT COLUMNS AND ROWS

Sometimes you might want to print portions of a large spreadsheet that are not adjacent. To do this, Works allows you to **hide cells** from view. Suppose you want to print only the Total and Percent columns of the Adventure Tours spreadsheet. To make those columns meaningful, you will also need to print column A, which contains the row labels. To accomplish this, you would need to hide columns B through M. Figure 7.20 shows the Adventure Tours spreadsheet after hiding columns B through M. To hide columns or rows, you select the desired columns (or rows) and set the column (or row) width to zero. Practice this technique by hiding columns.

1. **Point to and click on the column heading B.**

2. **Holding down the mouse button, drag the pointer to select columns B through M.**

3. **Choose Column Width from the Format menu.**

7.20

The spreadsheet after hiding columns B through M

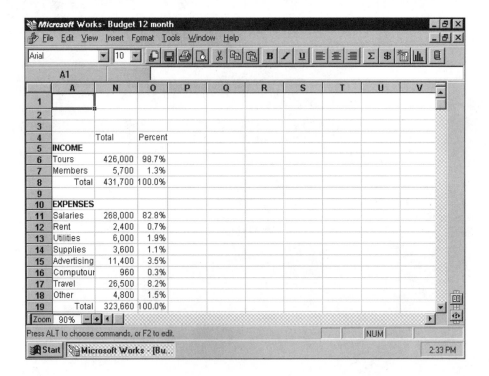

4. Type 0

5. Click on OK.

6. Press (HOME).

The spreadsheet appears with the selected columns hidden. You can also print the spreadsheet this way. Now view how the spreadsheet will print.

7. Click on .

8. After viewing the document, return to the spreadsheet.

To redisplay the hidden columns, you simply widen them. To widen all the hidden columns at once, you can select the entire spreadsheet.

9. Choose Select All from the Edit menu.

10. Choose Column Width from the Format menu.

11. With the column width set to 10, click on OK.

The columns reappear.

12. Close the spreadsheet without saving the changes.

LINKING DOCUMENTS AND OBJECTS WITHIN DOCUMENTS

Microsoft Works 4.0 allows you to transfer information from one document to another. One way to transfer information would be to use the copy and paste commands. This process could be used to copy information from a word processing document to another word processing document, or from a spreadsheet document to a word processing document. Another way to add information from one document to another is through **linking**. For example, you could link the information in a spreadsheet to a word processing document. The advantage of linking is that any change in the spreadsheet data would automatically be reflected in the word processing document.

Figure 7.21 shows a word processing document with data from a spreadsheet added to the document. To practice linking documents, you will duplicate this document and then make changes in the spreadsheet to see how the word processing document is automatically updated. Start by opening the two documents, Newsletter, and Travel industry expenditures.

1. Open the word processing document named *Newsletter*.

2. Open the spreadsheet named *Travel industry expenditures*.

Before you can add the spreadsheet data to the word processing document, you must identify the range of cells that are to be linked. This is done by selecting the cells and specifying a range name.

7.21

A word processing
document with data
added from a
spreadsheet document

ADVENTURE TOURS

TRAVEL INDUSTRY SHOWS STEADY INCREASE

As shown by Figure 1, the travel industry has enjoyed a steady increase over the last few years. Many reasons have been given for this increase. First, our economy has been on an overall upward trend for the past five years. The unemployment rate has been decreasing, and discretionary income has increased an average of 3% for the last four years. Second, the cost of travel has actually decreased. Led by the decline of oil prices, fuel costs have declined, which, in turn, allows airlines to decrease fares. Third, people have become more interested in exotic tours as their income has risen and remote locations have become accessible.

Travel Industry Expenditures				
	(in millions)			
1991	1992	1993	1994	1995
4,500	5,200	5,700	6,100	6,600

NEW MANAGER

Joanne Terry will be the manager of our new office in Gillman Village. Joanne has been with Adventure Tours for three years, the last two years as assistant manager in the North Seattle office. While Joanne has traveled extensively, she has focused on the Far East. After graduating from the University of Washington in International Studies, she spent two years in Malaysia as a Peace Corps volunteer. She is fluent in the Malaysian language, as well as Chinese. Joanne has led several tours, including to the base camps at Mt. Everest and K2. Each year she leads our staff on the annual Mt. Rainier climb. We feel very fortunate that Joanne will be managing our newest office.

TRAVEL TIP OF THE MONTH

Nothing is more annoying than arriving at your destination after a very long plane flight and being too tired to start enjoying your trip. Therefore, here are a few tips to help prevent jet lag: (1) Don't overeat or drink any alcohol on the flight; (2) start adjusting your sleep schedule several days before the flight.

GRAND OPENING OF NEW OFFICE

We are proud to announce the opening of our new office in the Gillman Village Business Park in Issaquah. This office is designed to serve the needs of our growing Eastside clientele. There will be an open house at 6:00pm on November 12th. Refreshments will be served, and door prizes, including an all-expense trip to Lhasa, Tibet, will be given away. Please join us to celebrate the opening of this new office.

3. Select cells B1 through F4.

4. Choose Range Name from the Insert menu.

The Range Name dialog box appears, allowing you to enter a name for the cell range.

5. Type Growth

6. Click on OK.

Now display the Newsletter document and insert the data from the spreadsheet.

7. Choose *Newsletter* from the Window menu.

8. Point to the line below the first paragraph of the document and click the mouse button to display the insertion point.

9. Choose Spreadsheet from the Insert menu.

The Insert Spreadsheet dialog box appears with the open spreadsheets listed. Once you choose a spreadsheet from the list, the range names for the selected spreadsheet will be displayed in the second list box.

10. Click on Travel industry expenditures.wks to select that spreadsheet.

11. Click on Growth (B1:F4) to select that range.

12. Click on OK.

The spreadsheet data is inserted into the document.

WORKING WITH LINKED OBJECTS

Linked data, such as a spreadsheet that has been inserted into a word processing document, is considered an **object**. The object can be moved, resized, edited, and deleted. In order to perform any of these operations, the object must be selected. An object is selected by placing the mouse pointer in the center of the object and clicking once. When an object is selected, boxes appear along the edges of the object. These boxes are called **handles**. The handles verify that the object has been selected, and they are also used to resize the object. Once an object is selected, it can be moved by placing the mouse pointer in the center of the object, holding the left mouse button and dragging the pointer to a new location. A selected object can be deleted by pressing (DELETE) on the keyboard or clicking on ✂.

Editing an object requires running the application that was used to create the object and displaying the object in the application window. Because the data is linked to the original application used to create it, you can run the application by double-clicking on the object. The action of double-clicking will start the application and display the object in the application window. When two different Works documents are linked, double-clicking on the object will display the data in the appropriate window and provide the appropriate menu and toolbar options for editing the object. Once the editing is complete, the original document can be saved and closed and the changes will appear in the linked object.

In this section you will work with objects. Start by moving the object down the page.

1. If necessary, click once on the object to select it.

Notice the sizing handles that appear, indicating that the object has been selected (see Figure 7.22). With the object selected, you can move the object up or down by dragging it. You point to the selected object and drag the pointer to the desired location; as shown in Figure 7.23.

2. Scroll the document so the spreadsheet and the blank area beneath the New Manager paragraph are both displayed.

3. Point to the middle of the object.

4. When the word "DRAG" appears, hold down the mouse button and drag the pointer to the position shown in Figure 7.23.

(*Note*: The word "DRAG" will change to "MOVE" as you reposition the object.)

5. Release the mouse button.

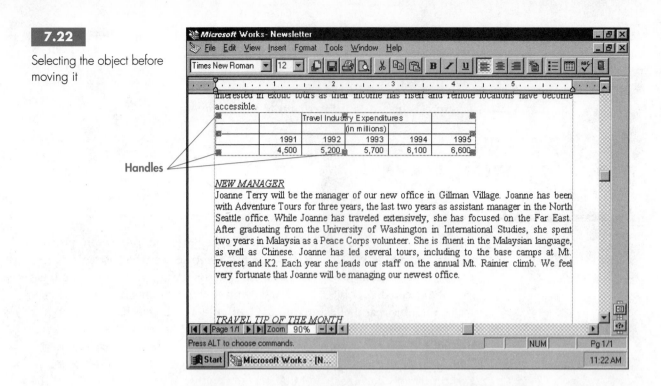

Handles

7.23

Dragging the object to a
new location in the
document

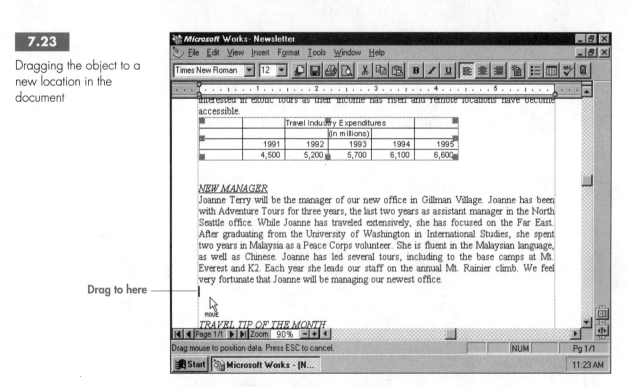

Drag to here

If you make a mistake while moving the object, or want to return the object to its previous location, use the Undo Drag and Drop command from the Edit menu.

6. **Choose Undo Drag and Drop from the Edit menu.**

There are three ways to move an object left or right across the page: the space-bar, the tab key, or the alignment commands and tools. To move the object when it *is not* selected, place the insertion point in front of the object and press the spacebar or the tab key. (*Note:* Do not use the spacebar or tab key when the object is selected, or the object will be deleted.) When the object *is* selected, you can use alignment commands or tools to align the object at the left, center, or right of the page. Center the selected object using the alignment commands.

7. Click on the object to select it.

8. Click on ▤.

To resize the object you drag a sizing handle.

9. Point to the lower-right corner sizing handle.

10. When the word "RESIZE" appears beneath the pointer, hold down the mouse button and drag the handle to the right about one inch.

11. Release the mouse button.

Before continuing, save the document.

12. Use the Save <u>A</u>s command from the <u>F</u>ile menu to save the document as *Newsletter 2*.

EDITING A LINKED OBJECT

In order to edit the linked object you must return to the application that created it, in this case, the spreadsheet application. Because you have linked the object using the Spreadsheet command from the Insert menu, you can return to the spreadsheet by double-clicking on the object. Then when you make a change in the spreadsheet data, the word processing document will be automatically updated.

1. Double-click on the spreadsheet object in the word processing document.

The spreadsheet appears.

2. Change the 1995 expenditure from 6,600 to 7,000.

3. Choose *Newsletter 2* from the <u>W</u>indow menu.

The word processing document appears with the changed data.

4. Close and save all documents.

LINKING A CHART WITH A WORD PROCESSING DOCUMENT

Many different kinds of documents can be linked, including spreadsheets, charts, word processing documents, and graphics. Adventure Tours uses many charts to track their business activity, so linking charts between documents is an important tool for them. Figure 7.24 shows a pie chart Adventure Tours president, Pat Flotten, would like added to a word processing document. The procedure to link the chart with the word processing document is similar to the process for linking spreadsheet data that you have just completed.

7.24

A word processing
document with a pie
chart added

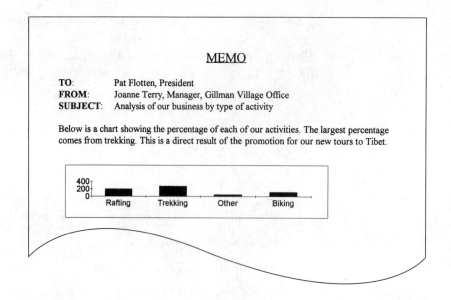

MEMO

TO: Pat Flotten, President
FROM: Joanne Terry, Manager, Gillman Village Office
SUBJECT: Analysis of our business by type of activity

Below is a chart showing the percentage of each of our activities. The largest percentage
comes from trekking. This is a direct result of the promotion for our new tours to Tibet.

1. Open Business analysis.

2. Open *Revenue by activity*.

3. Use the <u>W</u>indow menu to display the *Business analysis* document.

4. Press CTRL + END to move the insertion point to the end of the document.

5. Choose <u>C</u>hart from the <u>I</u>nsert menu.

The Insert Chart dialog box appears. First, you need to select the spreadsheet
that contains the chart and then select the chart.

6. Click on Revenue by activity.wks.

There is only one chart associated with the Revenue by activity spreadsheet.

7. Click on Chart1.

8. Click on OK.

The chart is now a linked object in the word processing document. Because it
is an object, it can be resized, moved, edited, and deleted. To change numbers
in the linked chart, you would change them in the application in which it was
created, the spreadsheet. This time you will close the word processing document before making the change to the chart. Then, when you reopen the
word processing document, the linked chart will be updated.

9. Save the word processing document as *Business analysis 2.*

10. Close the *Business analysis 2* document.

11. Verify that the *Revenue by activity* spreadsheet is displayed.

12. Choose <u>C</u>hart from the <u>V</u>iew menu.

13. Click on OK in the dialog box.

(*Note*: There is only one chart associated with this spreadsheet.)

Notice the amount for the rafting category—currently 150.

14. Choose <u>S</u>preadsheet from the <u>V</u>iew menu.

15. Change the rafting amount to 200.

16. Choose Chart from the View menu.

17. Click on Chart1 and click on OK.

Notice the change in the rafting category.

18. Choose Spreadsheet from the View menu.

19. Choose Save from the File menu.

Now open the word processing document.

20. Open *Business analysis 2*.

A message appears asking if you want to update links when opening the document.

21. Click on Yes.

The word processing document appears with the updated chart.

22. View the updated chart.

23. Close both documents and save the changes.

KEY TERMS

align data	font	linking
AutoFormat	handles	number format
bold	hide cells	object
border	italic	pattern
center across selection	line	type style

KEY COMMANDS

Alignment	Insert/Spreadsheet	Split
AutoFormat	Number	Undo Drag and Drop
Border	Page Setup	Undo Format
Column Width	Range Name	View/Chart
Font and Style	Select All	View/Spreadsheet
Gridlines	Set Print Area	Zoom
Insert/Chart	Shading	

REVIEW QUESTIONS

1. Entries in a cell can be _____, _____, and _____ aligned.

2. **T F** Data that is center aligned across several cells displays in the middle of the selected cells but remains in the original cell.

3. A cell can be outlined by choosing the _____ command in the _____ menu.

4. **T F** Choosing the Outline option in the Border dialog box places a border completely around the selected cells.

5. **T F** Fonts can be used to add variety to the appearance of a document.

6. **T F** The Split command allows you to view two non-adjacent parts of the spreadsheet at one time.

7. **T F** Cells that are hidden will not be displayed onscreen but they will print.

PROJECTS

1. Figure 7.25 shows a document that has been enhanced by:
   a. Increasing the column width for all columns (A–D) to 12
   b. Center-aligning the document heading across the document
   c. Changing the document heading to bold type
   d. Center-aligning the row headings
   e. Inserting single-line, double-line, and thick-line borders
   f. Inserting a pattern

   The original spreadsheet documents are shown in Figure 5.1. If you completed Project 1 at the end of Chapter 5, you would have saved this spreadsheet as *WKS Chapter 5 project 1*. If so, you can open the spreadsheet and make the changes. If not, you must first complete the original spreadsheet and then make the changes. Include your name at the bottom of the document. Save the spreadsheet as *WKS Chapter 7 project 1*, and then print the document. Close the document.

2. Figure 7.26 shows a document that has been enhanced by:
   a. Inserting blank rows
   b. Adding a document heading, SURVEY RESULTS

7.25

The income forecast document with several enhancements

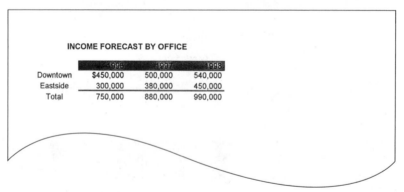

7.26

The survey document with several enhancements

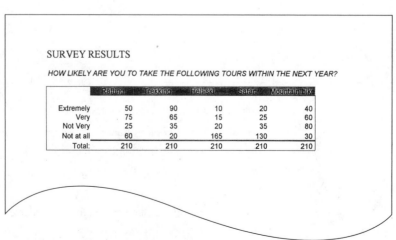

c. Changing the type style and enlarging the font for the document heading

d. Changing the subheading (the question) to italic type

e. Increasing the column widths for all columns (A–F) to 12

f. Center-aligning the column headings

g. Right-aligning the row headings

h. Inserting single-line, double-line, and thick-line borders

i. Inserting a pattern

The original spreadsheet is shown in Figure 5.1. If you completed Project 2 at the end of Chapter 5, you would have saved this spreadsheet as *WKS Chapter 5 project 2*. If so, you can open the spreadsheet and make the changes. If not, you must first complete the original spreadsheet and then make the changes. Include your name at the bottom of the document. Save the spreadsheet as *WKS Chapter 7 project 2*, and then print the document. Close the document.

On the data disk is a file called Great Wall trek. This spreadsheet contains the names and addresses of members who will be going on a trek of the Great Wall of China. The spreadsheet also contains the amounts each person has paid to date and what money, if any, is owed to Adventure Tours. You will use this spreadsheet to complete the following three projects.

3. Open Great Wall trek and complete the following:

a. Using the Zoom command:

- Which is the highest standard magnification option that can be used to view the entire document?

- Which column headings are displayed when you choose the 200% magnification?

b. With 100% magnification and using the print preview screen:

- What columns are displayed on the first page?

- What columns are displayed on the second page?

4. Open Great Wall trek. Preview the document, and print it with only the document title, column headings, and the names and addresses of members in Seattle displayed. Save the document as *WKS Chapter 7 project 3*. Close the document.

5. Using the word processing application, develop a memo from you to the company employees. In the memo refer to the survey results from a spreadsheet named Survey results. Then link the information from the Survey results spreadsheet to the memo. Save the memo as *WKS Chapter 7 project 4*, and then print the memo. Close the document without saving changes.

Working with Charts

- Define a chart

- Describe the relationship between spreadsheet data and a chart

- Use the New Chart button to create a chart

- Change chart types

- Save and print a chart

- Enhance charts

A **chart** is a drawing showing the relationships among numbers. The most common types of charts are column, line, and pie, as shown in Figures 8.1, 8.2, and 8.3, respectively. **Bar charts** are useful in comparing two sets of data such as last year's income and this year's income. Figure 8.1 shows Adventure Tours' quarterly income for the previous and current years. The bar chart makes it easy to compare the numbers quarter by quarter. **Line charts** are useful in analyzing trends. Figure 8.2 shows the same data as in the bar chart; however, because the data is illustrated graphically as a line chart, it is easy to spot the upward trend. **Pie charts** are useful in showing the relationship each part has to the whole. Figure 8.3 shows the part (percentage) each quarter's income is of the total yearly income. Notice that each quarter is distinguished by a different pattern in each "slice" of the pie.

Usually, when you create a chart you need to specify two things: numbers and labels. **Labels** provide context for the data, such as indicating the months or years. Thus, when you want to chart the income by month, the income is the numbers, and the months (January, February, March, . . .) are the labels. Normally, for bar and line charts the numbers are plotted vertically on the **y-axis**, and the labels are plotted horizontally on the **x-axis** (see Figure 8.4, which shows a chart of Adventure Tours' income by month). A pie chart does not use axes but rather divides the total pie (the "whole") into pieces according to each piece's relationship to the whole. Thus, as shown in Figure 8.3, if the first-quarter income is 17.6 percent of the year's total income, its slice is 17.6 percent of the pie. The "whole" may be designated as any unit you desire: for example, it may be the income for a year, a quarter, or a month, depending on what it is you are trying to analyze. Each slice of the pie then equals a percentage of that whole. In addition to its size, each slice may be further distinguished from other slices through the use of color or background pattern. (*Note*: If you are using a color monitor, the charts you create will be displayed in color. However, in this book, colors are represented by various shades of gray.)

8.1

A bar chart

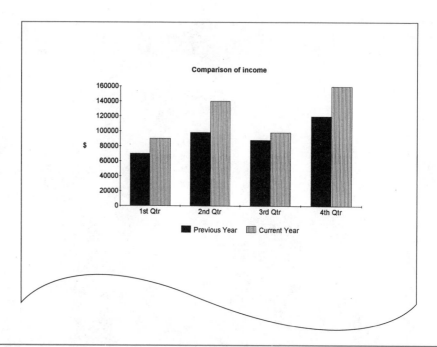

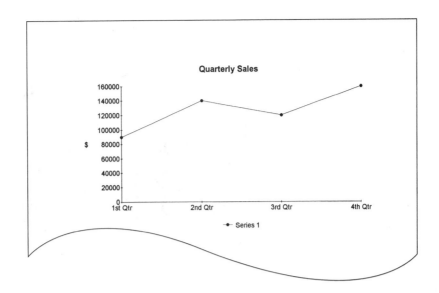

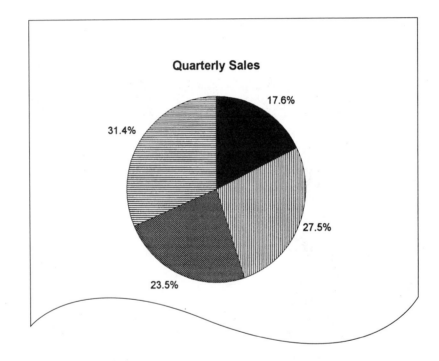

CREATING A CHART

To create a chart, you develop a new spreadsheet or open an existing one, select the cells that contain the data to be used in the chart; and use the New Chart dialog box to create the chart. Because spreadsheets are comprised of numbers, they can easily be used as a basis for creating charts. Figure 8.5 shows a spreadsheet with Adventure Tours' income for a four-month period. Pat Flotten, president of Adventure Tours, would like this data displayed in a series of charts and has asked you to develop these. To do so, you will do the following:

1. **Start Works.**

2. **On your own, create the spreadsheet shown in Figure 8.5.**

8.4

The X and Y axis

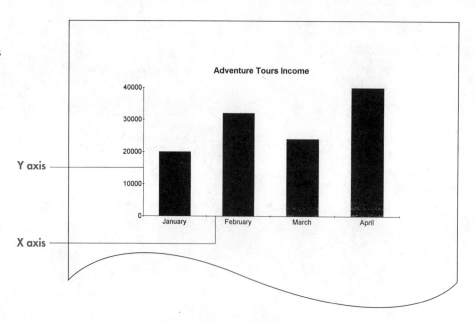

New Chart button

8.5

The spreadsheet used to create a chart

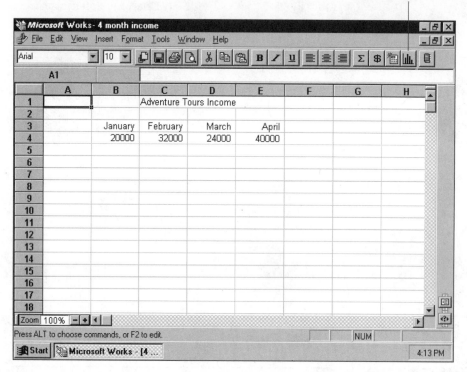

3. **Save the spreadsheet as *4 month income*.**

The New Chart ![button] button is found on the toolbar (see Figure 8.5). Before choosing the New Chart button, you must select the cell range that contains the data to be included in the chart. In this case, the data will be the month headings and the income data.

4. **Select cells B3 through E4.**

5. **Click on ![button].**

A First-time Help dialog box may appear offering instructions in creating a chart. Click on OK to bypass this help window.

6. If necessary, click on OK to bypass the First-time Help dialog box.

The New Chart dialog box appears, as shown in Figure 8.6. The dialog box shows how the chart would look as a bar chart. Take a moment to view the different chart types.

7. Click on the line chart box, which is second from the right in the top row of the chart options (see Figure 8.6).

The chart changes to a line chart, which shows an overall upward trend in income.

8. Click on the pie chart box, which is the rightmost option in the top row of the chart options (see Figure 8.6).

The pie chart shows the proportion each month represents of the total income for the quarter.

9. Change the chart type back to a bar chart.

10. Click inside the box under the word Title.

11. Type Adventure Tours Income

The title is automatically displayed as part of the chart.

12. Click on the Border checkbox.

13. Click on the Gridlines checkbox.

View the sample labeled "Your Chart" to see the results when a border and gridlines are added.

14. Remove the border and gridlines.

Your dialog box should resemble the one in Figure 8.6.

15. Click on OK to display the chart.

The chart is displayed in its own window, and the title bar reads "4 month income - Chart1." You can switch between the chart window and the document window using the Window menu.

16. Click on Window in the menu bar.

Notice there are two open windows, "4 month income" and "4 month income - Chart1." The check mark next to "4 month income - Chart1" indicates that it is currently displayed.

17. Click on "4 month income" to display the spreadsheet window.

The spreadsheet is displayed. Any changes you make in the area that was used to create the chart will change the chart.

Line chart option   Pie chart option   Mixed chart option

Bar chart option

3-D Bar chart option

Border option

Gridlines option

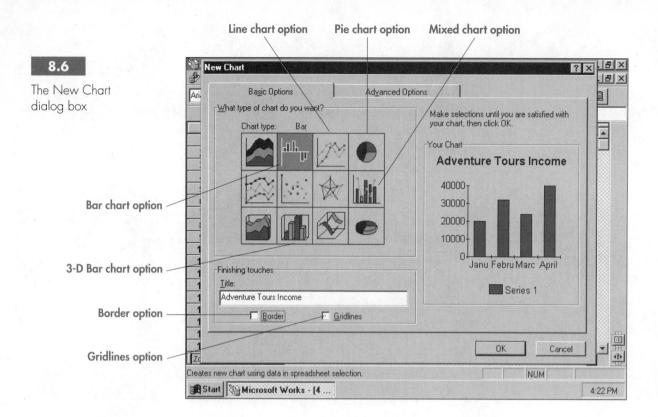

EDITING THE NUMBERS IN A CHART

You can change the numbers in the spreadsheet, and the chart will automatically be adjusted. Practice this by changing the January income to 60000.

1. Click on cell B4.

2. Type 60000 and press ⏎ ENTER .

3. Use the Window menu to display the chart.

Notice that the chart is adjusted to reflect the new number.

4. On your own, return to the spreadsheet and change the income for January back to 20000.

SAVING A CHART

After developing a chart, you can save the spreadsheet, and the chart will be saved with it. Later, when you open the spreadsheet, the chart will be opened also.

1. Choose Save from the File menu.

PRINTING A CHART

A chart is printed from the chart window. Before printing a chart you should preview how it will print.

1. Use the <u>W</u>indow menu to display the chart.

2. Click on 🔲.

The Print Preview window shows that the chart will be printed using the entire page. You could change the margins to reduce the size of the chart or you could specify that the chart be printed the size of the screen. Both of these options are in the Page Setup dialog box.

3. Click on [Cancel] to return to the chart window.

4. Choose Page Setup from the <u>F</u>ile menu.

5. Click on the <u>O</u>ther Options index tab.

6. Click on <u>S</u>creen Size.

7. Click on OK.

8. Click on 🔲.

The chart is reduced in size. Now print the chart.

9. Click on [Print].

CHANGING CHART TYPES

Works provides several different chart types. In this section, you will display some of these types using the Chart Type command in the Format menu.

1. Choose <u>C</u>hart Type from the F<u>o</u>rmat menu.

The Chart Type dialog box appears with the Basic Types index tab displayed. The selected chart type, Bar, is printed above the chart type options. Each of these types has several variations. After choosing a chart type in the Basic Types index tab, you can display the Variations index tab and select from additional options. Display the Variations index tab and see the options for the Bar chart type.

2. Click on the <u>V</u>ariations index tab.

The Variations index tab appears, showing six different types of bar charts. Some of these charts are used when you have more than one data series. For example, a chart of income for the current year and income for the previous year would have two data series. The top left chart would display these two data series side-by-side. Other charts display gridlines, or include the actual numbers in the chart. Take a moment to display these charts.

3. Click on the leftmost option in the bottom row.

4. Click on OK.

The chart is displayed with gridlines.

5. Choose Chart Type from the Format menu.

6. Click on the Variations index tab.

7. Click on the middle option in the bottom row and choose OK.

The numbers are displayed above the columns. Now choose another chart type.

8. Choose Chart Type from the Format menu.

9. Choose the line chart from the top row of options.

10. Display the Variations index tab.

As with bar charts, there are six types of line charts. The first three types are typical charts that show variations in the use of lines and markers. **Markers** are the small symbols that appear at each data point (that is, 20000, 32000, 24000, and 40000). To examine a line chart that uses markers, follow the steps below.

11. Click on OK to display the chosen line chart.

Take a moment to study the chart. Notice that the markers appear at each data point. You can remove the markers by choosing a different line chart option. Remove the markers from the chart.

12. Choose Chart type from the Format menu.

13. Display the Variations index tab.

This time use the shortcut for choosing a chart type: double-click on it.

14. Double-click on the middle line chart of the top row of chart options.

Notice that the markers are removed from this chart.

15. On your own, change the line chart so it shows only the markers.

16. On your own, change the line chart so it displays lines, markers, and gridlines.

Now display some of the pie charts. This time, use the toolbar buttons to display the Chart Type dialog box.

17. Click on .

18. Click on OK.

The pie chart is displayed with a title but no labels.

19. Click on and display the Variations index tab in the Chart Type dialog box.

20. Select the pie chart with labels only (bottom row, left box) and view the sample in the Your Chart box.

The labels appear.

21. On your own, select the pie chart that includes both the labels and the percentages and choose OK.

This chart shows the labels and the percentage that each slice is of the whole pie.

CREATING A CHART WITH TWO DATA SERIES

Until now you have been working with a single **data series** (income for January through April). Figure 8.7 shows a chart with a second data series (expenses for January through April) added to the spreadsheet and plotted on the chart. You will create another chart, this time using the New Chart command. Before creating the new chart, you need to add and select the words "Income" and "Expenses." These terms comprise the chart **legend**, which is a key to the various parts of a chart. In this case, the legend distinguishes between the two data series. Start by deleting the current chart.

1. With the pie chart displayed, choose Dele̲te Chart from the T̲ools menu.
2. Click on Chart1 in the list box, then click on D̲elete.
3. Click on OK.

A confirmation message appears advising you that you cannot undo the deletion. Choose OK.

4. Click on OK.

The chart disappears. Next enter the new data.

5. Select cell A4.
6. Type Income
7. Type Expenses into cell A5.
8. Select cell B5.
9. Type 18000
10. On your own, enter the other numbers (see Figure 8.8).
11. Select cells A3 through E5.
12. Choose Create N̲ew Chart from the T̲ools menu.
13. Click inside the T̲itle box.

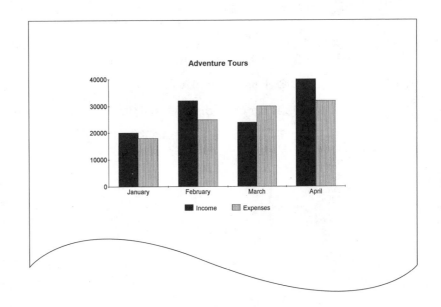

8.7

A chart with two data series

8.8

The spreadsheet used
to create a chart
with two series

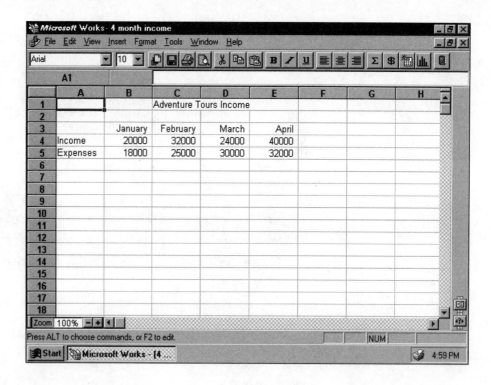

14. **Type** Adventure Tours

15. **Click on OK.**

The bar chart makes it easy to compare income and expenses month by month. Take a moment to view other chart types using the Chart Type dialog box.

16. **On your own, change this bar chart to a line chart.**

The line chart shows expenses moving up in a fairly gradual manner. But income fluctuates sharply, including a steep decline in March, where expenses were greater than income.

17. **Click on** ▦ **(see Figure 8.9).**

18. **Click on OK.**

This **mixed chart** combines a column and a line.

19. **Click on** ▦ **(see Figure 8.9).**

The 3-D bar chart displays as a three-dimensional object.

20. **Click on** ▦ **and choose OK.**

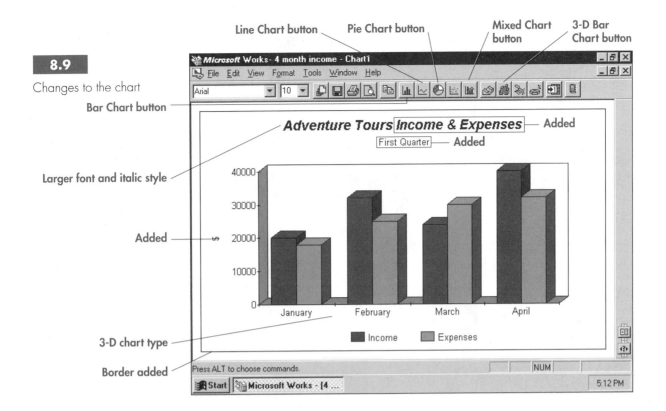

8.9

Changes to the chart

Line Chart button — Pie Chart button — Mixed Chart button — 3-D Bar Chart button

Bar Chart button

Larger font and italic style

Added

3-D chart type

Border added

Adventure Tours Income & Expenses — Added
First Quarter — Added

CHANGING THE APPEARANCE OF A CHART

Works provides several ways in which you can enhance the appearance of a chart and draw the reader's attention to a part of the chart. Figure 8.9 shows the chart with the following enhancements:

- The words "Income & Expenses" are added to the chart title to clarify its meaning; the title is italicized and displayed in a larger font.

- A subtitle "First Quarter," is added.

- The y-axis title is changed to a dollar sign ($).

- A border is placed around the chart.

- The chart is displayed in a 3-D format.

Start by changing the titles using the Titles command from the Edit menu.

1. **Choose Titles from the Edit menu.**

The Titles dialog box appears allowing you to change the chart title, add a subtitle and titles for the x- and y-axes. Figure 8.10 shows the completed dialog box.

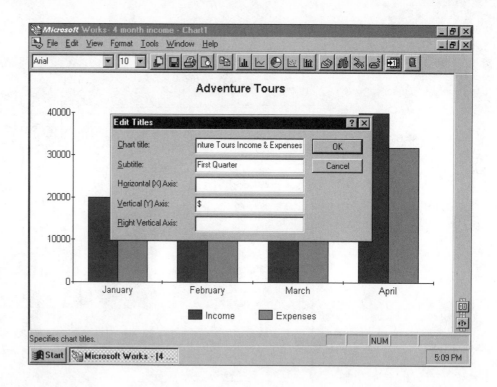

2. **Type** Adventure Tours

3. **Press Tab to move the insertion point to the Subtitle box.**

4. **Type** First Quarter

5. **Press** (TAB ⇄) **twice to move the insertion point to the Vertical (Y) Axis box.**

6. **Type** $

7. **Click on OK to return to the chart.**

Next you will increase the font size and italicize the title. This can be done by highlighting the title and using the Font and Style command from the Format menu.

8. **Click on the title to highlight it.**

(*Note*: the title is an object in the chart and a border with handles will appear when the title is properly selected.)

9. **Choose Font and Style from the Format menu.**

10. **Choose 14 from the Size list.**

11. **Click on Italic in the style box.**

12. **Click on OK.**

Now add a border around the entire chart.

13. **Point to below the *A* in *Adventure*.**

14. **Click the mouse button.**

15. **Choose Border from the Format menu.**

A border appears around the chart. Finally, display the chart in a 3-D format.

16. Choose 3-D from the Format menu.

Your screen should resemble Figure 8.9. Now print the spreadsheet and chart.

17. Use the Page Setup dialog box to change the chart size to screen size.

18. Print the chart.

This completes the section on creating and enhancing charts. Now save the document.

19. Save the spreadsheet as *4 month income and expense*.

20. Close the spreadsheet.

KEY TERMS

bar chart	legend	pie chart
chart	line chart	3-D bar chart
data series	markers	x-axis
labels	mixed chart	y-axis

KEY COMMANDS

3-D	Chart Type	Delete Chart
Border	Create New Chart	Titles

REVIEW QUESTIONS

1. A chart is a drawing showing the relationships among _____.

2. The most common types of charts are _____, _____, and _____.

3. Normally, the numbers are plotted vertically on the _____ axis of a chart.

4. To create a chart, you use the _____ _____ button.

5. The _____ menu is used to change chart types.

1. Develop the line chart shown in Figure 8.2. The numbers for the quarters are 1st Qtr, 90000; 2nd Qtr, 140000; 3rd Qtr, 120000; 4th Qtr, 160000. Include your name on the spreadsheet. Save the spreadsheet as *WKS Chapter 8 project 1*. Print the spreadsheet and the chart. Close the spreadsheet.

2. Using the spreadsheet from Project 1, develop the pie chart shown in Figure 8.3. Save the spreadsheet as *WKS Chapter 8 project 2*, and then print the chart only. Close the spreadsheet.

3. Develop a spreadsheet with the following data. Using the spreadsheet, create the bar chart shown in Figure 8.1. Save the spreadsheet as *WKS Chapter 8 project 3*, and then print the chart. Close the spreadsheet.

	1st Qtr	2nd Qtr	3rd Qtr	4th Qtr
Previous year	70000	98000	88000	120000
Current year	90000	140000	98000	160000

4. Enhance the chart created in Project 3 so that it duplicates the content and style of the chart in Figure 8.11. Save the spreadsheet as *WKS Chapter 8 project 4*, and then print the chart. Close the spreadsheet.

8.11

A chart with several enhancements

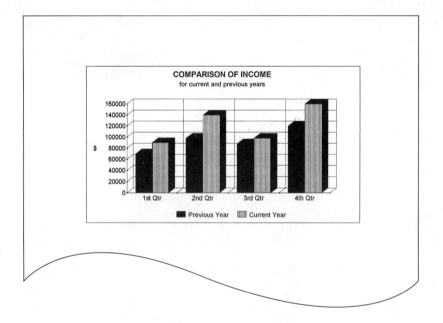

Introduction to Databases

IN THIS CHAPTER YOU WILL LEARN HOW TO:

- Create a database
- Enter data into a database
- Display data using a form
- Sort records
- Find and replace data
- Create a calculated field

A **database** is a collection of related information, such as a library card catalog or a college's course offerings. Other examples include a city's list of registered voters, a hospital's patient records, and a company's list of employees. Most companies have more than one database; it may have one database of employee information, another for inventory, and still another for suppliers. A company would maintain separate databases for each area of its business because a database ideally contains only related information. Thus, the employee database would only contain information about employees, the supplier database would only contain information about suppliers, and so forth. However, each database would contain similiar types of records (names, addresses, telephone numbers, and so on). The kind of information contained in a specific database is determined by its use. For example, a company such as Adventure Tours, may create a customer database to maintain such information as:

- Who their customers are and where they are located

- How long each customer has been buying from them

- Which customers are slow in paying their bills

- Which customers haven't purchased from them in a long time

- Who the top ten customers are

9.1

A database table

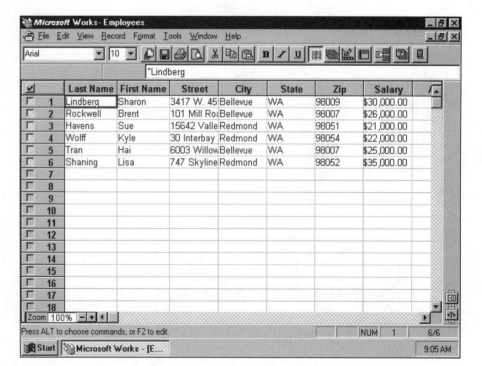

Many computer programs, such as Works, include an application for creating, organizing, and maintaining a database. To create a database, you first decide on the use of the database, which then helps you determine the specific information that must be included in it. Works lets you create a table in which you define the fields, or the specific units of information such as last name or salary that will make up each database record. Figure 9.1 shows such a table for a database created by Adventure Tours to keep track of employee information.

THE STRUCTURE OF A WORKS DATABASE

The basic organizational structure of the database is a table, and all activities involving a Works database depend on tables. A **table** consists of rows and columns, as shown in Figure 9.1. Each column contains a single item of information, called a **field**, such as a person's last name. In this case there are eight fields: Last Name, First Name, Street, City, State, Zip, Salary, and Age. Each row in the table contains the related information, called a **record**. That is, the name, address, and salary information would be that employee's record. After creating a database, Works allows you to search the records for specific information (such as which employees live in Bellevue), and to create, save, and print reports using the information.

CREATING A DATABASE

In this section you will develop a database to keep track of Adventure Tours' employees. The first step in creating a database is to determine the type of information that will be included in the database. In this case Adventure Tours wants to keep track of the names, addresses, salaries, and ages of their employees. This information is the basis for the fields that are included in the database. Begin by starting the Works program.

1. **Start the Works program.**

2. **Click on the Works Tools index tab in the Works Task Launcher dialog box.**

3. **Click on** ▨ **.**

(*Note*: The First-time Help dialog box may appear. This dialog box gives you access to Works' context-sensitive Help feature. You can bypass this dialog box.

4. **If the First-time Help dialog box appears, click on OK to bypass the help feature.**

The Create Database dialog box appears onscreen. This dialog box is used to create the **field names** that will be used in your database. The process for creating fields is to first type the field name, such as "Salary," in the Field name box, then select the format and click on Add. The dialog box remains open so you can continue to add fields to the database. The format options indicate the type of information that will be stored in the new field. So, for example, the field that stores salary information would be formatted as a number. Field names and the field format should be representative of the information to be included in the field. Thus, in the database you create for Adventure Tours, the fields and their formats will be:

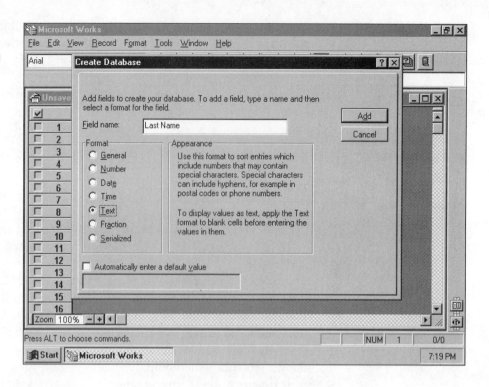

Field Name	Format
Last Name	Text
First Name	Text
Street	Text
City	Text
State	Text
Zip	Text
Salary	Number
Age	General

Figure 9.2 shows the Create Database dialog box with an entry for the Last Name field.

5. **Type** Last Name

6. **Click on** Text **under the Format options.**

Your screen should resemble Figure 9.2

7. **Click on Add.**

The Field is added to the database, and Field 2 appears in the Field name box. Continue by adding all the fields listed above.

8. **On your own, add the First Name, Street, City, State, and Zip fields, and format them as Text fields.**

9. **For the next field (Field 7), type** Salary **as the field name.**

10. **Click on Number in the Format area.**

When the Number format option is selected, a list of options is displayed in the Appearance list box. Choose the third option, which displays a dollar sign, comma, and two decimal places.

11. Choose the third option ($1,234.56) in the Appearance list box.

12. Click on Add.

13. Type Age in the Field name box.

14. Verify that the General format is selected.

15. Click on Add.

All the fields necessary for the new database have now been created. Click on Done to remove the Create Database dialog box and to see the results.

16. Click on Done.

The database in its current view, **List view**, is now in a table format, that is, it resembles a spreadsheet in that it is made up of rows and columns. The column headings are the field names you selected. The row numbers mark each new record in the database. Currently, there are no records in the database. Next you will add information to the database using the List view. This view allows you to see several records onscreen at once.

17. If necessary, maximize the database window.

ENTERING DATA INTO A DATABASE

Using List View

Entering data into the List view of the database is similar to adding information to a spreadsheet. The first field of the first record is selected. After typing information into the field, press the (TAB ⇆) key to move to the next field. When you have moved through all fields for one record, the (TAB ⇆) key takes you to the first field of a new record. Figure 9.3 shows the database in List view after one record has been added. Complete the following steps to duplicate Figure 9.3:

1. Type Lindberg

2. Press (TAB ⇆).

3. Type Sharon and press (TAB ⇆).

4. Continue to enter the following field data for this record, pressing (TAB ⇆) after each entry:

Street: 3417 W. 45th

City: Bellevue

State: WA

Zip: 98009

Salary: 30000

Age: 36

9.3

Data entered into the List view for the first record

List view button   Form view button

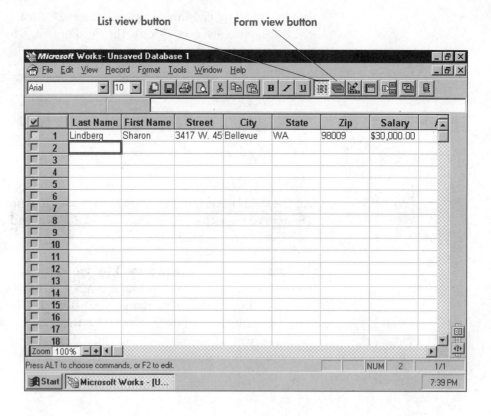

Your screen should resemble Figure 9.3. Notice that the Street information is not fully displayed and the Age field is off the screen. One way to fully view all fields and their contents onscreen is to use **Form view**. You can switch from List view to Form view using the Form command in the View menu or by clicking on 🗎 on the toolbar (see Figure 9.3). Next you will display database fields in Form view and add records using this view.

Using Form View

The Form view makes it easier to enter and read information because it displays only one record at a time.

1. Click on 🗎 (see Figure 9.3).

The fields and the first record are displayed in Form view. To show a blank form so a new record can be added, you either press (TAB ⇆) until the highlight moves through the current record and to the next form, or you click on the Last Record button ▶❙ on the left edge of the horizontal scroll bar (see Figure 9.4). Continue by displaying a blank form and entering the following records.

2. Click on ▶❙ (see Figure 9.4).

You enter data into a form in the same way that you enter it when you are in List view.

3. Type Rockwell in the Last Name field and press (TAB ⇆).

4. Type Brent in the First Name field and press (TAB ⇆).

Continue entering the data for Brent Rockwell until your screen resembles Figure 9.4.

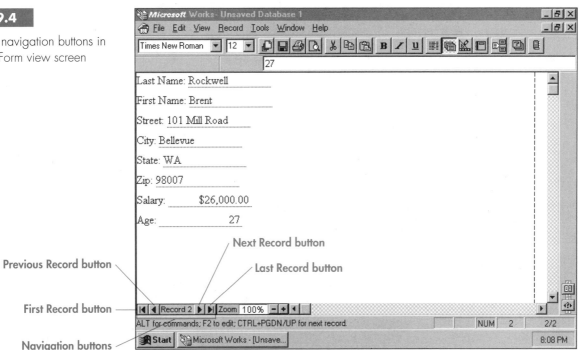

5. On your own, enter the remaining data for this record:

   Street: 101 Mill Road

   City: Bellevue

   State: WA

   Zip: 98007

   Salary: 26000

   Age: 27

Your screen should resemble Figure 9.4. To start a new record, press (TAB ⇄).

6. Press (TAB ⇄) to start a new record.

7. On your own enter the data for the following employees.

Enter the records in the following order: Havens, Wolff, Tran, and Shaning. Press (TAB ⇄) after making the last entry, which is Shaning's age.

Sue Havens	Kyle Wolff
15642 Valley St	30 Interbay Ave
Redmond WA 98051	Redmond WA 98054
21000	22000
24	38
Hai Tran	Lisa Shaning
6003 Willows Rd	747 Skyline Dr
Bellevue WA 98007	Redmond WA 98052
25000	35000
26	29

(*Note*: Press the (TAB ⇄) key after the final entry.)

DISPLAYING RECORDS IN FORM VIEW

You now have six records entered into the database. You can view different records, one at a time, using several different methods. Using the keyboard, CTRL + HOME displays the first record and CTRL + END displays the last record in the database. To use the mouse, you click on the navigation buttons to the left of the horizontal scroll bar. First, use the keyboard to display Sharon Lindberg's record.

1. Press CTRL + HOME .

Lindberg's record is displayed.

Records are numbered in the order in which they were entered into the database. Notice the words "Record 1" displayed near the lower-left corner of the screen, between the navigation buttons (see Figure 9.4). Take a moment now to practice using the navigation buttons.

2. Click on the ▶.

Record number 2 appears.

3. Click on the ▶ and notice that record 3 appears.

4. Click on the ◀ and notice that record 2 appears.

5. Click on the ◀ and notice that record 1 appears.

SAVING A DATABASE

Before continuing, save the database with the file name Employees.

1. Choose Save As from the File menu.

2. Type a:\Employees (or b:\Employees).

3. Click on Save.

Notice the file name, Employees, now appears on the title bar.

DISPLAYING RECORDS IN THE LIST VIEW

Form View is useful whenever you want to see only one record at a time. List view, in contrast, allows you to see multiple records simultaneously. Figure 9.5 shows the Employees database displayed in List view. Switch from Form view to List view.

1. Click on ▦ (see Figure 9.5).

The List view of the Employees database appears. Because List view format is very similar to a spreadsheet, much of what you have learned with the Works' spreadsheet application applies to the database information in List view. For instance, you can move around the table and enter, edit, delete, copy, move, and format data. You can also add, delete, and sort records. One difference between Form and List views is the field width. The List view displays all the fields with the same width, eleven characters. Again, notice that some of the data in the Street field does not display because the data is longer than eleven characters. You can change the width of the Street field to view all the data.

2. **Click on the column heading Street to select the column.**

3. **Choose Field Width from the Format menu.**

4. **Click on Best Fit in the Field Width dialog box.**

Another method for adjusting column widths, similar to the process used in formatting spreadsheets, is to point to the line between the column headings and drag the line to the desired position. Use this process to reduce the width of the State column.

5. **Point to the line between the State and Zip column headings.**

6. **When the word "ADJUST" appears, hold down the mouse button and drag the mouse to just after the e in State.**

7. **Release the mouse button.**

The column size for the State field is reduced. Remember, changing the column width in List view does not change the original field size created in Form view.

In addition to changing the column width, you can rearrange columns. Figure 9.6 shows the process for moving the Age field to the left of the Salary field. You move columns by selecting the column and dragging it to the new position.

List View button

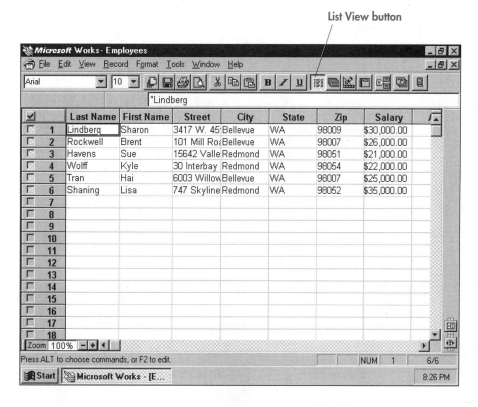

9.5

The Employees database displayed in the List view

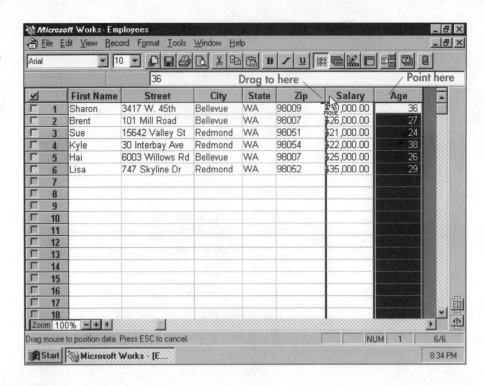

8. Click on the heading Age to select the column. (*Note*: You may have to scroll the list to see the Age field.)

9. Place the pointer on the field name Age.

10. When the word "DRAG" appears, hold down the mouse button and drag the pointer to the left of the Salary column. Note that the word "DRAG" changes to "MOVE" (see Figure 9.6).

11. Release the mouse button.

EDITING DATA IN A TABLE

As you work with a table, it may be necessary to change data due to a mistake in data entry or a change in the record information; for example, if an employee moves, a new address will have to be entered. To edit the data within a table, you highlight the desired field and retype it or otherwise make the change. Figure 9.7 shows four edits to the table:

- Lisa Shaning's zip code is changed to 98054.

- Kyle Wolff's salary is changed to $25,000.00.

- Sue Haven's street address is changed to 15642 Valley Dr.

- Brent Rockwell's street address is changed to 10151 Mill Road.

Start by changing Lisa Shaning's zip code.

1. Use the arrow keys or the mouse pointer to select the cell listing Lisa Shaning's zip code (98052).

2. Type 98054

Changes to the data
in the table

"51" added

"Dr" replaces "St"

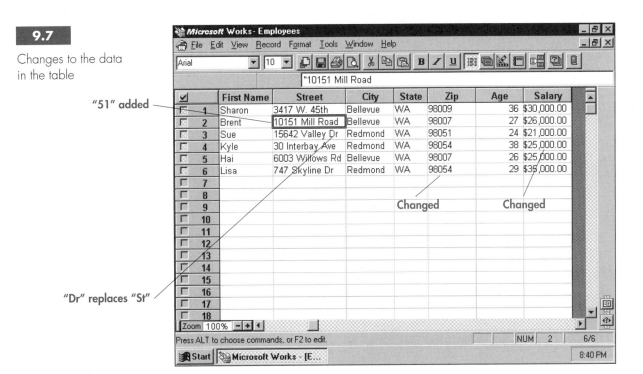

3. **Select Kyle Wolff's salary ($22,000).**

4. **Type** 25000

Next, correct Sue Haven's address. This time you will change part of the entry
rather than retyping the entire address.

5. **Click once on Sue Haven's street address to select it.**

6. **Point to the right of the address in the formula bar (see Figure 9.8).**

Pointing to the address in
the formula bar

Point here

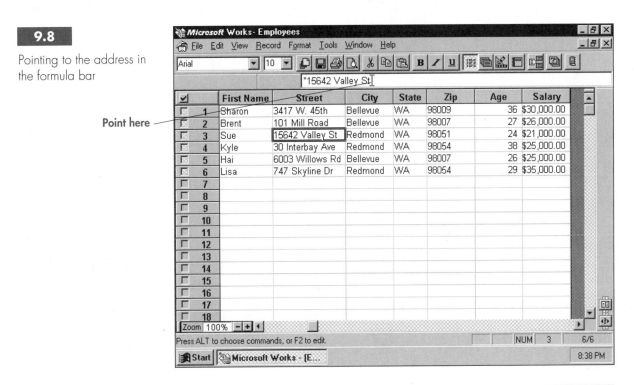

7. Click the mouse button.

Notice that a blinking vertical line appears where you clicked with the mouse. This is the insertion point, and it is used to add or delete characters from the field.

8. Press the (← BACKSPACE) key twice to delete the word *St*.

9. Type Dr

10. Press (↵ ENTER).

Now change Brent Rockwell's street address.

11. On your own, change Brent Rockwell's street field from 101 Mill Road to 10151 Mill Road.

Your screen should resemble Figure 9.7.

ADDING DATA IN A TABLE

Records can be added to the database using either List or Form views. To add another record to the list, click on the left field in the first empty row. Figure 9.9 shows a new record entered into row 7. Add that record information now.

1. Select the Last Name field in row 7.

2. Type Terry

3. Press (TAB ⇆).

9.9

A new record entered into row 7

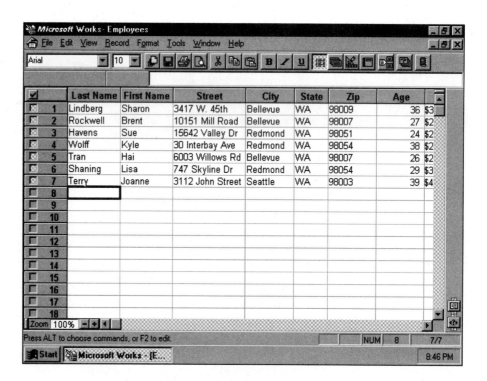

4. On your own, enter the rest of the record data:

First Name: Joanne

Street: 3112 John Street

City: Seattle

State: WA

Zip: 98003

Age: 39

Salary: 45000

5. Press (TAB ⇄) after the last entry, which is the Salary amount.

Your screen should resemble Figure 9.9.

SORTING RECORDS

Works allows you to **sort** the records in a database. Before sorting a table, you should save the database using a new name. That way, if you make a mistake during the sort, you can return to the original table.

1. Save the database with the name *Employees 2*.

To sort a database, you must specify the field used for the sort and the sort order. Records can be sorted in **ascending** order (A–Z, 0–9) or **descending** order (Z–A, 9–0). Complete the following to sort the records alphabetically in ascending order by last name.

2. Click on the column heading Last Name to select the Last Name field.

3. Choose Sort Records from the Record menu.

4. If necessary, click on OK to bypass the First-time Help dialog box.

The Sort Records dialog box appears. Works allows you to sort by more than one field. This is useful if you have two or more records with identical information in a particular field and need to determine which record comes first. For example, if more than one person has the same last name, you could sort records by both last name *and* by first name. To do this, you specify the last name as the first sort field, and the first name as a second sort field. The dialog box shows that Last Name is specified as the first field by which to sort and that the sort order is ascending.

5. To specify a second sort field, click on ▾ in the first Then by field box.

6. Click on First Name.

Your screen should resemble Figure 9.10.

7. Click on OK.

Note that the records are now sorted by last name.

8. If necessary, click on Havens to select that employee record.

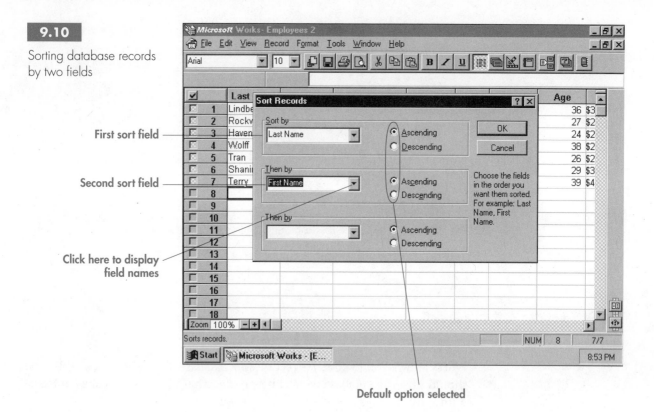

First sort field

Second sort field

Click here to display
field names

Default option selected

SEARCHING A TABLE FOR
RECORDS AND DATA

Works allows you to search a table in order to locate specific records or data. You can search using the Find command in the Edit menu. The Find command allows you to search for records that contain specific data. For example, you could search the Salary field for those employees who make $30,000 or search the City field for those employees who live in Redmond.

1. Choose **Find** from the **Edit** menu.

A dialog box appears asking for more information about the search you are conducting. The parts to this dialog box are explained below:

- Find what. Use this text box to type in the text or value for which you are searching. If you want to search for those employees who live in Bellevue, you would type *"Bellevue."*

- Next record. Choose this option if you want to move to the next record that contains the search value.

- All records. Choose this option if you want to display only all of the records that match the search value. The records are displayed in a table format.

Figure 9.11 shows the completed Find dialog box, which will locate those record(s) that have Bellevue entered in the City field.

2. Type Bellevue in the **Find** what box.

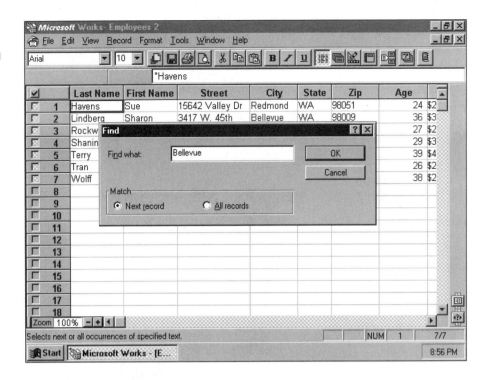

3. Verify that Next record is selected.

4. Click on OK.

The highlight will move to the first record that has Bellevue in the City field. You can use the Find dialog box to find the next occurrence of Bellevue.

5. Choose Find from the Edit menu.

Notice that the text from your previous search, Bellevue, is still displayed in the Find what box.

6. Click on OK.

The next record with Bellevue in the City field is selected. You can continue finding one record at a time or you can use the All Records option to display all of the records that have Bellevue in the City field.

7. Choose Find from the Edit menu.

8. Click on All records.

9. Click on OK.

The table now shows only the records of those employees who live in Bellevue. This is not a new database, but rather a different **view** of the Employees database. Notice the record numbers at the left of the screen. The numbers are 2, 3, and 6. These are the record numbers of those employees who live in Bellevue. Works has hidden the other records. You can switch to the hidden records or display all of the records again using the Show command in the Record menu. Try switching to the hidden records.

10. Click on the Record menu.

11. Point to Show.

12. Click on 4 Hidden Records.

All of the records *except* the employees who live in Bellelvue are displayed.

13. Display the Record menu and choose 4 Hidden Records from the Show command.

The records for the employees who live in Bellevue reappear and the other records are once again hidden. Now display all the records.

14. Choose 1 All Records from the Show command under the Record menu.

FINDING AND REPLACING DATA

Works allows you to search a table for specific information in order to replace or update that information. To do this, you use the Find feature in combination with the Replace feature. This process is particularly useful if you need to replace identical information in several records, such as changing a telephone area code.

Before replacing data, resize the Zip and Age columns so all fields are visible.

1. Point to the Zip column heading.

2. Double-click to resize the Zip field to Best Fit.

3. On your own, resize the Age field to Best Fit.

All columns should be fully displayed. If they aren't, maximize the document window and resize other fields.

4. If necessary, click on ▣ and resize other fields to fully display all data.

Now you are ready to perform the Find and Replace procedure. To start the Find and Replace procedure, choose Replace from the Edit menu.

5. Choose Replace from the Edit menu.

The Replace dialog box appears on the screen. Notice that this dialog box shares common elements with the Find dialog box. Also notice that the search term (Bellevue) from your last Find procedure still appears in the Find what box. In this Find and Replace procedure, you will change any salary amount of $45,000 to $47,000. To do this, type 45000 in the Find What box and type 47000 in the Replace box. When the command is executed, the changes will be made.

6. Type 45000 in the Find what box.

7. Press (TAB ⇆).

8. Type 47000 in the Replace with box.

After the dialog box is completed, select Find Next to go to the next record that lists $45,000 in the Salary field. When $45,000 is highlighted, click on Replace to enter $47,000.

9. Click on Find Next.

Notice $45,000 is highlighted in the table.

10. Click on Replace.

The new salary, $47,000, is entered into the record.

11. Close the Replace dialog box.

USING WILDCARD CHARACTERS

Suppose you need to find a record in the database but do not know the exact spelling of an entry. Works provides two **wildcard characters**, the question mark (?) and the asterisk (*), to help you find the desired record. The question mark is used when you are unsure of a single letter or number in a field. The asterisk is used to represent strings of unknown letters and numbers. The use of these two wildcard characters is explained below:

- Question mark (?). The question mark is used when you are unsure of a single letter or number in a text string. So, M?ll will locate Mill or Mall, or any other data that starts with an M, ends with two ls, and has one letter in between.

- Asterisk (*). The asterisk is used when you are unsure of two or more letters or numbers in a text string. So, Re* will find data entries such as Redmond, Renton, or Redondo.

Practice using wildcards to locate data in a field by searching for any zip codes that begin with the numbers 9805.

1. Choose <u>F</u>ind from the <u>E</u>dit menu.

2. Type 9805?

3. Click on <u>A</u>ll records.

4. Click on OK.

All the records that have zip codes beginning with 9805 are displayed.

5. Choose <u>1</u> All Records from the Sh<u>o</u>w command under the <u>R</u>ecord menu.

Now use the asterisk (*) to locate the employee who lives on Mill Road.

6. Choose <u>F</u>ind from the <u>E</u>dit menu.

7. Type *Mill* in the Fi<u>n</u>d what box.

8. Click on OK.

The street address is selected, and you can identify the employee as Brent Rockwell.

PRINTING A TABLE

A table can be printed like any other Works document. To ensure that the table will print on one page, you may need to change the page orientation to landscape.

1. Choose Page Setup from the <u>F</u>ile menu.

2. Click on the <u>S</u>ource, Size, and Orientation index tab.

3. Choose <u>L</u>andscape from the Orientation options.

4. Click on OK.

Before printing, you should use the Print Preview function to see how the table will print.

5. Click on 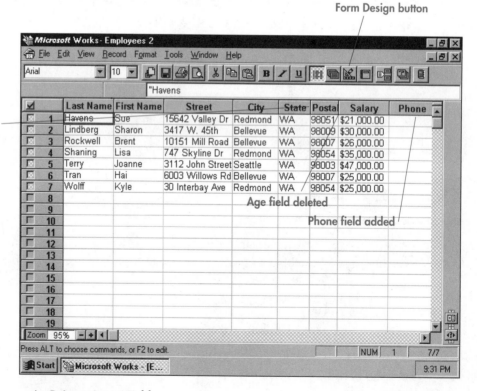.

6. Click on [Print].

The table is printed. Before continuing, change to the Form view.

CHANGING THE STRUCTURE OF A DATABASE

Works allows you to make changes in the design of a table, even after record data has been entered. Figure 9.12 shows the List view of the database design after deleting the Age field, adding a Phone field, and changing the Zip field name to Postal Code. To delete a field, you select it and choose the Delete Field command from the Record menu.

1. **Click once on the column heading Age to select the Age field.**

2. **Choose Delete Field from the Record menu.**

A confirmation message appears, asking if you want to permanently delete this information.

3. **Read the message then click on OK.**

To add a field, you choose Insert Field from the Record menu and specify the location of the field, either before or after the currently selected field.

4. **Verify that the Salary field is highlighted.**

5. **Click on the Record menu.**

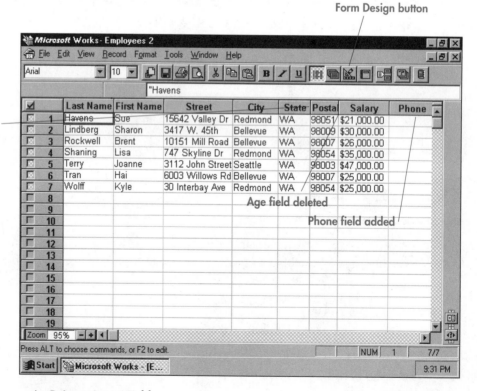

9.12

The database design after making changes to the fields

Field name changed to Postal Code

Form Design button

Age field deleted

Phone field added

6. **Point to Insert Field.**

7. **Click on 2 After.**

The Insert Field dialog box appears. This dialog box is similar to the Create Database dialog box you used earlier. The name of the field you are adding is Phone, and it is a text field.

8. **Type** Phone

9. **Click on** <u>T</u>ext **in the Format section.**

10. **Click on A**<u>d</u>**d.**

11. **Click on D**<u>o</u>**ne.**

To rename a field, you select the field name and choose Field from the Format menu.

12. **Click on the column heading Zip to select the Zip field.**

13. **Choose Fie**<u>l</u>**d from the F**<u>o</u>**rmat menu.**

The Format dialog box appears with the Field index tab displayed. The options in this tab resemble the ones displayed in the Insert Field and Create Database dialog boxes. Replace the field name Zip with Postal Code.

14. **Type** Postal Code **and click on OK.**

Your database should resemble Figure 9.12. (*Note:* The zoom has been changed to 95% to display all fields onscreen.)

CUSTOMIZING A FORM

You have been using List view to edit existing records, enter new records, and add and remove fields. Now you will learn how to make changes to the form to make it easier to enter data and to avoid data entry mistakes. Figure 9.13 shows Form view with the following changes:

- Several fields have been moved.
- The field names are aligned.
- The field names are in bold type.
- A border is placed around the field data.
- A graphic, the Adventure Tours logo, has been inserted.

To make changes to a form, you must display it in the Form Design view. You can switch to Form Design view by choosing Form Design from the View menu or by clicking on the Form Design button 📷 on the toolbar (see Figure 9.12). First view the form before making changes.

1. **Click on** 📄 **.**

Notice the placement of fields on the form. Now go to Form Design view.

2. **Click on** 📷 **.**

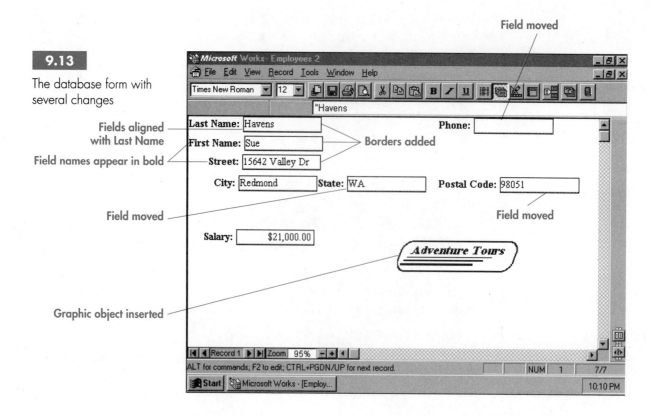

9.13

The database form with several changes

Field moved

Fields aligned with Last Name

Field names appear in bold

Field moved

Graphic object inserted

Borders added

Field moved

You will begin by moving fields so they match the arrangement shown in Figure 9.13. To move a field you point to the field name, hold down the mouse button, and drag the field to the new location. Figure 9.14 shows this process.

3. Point to the word *State*.

4. Hold down the mouse button.

5. Slowly drag the field to the location shown on Figure 9.14.

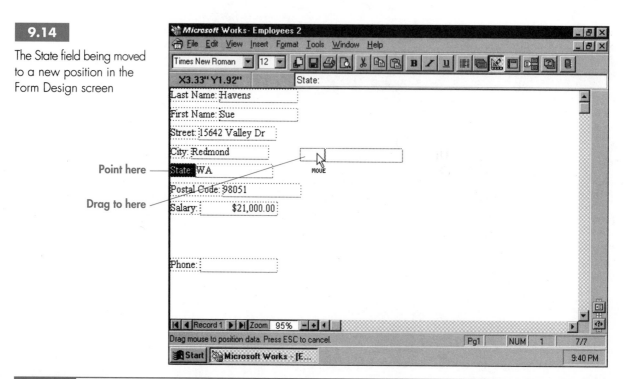

9.14

The State field being moved to a new position in the Form Design screen

Point here

Drag to here

6. Release the mouse button.

7. On your own, move the Postal Code and Phone fields as shown in Figure 9.13.

Now, align the Street, City, and Salary fields.

8. Move the Street field to align with the First Name field.

9. On your own, move the City and Salary fields to align with the First Name field.

Next use the bold button on the toolbar to bold the field names.

10. Click on Last Name to select it.

11. Click on ▣ in the toolbar.

12. On your own, bold the rest of the field names.

Now use the Border command to place a border around a data entry box.

13. Click on Havens to select the Last Name data entry box.

14. Choose Border from the Format menu.

The Format dialog box appears with the Border index tab displayed. The options in this index tab allow you to specify the line style and color of the outline. Currently a thin black line is selected.

15. Click inside the box labeled Outline. A single thin black line appears in the box.

16. Click on OK.

Notice an outline border has been placed around Havens.

17. Click on Sue to select the First Name data entry box.

18. On your own, place the same border around the data entry boxes.

Finally, insert the logo. The logo is saved on the data disk with the name Ati logo. You need to position the insertion point where the logo will appear and choose Object from the Insert menu.

19. Point to the location shown in Figure 9.13, then click the mouse button to display the insertion point.

20. Choose Object from the Insert menu.

21. If necessary, click on OK to bypass the First-time Help dialog box.

The Insert Object dialog box appears allowing you to specify the type of object. You need to indicate that this object is created from a file.

22. Click on Create from File.

The dialog box changes, allowing you to specify the file path and file name.

23. Delete the entry in the File box.

24. Type a:\Ati logo (or b:\Ati logo).

25. Click on OK.

The Microsoft Paint program opens, displaying the Paint tools and menu, and the Adventure Tours' logo graphic appears on screen. **Microsoft Paint** is part of the Windows 95 operating system and was used to create the logo. To complete the process of adding a graphic, click on a blank area in the form.

26. Click on a blank area on the form.

The Paint window disappears and the graphic is added. Change to Form view to see the changes.

27. Click on 🖼.

This completes the section on customizing a form. Your form should resemble Figure 9.14.

PRINTING A FORM

Now Print a form. If you print from the Form view all records will be printed unless you specify otherwise. The following instructions show you how to print just one form. First, change the print orientation from landscape, which you used to print the records in List view, to portrait.

1. Choose Page Setup from the File menu.

2. Display the Source, Size, & Orientation index tab, if necessary.

3. Click on Portrait.

4. Click on OK.

Now you can print a single record in Form view.

5. Choose Print from the File menu.

6. If necessary, click on OK to bypass the First-time Help dialog box.

The Print dialog box appears. Notice the setting called Current record only, which is near the bottom of the dialog box. By selecting this option, you print only the record that is showing on the screen, not the entire database of records.

7. Click on Current record only.

8. Click on OK.

9. Close the database and save the changes.

CREATING A DATABASE: A COMPREHENSIVE EXAMPLE

In this section you will work with a database called Clients, which is a list of Adventure Tours' customers. You will use the database to search for and replace data, customize a form, format the currency data to display a dollar sign, and create a calculated field.

1. Open *Clients* and maxmize the document window.

2. If necessary, click on 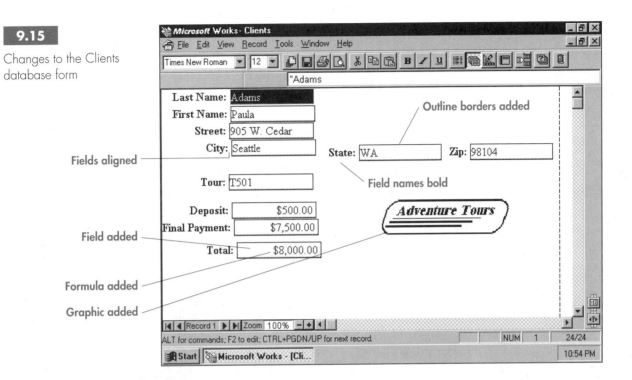.

3. Press CTRL + HOME to select record number 1.

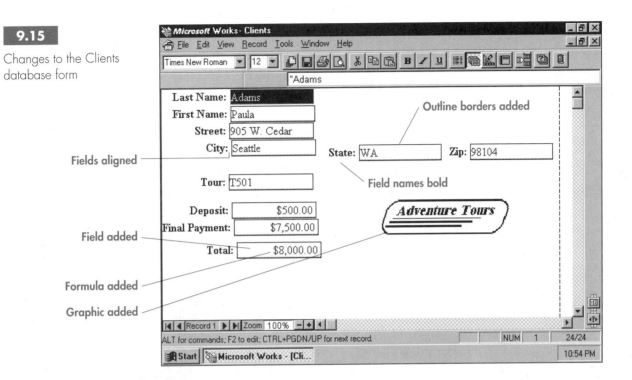

9.15

Changes to the Clients database form

Notice that the word "Bellevue" is spelled several ways and with different uppercase and lowercase combinations (Bellevue, Bellview, Bellvue, Belleview, BELLEVUE, bellevue). Use the Replace command to change all the spellings to "Bellevue."

4. Choose Replace from the Edit menu.

5. Type Bell* into the Find what box.

6. Type Bellevue into the Replace with box.

7. Click on Replace All.

Notice the changes made in the City field.

8. Click on .

Figure 9.15 shows the changes you will make to the Clients form to customize it. These include moving fields, formatting the field names to display in bold, placing a border around the field data, and inserting the logo.

9. On your own, duplicate the form shown in Figure 9.15 *except* the Total field.

In each record, the Total field will contain a different value, based on each client's deposit and the cost of his or her tour. Therefore, you must insert a formula into this field so that the Total amount can be calculated correctly for each client. You do this by adding a calculated field.

Works allows you to create a field that can be used to display the results of a calculation, called, simply enough, the **calculated field**. The calculation itself can involve more than one field. For example, in the clients' database a calculated field can be used to display the results of adding the Deposit and Final Payment fields. The process is to create the field and then enter a formula to perform the calculation.

1. Point to below the *F* in *Final Payment*.

2. Click the mouse button to display the insertion point.

3. Choose Field from the Insert menu.

4. Type Total

5. Choose Number from the Format options.

6. Choose the third option ($1234.56) in the Appearance list box.

7. Choose OK.

8. If necessary, align the Total field with the Final Payment and Deposit fields. Change the field name to boldface and add a single line outline border.

9. Click on a blank area of the form to view the changes.

Next you will add a formula to the Total field so that the results are automatically calculated whenever a new record is entered. To make changes to the content of this field, you must be in List view.

10. Click on ▦.

11. Click on the Total column heading to select this field. (*Note:* You may have to scroll to view this field.)

12. Type =Deposit+Final Payment

Notice that the formula appears on the Formula bar, as shown in Figure 9.16.

13. Press (↵ ENTER).

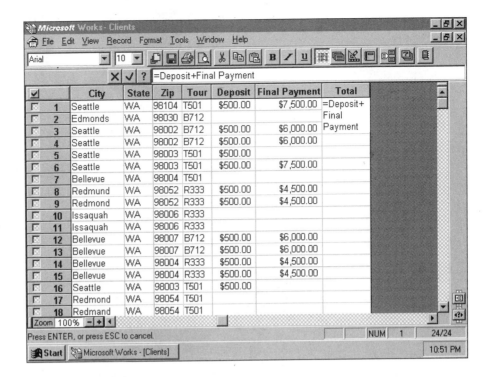

The formula is added to the calculated field and the calculations are performed. Now view the database in Form view. First display record 1.

14. Press (CTRL) + (HOME).

15. Click on 🖻.

Your screen should resemble Figure 9.15.

16. Save the database as *Clients 2* and close the database.

KEY TERMS

ascending	field name	sort
calculated field	Form view	table
database	List view	view
descending	Microsoft Paint	wildcard characters
field	record	

KEY COMMANDS

<u>1</u> All Records

<u>B</u>order

D<u>e</u>lete Field

Field <u>W</u>idth

<u>F</u>ind

F<u>o</u>rm

Form <u>D</u>esign

F<u>o</u>rmat/Fie<u>l</u>d

<u>4</u> Hidden Records

<u>I</u>nsert Field

<u>L</u>ist

<u>O</u>bject

Page Setup

R<u>e</u>place

Sh<u>o</u>w

<u>S</u>ort Records

REVIEW QUESTIONS

1. A(n) _____ is a collection of related information.

2. **T F**   A table consists of rows and columns.

3. A column in a table contains a single item or category of information called a(n) _____ .

4. A row in a table contains related information called a(n) _____ .

5. **T F**   Form view allows you to make changes in the table design.

6. The _____ _____ keys are used to move to the beginning of a table.

7. **T F**   The Find command from the Edit menu can be used to find specific data in a table.

8. To find all last names starting with T, you would enter _____ in the Find dialog box.

9. **T F**   You should save the table before sorting the records.

PROJECTS

1. Make the following changes to the Employees 2 database.

   a. Add the following phone numbers:

Record	Phone Number
Havens	555-2934
Lindberg	555-8937
Rockwell	555-4581
Shaning	555-9008
Terry	555-0003
Tran	555-3388
Wolff	555-4411

   b. Add the following records:

      Connie Venitou
      12235 Spokane
      Seattle, WA 98102
      555-0002
      $26,000

      Brad Johnson
      901 185th Place
      Bellevue, WA 98007
      555-7773
      $24,000

   c. Change Lisa Shaning's address to 474 Skyline Drive.

   d. Change Joanne Terry's phone number to 555-1226.

   e. Add a field to the table to list each employee's second language. You decide on the field name and sizes.

   f. Update all records with the following information:

Record	New Data
Havens	Spanish
Johnson	Chinese
Lindberg	French
Rockwell	Spanish
Shaning	German
Terry	Russian
Tran	Chinese
Venitou	Greek
Wolff	Spanish

   g. Search for those employees who speak Spanish, and display them in List view.

   h. Save the database as *Employees 3* and print a table showing all records. Close the database.

2. Develop a database of independent tour guides and enter the following data. You decide on the field names and sizes. Save the database as *Guides*.

Alan Taylor	Carole Scholl	Mark Garcia
1962 Shrader St	25403 Tiger Mt Road	77 Mill Creek Dr
Seattle WA 98105	Issaquah WA 98031	Redmond WA 98052
(206) 555-9835	(206) 555-8933	(206) 555-0011
Rafting	Trekking	Biking
Jerry Mason	Curtis Rush	Diane Skinner
1508 NE 187th	8864 Somerset Dr	33114 Mt Hood Dr
Woodinville WA 98061	Bellevue WA 98009	Bothell WA 98033
(206) 555-8883	(206) 555-0582	(206) 555-4450
Heli-skiing	Trekking	Biking
Russ Chen	Cheryl Eaton	Pat Landry
808 133rd St	3854 Greenbrier	122 Bear Creek
Redmond WA 98010	Spokane WA 98081	Spokane WA 98081
(206) 555-3242	(509) 555-7491	(509) 555-1998
Trekking	Biking	Rafting

Print the table.

Search for, and display in the List view, the tour guides who:

- specialize in trekking
- specialize in biking
- live in Spokane
- have the last name Garcia
- live on Somerset Drive

Close the database.

3. Develop a personal database and create within it a table for organizing one of the following:

- Information on friends and relatives (name, address, birthdays, and so on.)
- Information on an organization you belong to
- Information on a collection you maintain (trading cards, stamps, CDs, and so on.)

Enter at least six records. Save the database as *My database* and print the table.

Close the database.

10

Developing Filters and Reports Using a Database

- Create a filter

- Apply a filter

- Use a filter in List view

- Use a filter in Form view

- Develop reports

- Create reports using a filter

In Chapter 9 you used the Find command to search a database for specific data. The search generated one of two results. Using Find with a Next Record match, the desired data was highlighted in the next record in which it appeared. Using Find with an All Records match, only those records that contained the data appeared in List view. In this chapter you will learn how to use another technique—a **filter**—to search a database and display the results as a table. Think of a filter as a question. Using the filter process, Adventure Tours could ask questions of its database, such as:

- Which clients live in Seattle?

- Which clients live in Seattle or Redmond?

- Which clients have not paid a deposit?

- Which clients are registered for the Trekking in Nepal tour?

The difference between using the filter process and the Find command is that a filter is more flexible. It allows you to search in two or more fields at the same time. For example, you could search for those clients who live in Seattle and who are registered for the Trekking in Nepal tour. In addition, you could search for two values in the same field. For example, you could search the City field for those clients who live in Bellevue or Redmond.

To filter a database you use the Filters command from the Tools menu or click on the Filters button ▣ on the toolbar. Figure 10.1 shows the completed Filter dialog box that will display all of the records for clients who live in Seattle. When you use the Filter dialog box you need to specify three things: 1) the field to compare (in this case, City); 2) how the comparison should be defined (in this case, "is equal to"); 3) the value the field will be compared with (in this case, Seattle). You can also assign a name to a filter so it can be used repeatedly. Works allows you to create up to eight filters at one time and to search on as many as three fields at a time.

In this example, Works searches the City field of each record and compares the value in the field with the word "Seattle." If Seattle is in the field, the record is displayed in List view. Complete the following process to duplicate Figure 10.1.

1. Open the *Clients tour info* database.
2. If necessary, click on ▣ and maximize the database window.
3. Choose **F**ilters from the **T**ools menu. (If necessary, click OK to remove the First-time Help dialog box.)

The Filter dialog box appears, followed by a smaller dialog box, titled Filter Name. Once you assign a name to a filter, it will be saved with the database and you can use it over and over. Type the filter name now.

4. **Type** Seattle Clients
5. Click on OK.

The Filter dialog box remains onscreen, and "Seattle Clients" appears in the Filter name box. Next you need to choose the Field name, which will be City for this filter.

6. Click on ▾ in the Fie**l**d name list box.

The complete Filter dialog box that will display all the records containing Seattle in the City field

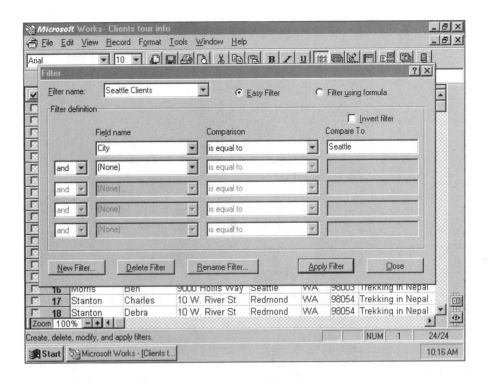

7. **Click on City** (*Note*: You may need to scroll the list to find the City field name.)

The comparison statement is automatically set for "is equal to." Because we want to find only records that have Seattle in the City field, we can keep the "is equal to" comparison. The final step is typing Seattle in the Compare To text box.

8. **Click inside the box under Compare To.**

9. **Type** Seattle

Your screen should resemble Figure 10.1.

10. **Click on** Apply Filter **near the bottom of the dialog box.**

List view displays only the records of those clients who live in Seattle. Now display all the records.

11. **Choose Show from the Record menu.**

12. **Choose 1 All Records from the Show command.**

All the records are displayed.

It is important to understand that, regardless of the type of filter you create, each filter is saved with the database. Whenever you apply a filter, it will display the desired records. Thus, if a new Seattle client was added to the database and the Seattle Client filter was applied, the new client's record would be displayed.

The Or Operator

What if Adventure Tours wants to know which clients live in Seattle or in Redmond? In this case, Works would search the City field to see if Seattle or Redmond appears. Figure 10.2 shows the filter. Notice that the two values— Seattle and Redmond—are each entered in a Field name box, and that the Or statement between the two values is selected, indicating that if *either* Seattle *or* Redmond is in the City field, the record will be displayed. When you use the **Or operator**, only *one* of the conditions needs to be true for a record to be displayed.

1. Click on ▨.

2. Click on [New Filter...] in the lower-left corner of the dialog box.

3. Type Sea or Redmond

4. Choose OK.

5. Click on City in the Field name list box.

6. Type Seattle in the Compare To box.

7. Press (TAB ⇄).

8. Click on ▾ next to the "and" option (see Figure 10.2).

9. Choose "or".

10. Complete the second line of the filter (i.e., City is equal to Redmond).

Your dialog box should resemble the one in Figure 10.2.

11. Click on [Apply Filter].

List view appears, displaying the records of those clients who live in Seattle or Redmond.

The And Operator

As you have seen, using the Or operator, you can search the City field for those clients who live in Seattle, Redmond, or Bellevue. Until now you have been searching on one field, City, but with the filter dialog box, you can search up to three different fields. For example, you could search for those who live in Seattle *and* have paid their deposit. Or you could search for those who are on the Trekking in Nepal tour *and* have not made their final payment. Figure 10.3 shows the completed dialog box that will display those clients who live in Seattle and are on the Trekking in Nepal tour. Notice the **And operator** is selected. When you use the And operator, *both* of the conditions must be satisfied for a record to be displayed.

Click here to choose the OR option

1. Click on 🔳 button.

2. Click on New Filter....

3. Type Sea/Trek Nepal in the Filter name box.

4. Choose OK.

5. Complete the first line of the filter (City is equal to Seattle).

6. Make sure that the "and" option to the left of the second Field name box is selected.

7. Complete the second line of the filter (Tour is equal to Trekking in Nepal).

Your dialog box should resemble the one in Figure 10.3.

8. Click on Apply Filter.

Clients who live in Seattle and are registered for the Nepal trek are displayed.

Greater than, Less than Comparison Statements

Using the greater than and less than comparison statements you can search for a range of values. Figure 10.4 shows the completed Filter dialog box that will display the records of clients who live in zip codes 98003 to 98006, inclusive. Using the And operator, both conditions you specify must be met in order for a record to display. In this case, the entry in the Zip field must be greater than or equal to 98003 and less than or equal to 98006. To create a filter for selecting these zip codes, you must change the Comparison from "is equal to" to "is greater than or equal to." You choose the desired comparison statement by clicking on the down arrow and selecting it from the list. Again, note that Figure 10.4 shows the completed dialog box.

10.3

A filter that will display records of clients who live in Seattle and are on the Trekking in Nepal tour

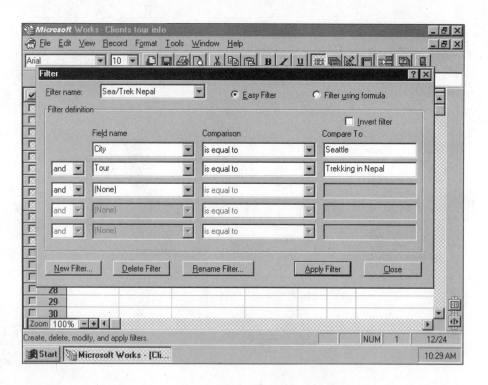

10.4

A filter that selects records within a range of values (zip codes 98003 through 98006)

Click here to select a Comparison statement

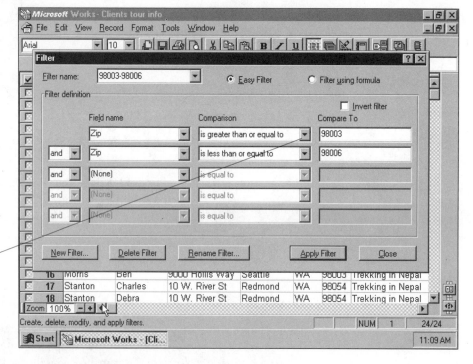

1. Click on ![icon].

2. Click on [New Filter...].

3. **Type** 98003-98006

4. Click on OK.

5. Complete the first line of the filter (see Figure 10.4).

6. Complete the second line of the filter.

7. Click on [Apply Filter].

The records that meet the comparison conditions are displayed. You can print the results of a filter as you would any table.

DELETING AND RENAMING FILTERS

Remember, in Works you can create up to eight filters at one time and all filters are saved with the database. Undoubtedly, there will come a time when you will want to modify, rename, or delete a filter. To modify a filter, you display it in the Filter dialog box and change the field names, comparison statements, or Compare To text boxes. The changes are automatically saved under the filter name. You can also rename a filter to more accurately reflect the type of comparison being performed, and you can delete a filter. Next, you will practice renaming and deleting filters.

1. Click on [icon].

Notice the Delete Filter and Rename Filter option buttons on the bottom of the dialog box.

2. Click on [Rename Filter...].

The Filter Name dialog box appears, displaying the name of the most recently used filter, the one that searched for a range of zip codes. You need to rename this filter.

3. Type Zips 98003-006

4. Click on OK.

The new Filter name is displayed. Now delete the Sea or Redmond filter.

5. Click on the [▾] in the Filter name list box to display all of the filters associated with this database.

6. Choose the Sea or Redmond filter from the list.

7. Click on [Delete Filter].

A message appears advising you that this operation cannot be undone or reversed.

8. Read the message and then choose Yes.

9. Click on Close to return to the List View.

Before continuing, display all of the records.

10. Choose Show from the Record menu.

11. Choose 1 All Records from the Show command.

12. Press (CTRL)+(HOME) to select the Last Name field of the first record.

The Filter dialog box provides a great deal of flexibility in creating a filter to search a database and display selected records. One way to quickly apply a filter is by using the Apply Filter command in the Record menu. Try using this command now.

13. Click on Record.

14. Point to Apply Filter.

The available filters are displayed in the menu.

15. Click on 1 Seattle Clients.

16. On your own, display all records.

APPLYING FILTERS IN FORM VIEW

Filters can also be used when the data is displayed in Form view. Using a filter in Form view gives you the advantage of displaying each of the selected records individually. The process for applying a filter in Form view is identical to the one used in List view. First, switch to Form view and then apply the Sea/Trek Nepal filter.

1. Click on .

2. Choose Apply Filter from the Record menu.

3. Click on 2 Sea/Trek Nepal.

4. Use the navigation arrows at the bottom of the screen to display the filtered records.

5. On your own, display all records.

6. Click on to return to the List View.

USING WILDCARD CHARACTERS IN A FILTER

As you may remember from Chapter 9, when you do not know the exact data to search for, Works allows you to use wildcards. Wildcards are permitted in filters. The asterick symbol (*) is used in place of a string of unknown characters, whereas the question mark symbol (?) is used in place of single unknown characters. Some examples are:

Entry	Field	Locates
M*	Last Name	Those whose last names start with M
Hill	Street	Those whose street address includes the characters Hill
Redm?nd	City	Those who live in Redmond or Redmand

Figure 10.5 shows a filter that will display the records of clients whose last name starts with M.

10.5

A filter that will display
records of clients whose
last name starts with M

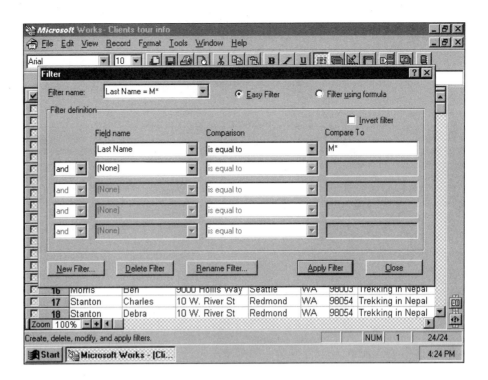

1. Click on 🖾.

2. Click on ⟦ New Filter... ⟧.

3. **Type** Last Name = M* **in the Filter Name dialog box.**

4. **Choose OK.**

5. **Choose Last Name from the Field Name list box.**

6. **Type** M* **in the Compare To box.**

Your dialog box should resemble the one in Figure 10.5.

7. Click on ⟦ Apply Filter ⟧.

Clients whose last name starts with M are displayed.

8. **Choose Show from the Record menu.**

9. **Choose 1 All Records from the Show command.**

10. **Press** ⟮ CTRL ⟯+⟮ HOME ⟯ **to move to the first record.**

DEVELOPING REPORTS

Until now you have been printing the information in a database in the form
of tables. However, Microsoft Works provides an easy way for you to develop
reports using the information from a database. Figure 10.6 shows a **report**
created using the information in the Clients tour info database and the report
definition that generates the report. A **report definition** is similar to a tem-
plate in that it determines how the report will appear. The report is made up
of four sections, each with one or more rows. These four sections of the report
definition are explained below.

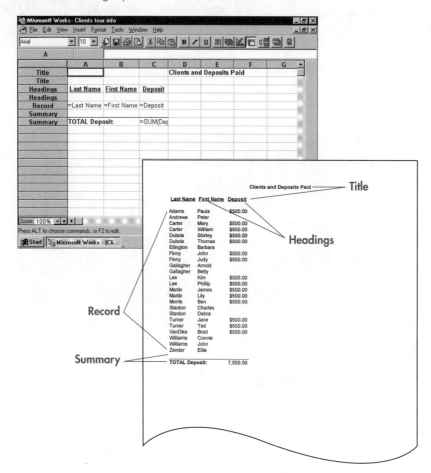

- Title: The **Title section** has two rows. The first row is used to enter a title for the report. In this case the title is Clients and Deposits Paid. The second title row is blank and can be used for a subheading or to create a blank line in the report.

- Headings: The **Headings section** is made up of two rows. The first Headings row contains the field names. The second Headings row is blank and is used to separate the field names from the field data.

- Record: The **Record section** is where record data is displayed. The report definition shows only one Record row. However, Works will use as many rows as necessary to display all of the desired records. Notice the finished report has 24 records (rows), one for each client.

- Summary: The **Summary section** contains the summary information for the report. In this case there are two Summary rows. The first Summary row is blank and separates the summary information from the record information. The second Summary row displays the words "TOTAL Deposit" and a function (SUM) that will calculate the total for the values in the Deposit column.

When creating a report, you decide on the fields to be included in the report and how the information will be summarized. To do this, you use the ReportCreator dialog box. When you have selected the desired options, such as fields to be displayed, the report title, and sorting and summary information, Works builds the report definition for you. Although you do not have to build the report definition yourself, it is advisable to study the report definition so you can customize the report layout. Examine Figure 10.6 until you understand the relationship between the report definition and the finished report.

CREATING A REPORT

To create a report, choose ReportCreator from the Tools menu or click on the Report View button 🖺 on the toolbar. A dialog box appears asking you to provide a name for the report. The next dialog box that appears is titled ReportCreator. This dialog box has six index tabs, each providing different options for designing a report. The options enable you to add a title and fields to the report, sort and group the information, filter the records, and provide summary information, such as a total calculation for a numeric field. You will be using four of the six index tabs—Title, Fields, Sorting, and Summary—in creating the report shown in Figure 10.6.

1. If necessary, click on 🖺.

2. Choose ReportCreator from the Tools menu. (*Note*: You may have to bypass the First-time Help dialog box by clicking on OK.)

3. Type Deposits Paid as the report name.

4. Click on OK.

The ReportCreator dialog box appears. Notice that the report name, Deposits Paid, appears in the title bar along with the name of the database. The Title index tab is displayed and the Report title box is highlighted. Begin by adding a title to this report.

5. If necessary, click on the Title index tab.

6. Type Clients and Deposits Paid in the Report title box.

Next, add fields to the report. You can do this by clicking on the Fields index tab or by clicking on the Next button.

7. Click on the Fields index tab or click on ⬚ Next > ⬚.

The list on the left indicates the available fields for the open database. To add data to the report, you must choose the fields and click on the Add button. The fields will appear in the list on the right. *You must be sure to add the fields in the order that you want them to appear on the report.* Figure 10.7 shows the Fields index tab after field names have been selected for the report. Complete the following steps to duplicate Figure 10.7.

8. Verify that the Last Name field is highlighted.

9. Click on ⬚ Add > ⬚.

Notice that the highlight moves to the First Name field. A shortcut method for adding a field to a report is double-clicking on the field name. Try this method of adding fields to the report.

10. Double-click on First Name.

11. Using either method, add the Deposit field to the report.

Your dialog box should resemble the one in Figure 10.7. Now you are ready to determine the sorting order for the records. You can click on the Sorting index tab or on ⬚ Next > ⬚. Either choice will display the Sorting options.

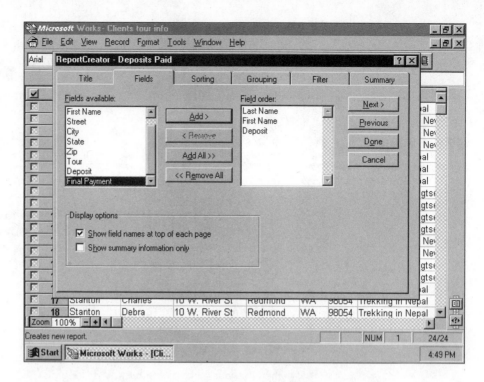

12. **Click on the Sorting index tab or click on** Next > .

You will sort records by the Last Name field only. Click on ▼ next to the Sort by box, and select the Last Name field.

13. **Click on** ▼ **in the Sort by list box.**

14. **Click on Last Name.**

You will not need the grouping or filter options for this report, so you can bypass these index tabs. To move directly to the summary options, use the Summary index tab.

15. **Click on the Summary index tab.**

The Summary options allow you to select a field and perform a calculation. Only one of the chosen fields contains numeric information, the Deposit field. You want to see the total amount for the deposits made, so you will select the Sum option.

16. **Click on Deposit to select that field.**

17. **Click on Sum from the Summaries options.**

Your dialog box should resemble the one in Figure 10.8. Notice the options for displaying summary information. If you were grouping records, you could provide summary information for each group. The default option places the summary information at the end of the report. This is the option you want to select. When you are finished choosing options, click on the Done command button and the report will be created.

18. **Click on** Done .

A dialog box appears informing you that the report definition has been created and asking if you want to preview the report or display the report definition. For now, preview the report.

10.8

The Summary section of the
ReportCreator dialog box
after choosing the Sum
option for the Deposit field

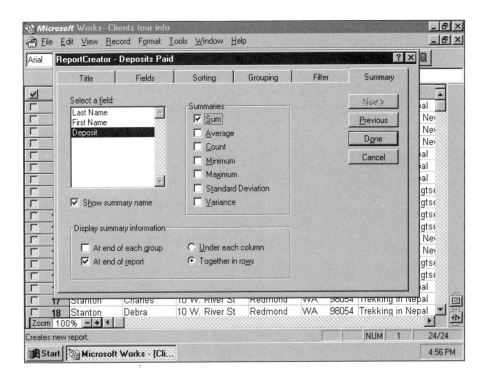

19. Click on **Preview**.

The report is displayed in the Print Preview screen. Use the zoom feature to
see the details of the report.

20. Point to the report and click the mouse button.

Notice that the clients are listed in alphabetical order and that the Deposit
field is totaled at the end of the report. Next you will go into the Report
Design view to make changes to the report.

21. Click on Cancel to display the report definition.

MODIFYING THE REPORT DEFINITION

The report definition can be used to modify the report layout. There are two
changes you will make to the report definition to make the report more readable. First you will move the heading and center it across the field names.
Next you will change the words "TOTAL Deposit" to "TOTAL:" and move this
text to column B.

1. **Click on the report title located in the first Title row in column D.**

2. **Choose Cut from the Edit menu or click on** ✂.

3. **Point to the cell column A in the top Title row.**

4. **Click the mouse button to select the cell.**

5. **Choose Paste from the Edit menu or click on** 📋.

Now center the heading across the columns using the Alignment command from the Format menu.

6. Highlight the first three cells in the top row (columns A, B, and C in the first title row).

7. Choose Alignment from the Format menu.

8. Verify that the Alignment index tab is displayed.

9. Choose Center across selection under the horizontal positioning options.

10. Choose OK.

The title now appears centered across all columns. The next change will be to delete the words "TOTAL Deposit:" and enter the word "TOTAL:" into column B of the second summary row.

11. Click on TOTAL Deposit:.

12. Press (DELETE).

13. Click on the cell Column B of the second Summary row (next to the =SUM function).

14. Type TOTAL:

15. Press (↵ ENTER).

16. If not already selected, click on **B** to make the text boldface.

You screen should resemble the report definition shown in Figure 10.9.

17. Click on ▢.

18. View the changes to the report and click on [Cancel].

Figure 10.10 shows a report with the clients' names, deposits, and final payments, and the report definition used to create it. Complete the following steps to duplicate this report.

10.9

The report definition for the Deposits Paid report

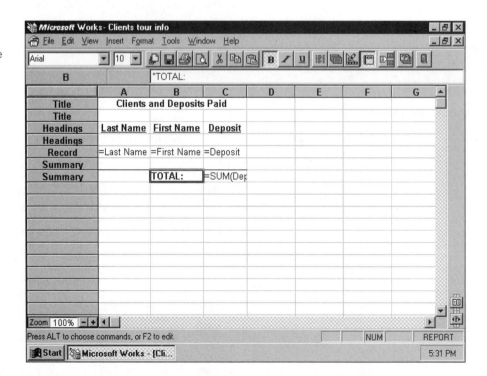

Title moved and centered across columns

Total moved

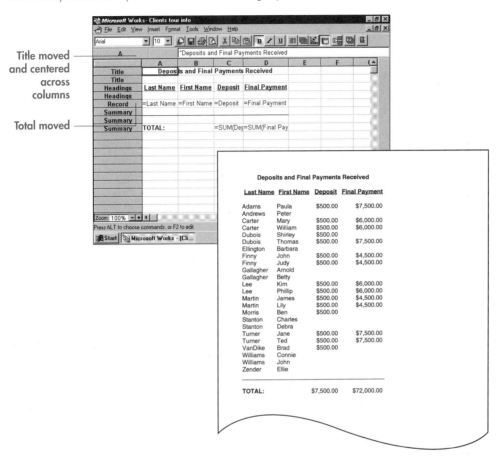

1. Choose <u>R</u>eportCreator from the <u>T</u>ools menu.

2. Type Money Received for the report name and click on OK.

3. Verify that the Title index tab is displayed.

4. Type Deposits and Final Payments Received in the <u>R</u>eport title box.

5. Click on <u>Next ></u>.

6. Verify that the Fields index tab is displayed, then add the Last Name, First Name, Deposit, and Final Payment fields in this order.

7. Click on <u>Next ></u>.

8. Verify that the Sorting index tab is displayed. Choose Last Name from the <u>S</u>ort by list box.

9. Click on the Summary index tab.

10. Click on the Deposit field to select this field.

11. Click on <u>S</u>um to select this Summaries option.

12. Under "Display Summary information," click on <u>U</u>nder each column.

(*Note:* This summary information display option will put the total deposit in the same column as the deposit information for each record. This choice affects the position of the Final Payment summary information as well.)

13. Click on the Final Payment field to highlight it and select this field.

14. Click on Sum to select this Summaries option.

15. Verify that Under each column is selected in the Display Summary information section.

16. Click on [Done].

17. Click on [Preview].

18. Click the mouse to zoom in on the report.

Notice that the word "SUM:" appears twice. You will return to the report definition and change the word from "SUM:" to "TOTAL:" and display it to the left of the total figures. Also notice that the title is not centered across the columns. You will move the title and choose the Center across alignment option.

19. Click on [Cancel].

20. Drag the mouse pointer across the two cells that contain the word "SUM:".

21. Press [DELETE].

22. Click on the cell Column A of the third Summary row.

23. Type TOTAL:

24. Click on **B** to make *TOTAL:* boldface.

25. Move the report title from column D to column A.

26. Highlight Columns A through D in the top Title row.

27. Choose Alignment from the Format menu.

28. Click on the Center across selection alignment option.

29. Choose OK.

Your screen should resemble the report definition in Figure 10.10.

30. Click on 🔍.

View the report and return to the report definition.

31. View the report, then click on [Cancel].

CREATING A REPORT USING A FILTER

Works allows you to create a report using a filter to select the report records. This is useful if you want to display only certain records in your report. Figure 10.11 shows a report that contains the names, city, and amounts paid for clients who live in Seattle, and the report definition used to create the report. To filter a report, you must create the filter first; then you select it from the Filter index tab in the ReportCreator dialog box. Earlier you created a filter called Seattle Clients. You will use that filter to design this report.

1. Choose ReportCreator from the Tools menu.

2. Type Seattle Clients, then click on OK.

3. Verify that the Title index tab is selected and that the Report title box is highlighted.

4. Type Seattle Clients - Deposits and Final Payments

A report definition and resulting report created using a filter

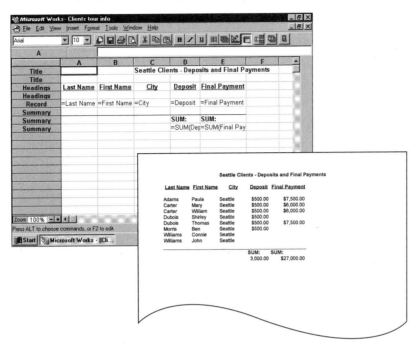

5. Click on **Next >** .

6. Add the **Last Name, First Name, City, Deposit,** and **Final Payment** fields to the report.

(*Note*: If you add a field by mistake, highlight it in the Field order list box and click on the Remove button.)

7. Click on **Next >** .

8. Choose **Last Name** from the **S**ort by list box.

9. Click on the **Filter** index tab.

10. Choose **Seattle Clients** from the filter list.

11. Click on **Next >** .

12. Choose **Deposit** from the field list.

13. Choose **S**um from the Summaries options.

14. Click on **U**nder each column to choose that Summary information display option.

15. On your own, create a sum formula for the **Final Payment** field.

16. Click on **Done** .

17. Click on **Preview** .

Your report should match the one in Figure 10.11. Notice that the word "SUM" appears twice and that the title is not centered across the report. In addition, the City field displays information that is repetitive. You will change the report definition so the title is centered, the word "TOTAL:" replaces the two occurrences of "SUM:," and the City column is removed. Your report and the corresponding report definition should match those pictured in Figure 10.12.

18. Click on **Cancel** .

The Seattle Clients report definition and resulting report with changes

Title moved
and centered
across
columns

Total added

City column
deleted

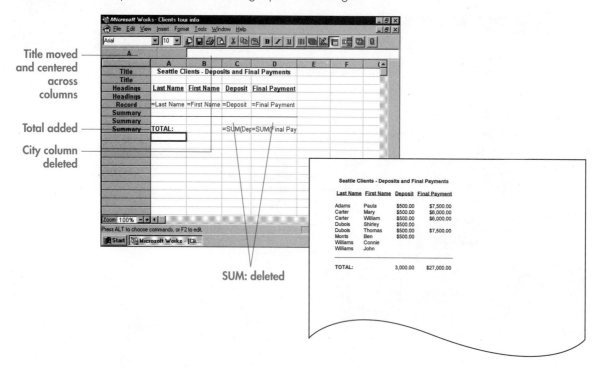

SUM: deleted

Compare the report definition to the one shown in Figure 10.11, then make the following changes to duplicate the report definition in Figure 10.12.

19. Center the report title across columns A through E.

20. Delete both occurrences of the word "SUM:." Type TOTAL: in the cell in Column A of the third Summary row.

21. Format *TOTAL:* in the bold style.

Now you will delete the column that contains the City information (Column C).

22. Click on the column header C to highlight the column.

23. Choose Cut from the Edit menu or click on [✄].

The City column is removed. Your report definition should match the one in Figure 10.12. Preview the report.

24. Preview the report, then return to the report definition.

CREATING A REPORT THAT GROUPS DATA

An important feature of the Works database application is the ability to create reports that group data. Figure 10.13 shows a report that is grouped by tour. A Summary row indicating the number of people on the tour is provided for each grouping. In order to create a report that groups data, you use the Grouping index tab in the ReportCreator dialog box. Complete the following to create the report in Figure 10.13.

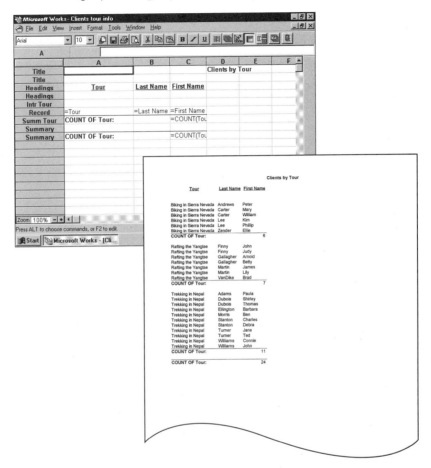

1. Choose ReportCreator from the Tools menu.

2. Type Clients by Tour for the report name and choose OK.

3. Type Clients by Tour for the report title.

4. Display the Fields index tab. Add the Tour, Last Name, and First Name fields to the report in this order.

5. Display the Sorting index tab, then choose Tour from the Sort by list box.

6. Click on the Grouping index tab or click on Next >.

The Grouping index tab shows only one available option, When contents change. This indicates that a new group will be created whenever the tour type changes. You can select this option by clicking in the checkbox.

7. Click in the When contents change checkbox.

8. Click on the Filter index tab or click on Next >.

You will choose the All Records option in the filter list to make sure that *all* database information is included in the report. This is a precautionary step, because the last report you created used a filter.

9. Click on (All Records).

10. Click on the Summary index tab or click on Next >.

For this report you want to find out the number of people signed up for each tour. Because the report is grouped by tour, you can select the Tour field and click on the Count option. To display the information at the end of each grouping, you will want to select the At end of each group display option.

11. Verify that Tour is highlighted, then click in the **C**ount checkbox.

12. Click on At end of each **g**roup in the Display Summary information section.

13. Click on **D**one to display the report in the Print Preview screen.

Your report should resemble the one shown in Figure 10.13. Return to the report definition and compare it to Figure 10.13.

14. On your own, return to the report definition.

ENHANCING A REPORT

Until now you have been making relatively few style changes to the layout of a report. Additional design changes are possible, including changes to the font, column width, and type styles. Figure 10.14 shows the Clients by Tour report with some additional formatting changes. These changes include some procedures you are familiar with and some that you have not yet practiced. The changes are:

- The title is centered across the report

- The Times New Roman font is applied to the title

- The font size for the title is increased

- Underlining is removed from the column headings

- A solid, double underline is placed under all three column headings

- Column headings are formatted with the italic style

- The word TOTAL replaces the words COUNT OF Tour: on the Summ Tour line

- The words TOTAL ALL TOURS: replaces the words COUNT OF Tour: on the bottom Summary line

Complete the following style changes to duplicate Figure 10.14.

1. Select *Clients by Tour* and move it to column A.

2. Using the **A**lignment command, center the title across columns A through C.

3. Use the Font Name list box to change the title font to Times New Roman.

4. Use the Font Size list box to change the title font to 16 point.

5. Select cells A, B, and C in the first headings row and click on ⓤ to remove the underlining.

Next you will add a border below the cells containing the column headings. To do this, you use the Border command in the Format menu. You will choose a double line from the border options.

6. Verify that the three column headings remain selected.

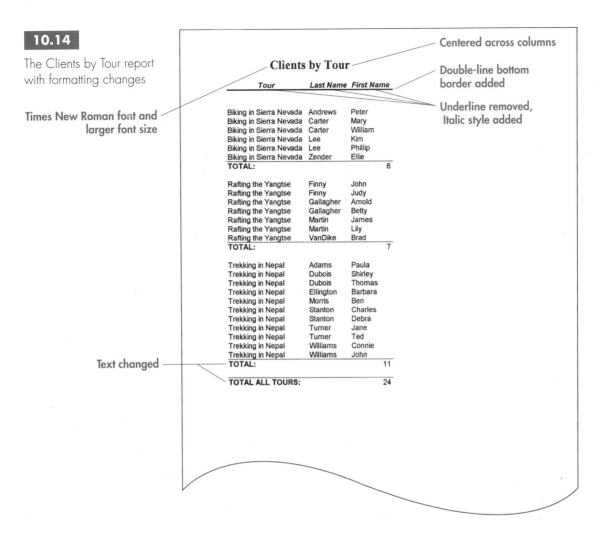

10.14

The Clients by Tour report with formatting changes

Times New Roman font and larger font size

Centered across columns

Double-line bottom border added

Underline removed, Italic style added

Text changed

Clients by Tour

Tour	Last Name	First Name
Biking in Sierra Nevada	Andrews	Peter
Biking in Sierra Nevada	Carter	Mary
Biking in Sierra Nevada	Carter	William
Biking in Sierra Nevada	Lee	Kim
Biking in Sierra Nevada	Lee	Phillip
Biking in Sierra Nevada	Zender	Ellie
TOTAL:		6
Rafting the Yangtse	Finny	John
Rafting the Yangtse	Finny	Judy
Rafting the Yangtse	Gallagher	Arnold
Rafting the Yangtse	Gallagher	Betty
Rafting the Yangtse	Martin	James
Rafting the Yangtse	Martin	Lily
Rafting the Yangtse	VanDike	Brad
TOTAL:		7
Trekking in Nepal	Adams	Paula
Trekking in Nepal	Dubois	Shirley
Trekking in Nepal	Dubois	Thomas
Trekking in Nepal	Ellington	Barbara
Trekking in Nepal	Morris	Ben
Trekking in Nepal	Stanton	Charles
Trekking in Nepal	Stanton	Debra
Trekking in Nepal	Turner	Jane
Trekking in Nepal	Turner	Ted
Trekking in Nepal	Williams	Connie
Trekking in Nepal	Williams	John
TOTAL:		11
TOTAL ALL TOURS:		24

7. Choose <u>B</u>order from the <u>F</u>ormat menu.

8. Verify that the Border index tab is displayed.

9. Select on the Botto<u>m</u> option under Border.

10. Click on the double-line option under <u>L</u>ine style.

11. Choose OK.

12. On your own, format the column headings in the italic style.

Next you will replace the words "COUNT OF Tour:" with "TOTAL:" and "TOTAL ALL TOURS:" Notice that the COUNT OF Tour: heading appears on both the SUMM Tour line and the bottom Summary line. Each line represents the location in the report where these words will appear. You can remove the existing text simply by clicking on the cell and typing the new text.

13. Click on *COUNT OF Tour:* on the Summ Tour line.

14. Type TOTAL:

15. On your own, change the other *COUNT OF TOUR:* line to *TOTAL ALL TOURS:*

16. Preview the report.

Your report should resemble the one in Figure 10.14.

17. Click on [Cancel].

18. Save the database with the name *Clients tour info revised* and close the database.

KEY TERMS

and operator	or operator	report definition
heading section	record section	summary section
filter	report	title section

KEY COMMANDS

Alignment	Border	ReportCreator
Apply Filter	Filters	

REVIEW QUESTIONS

1. A filter is a(n) _____.

2. When you create a filter you specify the _____ (s) that are to be displayed as a result of the filter.

3. **T F** A filter can be used to display records in either Form view or List view.

4. **T F** In Works you can create and store up to ten filters.

5. A maximum of _____ filters can be saved in the database at one time.

6. **T F** The Or operator in a filter allows you to search the same field for more than one value.

7. **T F** A filter can be used in creating a report.

8. **T F** To group data in a report, you must select a field to group on.

9. The _____ section is the part of the report definition that will display the data from a table.

PROJECTS

1. Using the Clients tour info revised database, develop the following filters. (*Note*: you will need to delete existing filters to keep within the eight-filter maximum.)
   a. Clients who live in Bellevue, Redmond, or Edmonds.
   b. Clients who have paid a deposit but not paid the final payment.
   c. Clients who have zip codes less than 98010.
   d. Clients who live on River Street.

   Develop a filter, called *Deposit*, of clients who have paid a deposit. Sort the resulting table by zip code, in descending order. Print the table. Close the database without saving changes.

2. Using the Guides database you created in Project 2 of Chapter 9, develop the following filters:
   a. Clients living in Spokane.
   b. Clients specializing in trekking.
   c. Clients living in Redmond, Bellevue, or Bothell.
   d. Clients specializing in biking or rafting.
   e. Clients with 206 area codes.

3. On the data disk is a database named Books, which contains information about publications sold by Adventure Tours. Open this database and browse through it to see the type of information it contains. Then develop the following filters.
   a. The books distributed by Outdoor Press.
   b. Books costing under $10.00.
   c. Books written by Messner.
   d. Books ranging in price from $10.00 to $20.00, inclusive.
   e. Books on biking. (*Hint*: Use the * wildcard to search the Title field.)
   f. Books about kayaking or rafting.

4. Using the Books database, develop a report that groups records by distributor. Include a total count of the records. Print the report.

5. Using the Books database, develop a filter for those books that cost more than $10.00. Name the filter Books Over $10. Using another filter, develop an additional report in which the books that cost more than $10 are grouped by distributor. Include the book's price and title in this report. Also include a count of each group of records and a total count of all records. Print the report. Close the database without saving changes.

6. Develop a report using the Guides database. Group the records in the report by specialty areas. Include a count of the records for each group and a total count of all records. Print the report. Close the database without saving changes.

11

Developing Form Letters, Addressing Envelopes, and Creating Mailing Labels

- Create a form letter

- Merge a form letter with database records to create a finished letter

- Use a filter to select database records for merging with a form letter

- Use mail merge for addressing envelopes

- Use mail merge for creating mailing labels

One of the most important tasks for many businesses is to send letters, such as advertisements or announcements, to its customers. Works allows you to create a document and merge it with names and addresses to create **form letters**. This is called **mail merge** and involves combining database records with a word processing document to create a finished letter. Figure 11.1 shows a letter that will be sent to each Adventure Tours client. The basic letter, an invitation to the grand opening of the new office, is the same letter for each client. Only the client's name and address change. The client information comes from a database and is merged with the word processing document, called the **main document**.

As just explained, there are two files involved when working with form letters: the database file containing the names and addresses, and the main document file created using the word processing application. Figure 11.2 shows these two files and the form letter that results from merging them. Notice the main document file has **placeholders** with the names of the fields in the database. Wherever a placeholder appears in the main document, the database information will print in the finished letter. Thus, you use the word processing application to create the main letter and the database to supply the variable information. Complete the following steps to create the main document shown in Figure 11.2.

1. Start Works and choose the <u>W</u>ord Processor tool from the Works Task Launcher dialog box.

2. If necessary, maximize the document window.

3. Type the current date.

4. Press (↵ ENTER) three times to add two blank lines.

At this point you need to add a field placeholder for the client's first name.

5. Choose Database <u>F</u>ield from the <u>I</u>nsert menu.

6. If necessary, click on OK to bypass the First-time Help dialog box.

11.1

A letter created by merging database information with a word processing document

October 15, 1996

Paula Adams
905 W. Cedar
Seattle, WA 98104

Dear Paula:

We would like to invite you to attend a reception to celebrate the opening of our new Eastside office located at Gillman Village Business Park on November 10th. The reception will start at 6:00pm.

There will be door prizes, including an all-expense-paid trip to Lhasa, Tibet. Come and meet our professional tour consultants and the manager, Joanne Terry.

The database file and the form letter used to create the merged letter

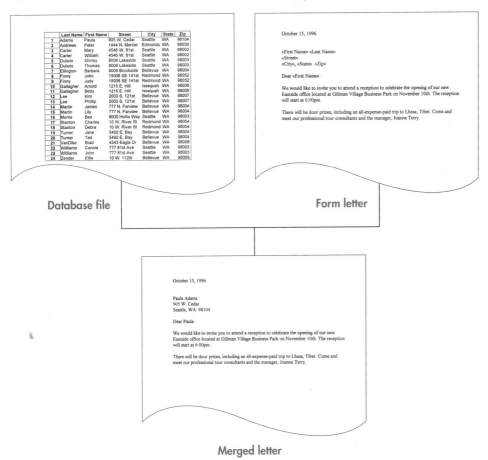

Database file

Form letter

Merged letter

The Insert Field dialog box appears, allowing you to choose which field to insert. First, you must specify which database to use. Your dialog box may or may not have a database specified. You need to specify the Clients database.

7. **Click on the ▦ button labeled "Use a different database."**

The Use Database dialog box appears. The Clients database may appear in this list if you recently viewed that file. You can select Clients from the list and click on OK. If Clients does not appear in the list, you need to select the Open a database not listed here button. For this exercise, we will assume that the database does not appear in the list.

8. **Click on the ▦ button labeled "Open a database not listed here."**

The Use Another File dialog box appears. This dialog box is similar to the Open dialog box.

9. **Type** a:\Clients **(or** b:\Clients**) in the File name box and choose Open.**

11.3

The Insert Field dialog box
with the First Name field
selected

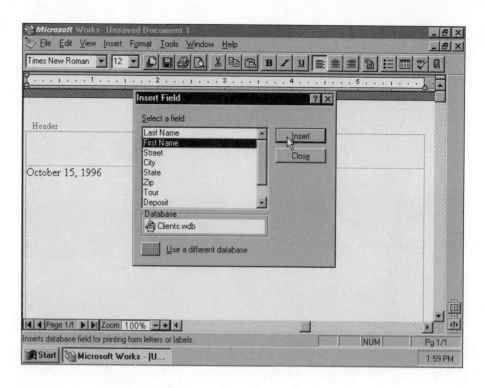

The database file is opened and the Insert Field dialog box displays the available field names for the Clients database.

10. **Click on First Name.**

Your screen should resemble Figure 11.3.

11. **Click on Insert.**

The placeholder <<First Name>> is inserted in the main document at the insertion point.

When you use placeholders for adding text to a document, you need to add spacing and punctuation before or after the field names. In this case, you need to add a space between the First Name and Last Name fields. Punctuation and spacing can be added only using the keyboard, so you need to close the Insert Field dialog box.

12. **Click on Close.**

13. **Press** (SPACEBAR) **once.**

14. **Choose Database Field from the Insert menu.**

15. **Verify that Last Name is highlighted, then click on Insert.**

16. **Close the dialog box and press** (↵ ENTER) **once.**

17. **On your own, continue to add the fields, punctuation and spacing, and text as shown in Figure 11.4.**

Your letter should resemble the one shown in Figure 11.4. Next you will merge the database information with the main letter using the Print Preview screen.

18. **Click on** 🔲.

19. **Choose OK to preview all records.**

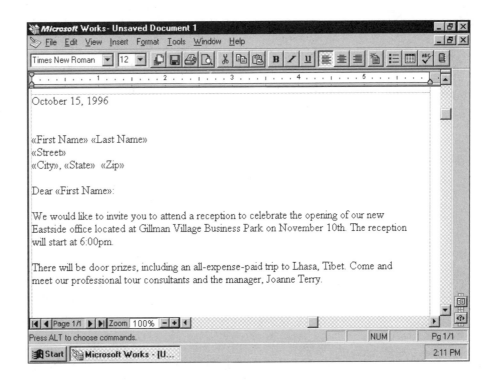

The Print Preview screen appears, showing the first merged letter.

20. Use the Zoom feature to view the name and address.

21. Click on [Next] to view the remaining letters.

22. Click on [Cancel] to return to the main document.

23. Save the main document with the name *Invitation - main document*.

At this point, the basic form letter process is complete, and you can edit the main document, print all of the finished letters, or print selected letters by creating a filter.

SELECTING RECORDS TO MERGE

At times, a company may not want to send the same form letter to all the clients in the database. In the current example, the form letter is an invitation to the grand opening of the Eastside office, so Adventure Tours may decide to send the letters only to clients who live close to that office. This selected mailing could be accomplished by creating a filter for the database and then merging the filtered records into a form letter. For example, Adventure Tours could select those records with certain zip codes, such as between 98004 and 98009. As you've already learned, to select specific records you create a filter. You will create a filter to be used specifically for performing a mail merge.

1. Open the *Clients* database.

2. Create a filter that will display records with zip codes between 98004 and 98009, inclusive.

3. Apply the filter.

The List view should show only clients who live in Issaquah and Bellevue, cities close to the new Eastside office.

4. Use the Window menu to switch to the *Invitation - main document*.

In order to perform the merge using the filter, you need to choose the Form Letters command from the Tools menu and select a filter from the list. Do this now to perform the merge.

5. Choose Form Letters from the Tools menu.

6. Click on the Recipients index tab.

7. Click on the Filtered records in the database.

The filter you just created and applied is automatically selected.

8. Click on Close.

9. Click on ▣ to view the letters that will print using the specified filter. (*Note*: A message will appear asking if you want to preview all records based on the selected filter. Choose OK to proceed with the preview.)

10. View the documents and then click on [Cancel] to return to the main document.

You can also use a filter to select a single record and merge the database information into a form letter. To do this, create a filter that will select a single client, Betty Gallagher, and print out a form letter for her.

11. Use the Window menu to switch to the Clients database.

12. Create a filter to display Betty Gallagher's record.

13. Apply the filter. Verify that only Betty Gallagher's record appears in List view.

14. Use the Window menu to switch to the main document.

15. Choose Form Letters from the Tools menu.

16. Click on the Recipients index tab.

Notice that the previous filter is still displayed in the Current Filter box. You can select another filter by clicking on the down arrow to display the list of available filters and choosing one from the list. Try this now.

17. Click on ▾ next to the Current filter box.

18. Choose the filter that you created to select Betty Gallagher's record.

19. Click on Close.

20. Click on ▣ to view the letter that will print using the specified filter. (*Note*: The Next button is inactive because there is only one letter to view.)

21. Click on [Cancel] to return to the main document.

22. Print the letter.

ADDRESSING ENVELOPES

After developing a form letter, you may want to address envelopes using the names and addresses in a database. An **envelope** can be created and attached to a main document, so that when you print the letters, the envelopes also print. The envelope contains field placeholders just as the main document does. Figure 11.5 shows the Envelopes dialog box with the field placeholders.

Complete the following steps to duplicate Figure 11.5.

1. **Verify the main document is displayed.**

2. **Choose Envelopes from the Tools menu.** (*Note*: **You may have to bypass the First-time Help dialog box.**)

The Envelopes dialog box contains several index tabs to assist you in creating envelopes. Most are self-explanatory from their names. The Main Address index tab is used to add database fields to the envelope.

3. **Click on the Main Address index tab.**

Notice that an insertion point appears in the box labeled "Main address." If you were not performing a mail merge, you could simply type in the addressee. However, because you are sending a form letter to each client using a mail merge, you need to use field placeholders. The Add Field button is used to insert the field placeholders one at a time.

4. **Use the ⌈ Add Field ⌉ button to create the main address placeholders for the envelope, as shown in Figure 11.5.**

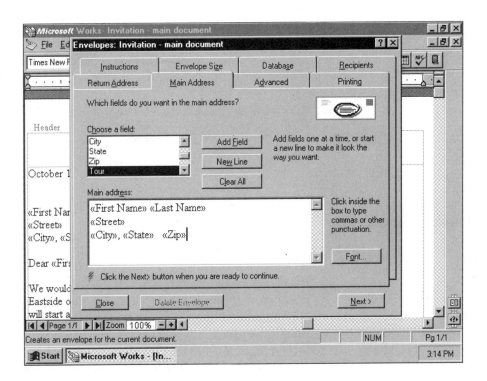

Now type in the return address.

5. **Click on the Return Address index tab.**

6. **Type** 1400 Rainier Place, Seattle, WA 98104

Notice the Envelope size index tab. You can use this list box to choose the size of envelope to print. Size 10 is the standard size for a business document.

7. **Click on the Envelope Size index tab.**

8. **Verify that Size 10 is selected.**

Now preview the envelope using the Printing index tab.

9. Click on the Recipients index tab.

10. If necessary, select the filter for Betty Gallagher's name and address.

11. Click on the Printing index tab.

12. Choose the Preview button in the dialog box.

13. Choose OK to preview the filtered records.

The envelope appears as it will print. Because you are working with a filter, only Betty Gallagher's envelope will print. Take a moment to return to the database, deselect the filter in order to show all records, and then preview all of the merged envelopes.

14. Click on [Cancel] to return to the dialog box.

15. Click on the Recipients index tab.

16. Click on All records in the database.

17. Click on the Printing index tab.

18. Click on [Preview].

19. Click OK to view all records.

20. View the envelopes by clicking on [Next >] and then click on [Cancel].

21. Close the Envelopes dialog box.

22. Save the document as *Invitation - main document with envelope*.

23. Close the main document.

CREATING MAILING LABELS

Very often, when a business is initiating a large mailing, it is more efficient to print mailing labels than it is to print individual envelopes. Figure 11.6 shows the names and addresses printed out as mailing labels. Creating mailing labels is similar to creating envelopes in that you use field placeholders. One of the most important considerations in preparing mailing labels is to correctly specify the dimensions of the labels. To help you, Works allows you to choose from several preset label sizes or to specify a custom label size. Notice the Label Style box in Figure 11.7 displays Avery 5660 (2 5/6" X 1"). Selecting this style and size will generate three labels across a page and up to ten labels down a page. Using the Avery 5660 label type, create mailing labels for the Invitation - main document file. Complete the following steps to duplicate Figure 11.7.

1. Open the file *Invitation - main document*.

2. Choose Labels from the Tools menu. (*Note*: you may have to bypass the First-time Help dialog box.)

The Labels dialog box appears, asking you to click on one of two buttons to set up the desired label type. You can choose Labels to create one label for each record in the database, or Multiple copies of one label to create a page or pages of labels for a single record in the database. Choose the Labels button.

3. Click the button next to Labels.

The Labels dialog box that appears onscreen is similar to the Envelopes dialog box: Steps are outlined on the Instructions index tab, and a Next button appears at the bottom of the dialog box. Use the Next button to move through the index tabs.

4. Click on [Next >].

The Label Size index tab appears listing the available label sizes. For this exercise, choose Avery 5660.

5. Scroll the list to display Avery 5660 (see Figure 11.7)

6. Click on Avery 5660.

Your dialog box should resemble the one shown in Figure 11.7.

7. Click on [Next >].

You are returned to the Instructions index tab. Notice that a check mark now appears next to the second item in the list indicating which index tabs you have displayed. Choose [Next >] to view the next dialog box.

8. Click on [Next >].

The Recipients index tab is displayed. The options in this tab allow you to select the records you want to print. You can choose to print records currently visible, records currently marked, records selected by using an existing filter or even all records in the database. The option you want is All records in the database, which is the current setting.

9. Review the Recipients index tab. Verify that All records in the database is selected, then click on [Next >].

10. Click again on [Next >].

The Label Layout index tab is displayed. Use the Add Field button to create the address in the Label Layout box. (*Note*: Your placeholders should match those created for the envelope as shown in Figure 11.5).

11. Use [Add Field] to create the label placeholders.

12. Click on [Next >].

13. Click again on [Next >].

The Printing index tab appears. Take this opportunity to preview the records/mailing labels.

14. Click on [Preview].

Paula Adams
905 W. Cedar
Seattle, WA 98104

Peter Andrews
1444 N. Mercer
Edmonds, WA 98030

Mary Carter
4546 W. 81st
Seattle, WA 98002

William Carter
4546 W. 81st
Seattle, WA 98002

Shirley Dubois
8008 Lakeside
Seattle, WA 98003

Thomas Dubois
8008 Lakeside
Seattle, WA 98003

Barbara Ellington
9009 Brookside
Bellevue, WA 98004

John Finny
15006 SE 141st
Redmond, WA 98052

Judy Finny
15006 SE 141st
Redmond, WA 98052

Arnold Gallagher
1215 E. Hill
Issaquah, WA 98006

Betty Gallagher
1215 E. Hill
Issaquah, WA 98006

Kim Lee
2003 S. 121st
Bellevue, WA 98007

Phillip Lee
2003 S. 121st
Bellevue, WA 98007

James Martin
777 N. Farview
Bellevue, WA 98004

Lily Martin
777 N. Farview
Bellevue, WA 98004

Ben Morris
9000 Hollis Way
Seattle, WA 98003

Charles Stanton
10 W. River St
Redmond, WA 98054

Debra Stanton
10 W. River St
Redmond, WA 98054

Jane Turner
5492 E. Bay
Bellevue, WA 98004

Ted Turner
5492 E. Bay
Bellevue, WA 98004

Brad VanDike
4343 Eagle Dr
Bellevue, WA 98008

Connie Williams
777 81st Ave
Seattle, WA 98003

John Williams
777 81st Ave
Seattle, WA 98003

Ellie Zender
10 W. 112th
Bellevue, WA 98009

11.7

Choosing Avery 5660 in the Label Size index tab of the Labels dialog box

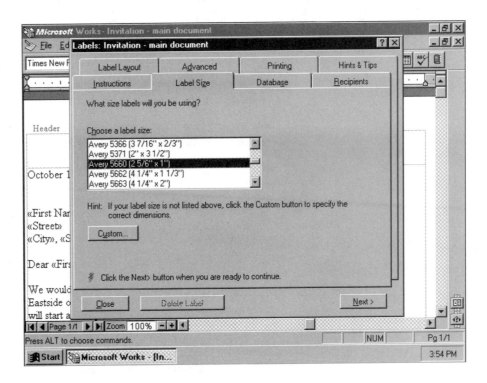

15. Click on OK to view all records.

The mailing labels appear as they would be printed.

16. Click on Cancel to return to the Labels dialog box.

17. Click on the Close button in the dialog box.

This completes the section on addressing envelopes and creating mailing labels.

18. Save the document as *Invitation - main document with labels*.

19. Close the main document and the database without saving changes.

KEY TERMS

envelopes	mail merge	main document
form letters	mailing labels	placeholders

KEY COMMANDS

Database Field	Envelopes	Labels
	Form Letters	

REVIEW QUESTIONS

1. **T F** The main document is created in the word processing application and is merged with a database file to create form letters.

2. Field _____ indicate the location on the main document where database information will be printed.

3. A(n) _____ can be used to select the records that are merged with a main document.

4. **T F** An envelope with placeholders can be saved with a main document.

PROJECTS

Using the Clients database create the following form letters:

1. A form letter to be sent to all clients. Thank the person for signing up for a specific tour. Use placeholders for the name, address and tour fields. Save the letter as *WKS Chapter 11 project 1*. Close the document.

2. A form letter to be sent to clients who have paid a deposit. Create a filter to select only those clients who have paid a deposit. In the form letter thank the person for the deposit and use placeholders for name, address, and deposit fields. Print the main document. Save the letter and envelope as *WKS Chapter 11 project 2*. Close the document.

3. A form letter to clients who have signed up for a specific tour but have not yet paid a deposit. Create a filter to select those clients. In the form letter indicate that a deposit is due and use placeholders for the name and address fields. Create mailing labels for the merged letters. Save the letter and label as *WKS Chapter 11 project 3*. Close the document.

Appendix
Works 4.0 for Windows 95 Quick Reference

This appendix contains a quick reference to Microsoft Works 4.0 for Windows 95. It describes the procedures most frequently used by the various tools in Microsoft Works. The appendix also includes information on the toolbars.

COMMON COMMANDS

Closing a file
- choose Close from the File menu

Creating a file
- choose New from the File menu (or click on the Task Launcher button)
- choose the Works Tools index tab
- choose the application tool button

Exiting Works
- choose Exit Works from the File menu (or click on the Task Launcher button and choose Exit Works)

Help, Getting
- click on the Shrink Help button
- choose a topic from the list

  or

  click on the Index button

  type a term in the text box and click on the related word in the list

Opening a previously created file
- choose Open from the File menu
- type the disk drive and file name (for example, a:\employees)
- choose open

  or

- click on the Task Launcher button
- choose the Existing Documents index tab
- click on the Open a document not listed here button
- type the disk drive and file name (for example, a:\clients)
- choose open

Previewing a file before printing

- choose Print Preview from the File menu or click on the Print Preview button

Printing

- choose Print from the File menu

Saving a file

- choose Save As from the File menu
- type the disk drive and file name (for example; a:\employees)
- choose OK

Starting Works

- start Windows 95
- click on the Start button
- point to Programs in the menu
- point to the appropriate program group
- click on Microsoft Works 4.0

CHARTS

Changing the type

- click on the toolbar button for the desired chart type
- complete the Chart Type dialog box
- choose OK

Creating

- select the cells with the data to be used in the chart
- click on the New Chart button
- complete the New Chart dialog box
- choose OK

Deleting

- choose Delete Chart from the Tools menu
- select the chart from the list
- choose Delete
- choose OK
- choose OK to confirm deletion

Displaying

- choose Chart from the View menu
- select the chart from the list
- choose OK

Help, Getting

- click on the Shrink Help button
- choose a topic from the list

  or

  click on the Index button

  type a term in the text box and click on the related word in the list

Printing

- choose Print from the File menu

DATABASE

Adding records to a database in Form view

- choose Insert Record from the Record menu (or click on the Insert Record button)
- type the field information, pressing (TAB ⇆) to move to the next field

Adding records to a database in List view

- choose Insert Record from the Record menu (or click on the Insert Record button)
- type the field information, pressing (TAB ⇆) to move to the next field

  or

- choose the first blank record in the list
- type the field information, pressing (TAB ⇆) to move to the next field

Closing a database

- choose Close from the File menu

Creating a database

- choose New from the File menu (or click on the Task Launcher button)
- choose the Works Tools index tab
- choose the Database button
- enter the field names into the Create Database dialog box and select the field format
- choose Done when all field names are entered

Creating a database filter

- choose Filters from the Tools menu (or click on the Filters button)
- enter a name in the Filter Name dialog box
- choose OK
- complete the Field Name, Comparison, and Compare To boxes in the Filter dialog box
- choose Apply Filter

Creating a database report

- choose ReportCreator from the Tools menu (or click on the Report View button)
- enter a name in the Report Name dialog box
- move through the dialog boxes; Title, Fields, Sorting, Grouping, Filter, Summary
- choose Done
- choose Preview to display the report

Deleting database records in Form view

- display the record
- choose Delete Record from the Record menu

Deleting database records in the List view

- select (highlight) the record
- choose Delete Record from the Record menu or press (DELETE)

Displaying all database records

- choose Show/All Records from the Record menu

Help, Getting

- click on the Shrink Help button
- choose a topic from the list
  or
  click on the Index button
  type a term in the text box and click on the related word in the list

Opening a previously created database

- choose Open from the File menu
- type the disk drive and file name (for example, a:\employees)
- choose open
  or
- click on the Task Launcher button
- choose the Existing Documents index tab
- click on the Open a document not listed here button
- type the disk drive and file name (for example, a:\clients)
- choose open

Printing database information from the Form or List views

- choose Print from the File menu (or click on the Print button)
- choose OK

Printing a report

- choose Report from the View menu
- select a report from the list
- choose Preview
- choose Print

Viewing a database in Form view

- choose Form from the View menu or click on the Form view button

Viewing a database in List view

- choose List from the View menu or click on the List view button

Viewing a report

- choose Report from the View menu
- select a report from the list
- choose Preview

Saving a database

- choose Save As from the File menu
- type the disk drive and file name (for example; a:\employees)
- choose OK

SPREADSHEET

Centering a heading across the worksheet

- select the heading and the cells it will be centered across
- choose Alignment from the Format menu
- choose the Alignment index tab
- click on Center across selection
- choose OK

Centering data within a cell

- select the cell
- click on the Center alignment button on the Formatting toolbar

Column widths, changing

- click on the column letter
- choose Column Width from the Format menu
- type in the desired column width
- choose OK

or

- point to the line between the column letters
- when the pointer changes to a double arrow and displays the word "ADJUST," hold down the mouse button and drag the column line to the desired position

Copying text and numbers

- select the data
- hold down the (CTRL) key

- hold down the mouse button and drag the data to the desired location
- release the mouse button

or

- select the data
- choose Copy from the Edit menu (or click on the Copy button)
- select the new location
- choose Paste from the Edit menu (or click on the Paste button)

Copying formulas

(*Note*: Cell addresses will automatically be changed as the formula is copied to a new location. If a part of the formula needs to remain the same, you must specify an absolute cell address by using $ signs in the cell address, e.g. $A$5.)

- use the process specified for copying text and numbers

Creating a new (blank) spreadsheet

- choose New from the File menu (or click on the Task Launcher button)
- choose the Works Tools index tab
- choose the Spreadsheet button

Deleting data in a spreadsheet

- select the cell(s)
- press (DELETE)

Formatting numbers

- select the cell(s)
- choose Number from the Format menu
- specify the desired format
- choose OK

Help, Getting

- click on the Shrink Help button
- choose a topic from the list

  or

  click on the Index button

  type a term in the text box and click on the related word in the list

Inserting a column

- click on the column letter
- choose Insert Column from the Insert menu

Inserting a row

- click on the row number
- choose Insert Row from the Insert menu

Moving text and numbers

- select the data
- hold down the mouse button and drag the data to the new location
- release the mouse button

or

- select the data
- choose Cut from the edit menu

- select the new location
- choose Paste from the Edit menu

Opening a previously saved spreadsheet

- choose Open from the File menu
- type the disk drive and file name (for example, a:\budget)
- choose open

or

- click on the Task Launcher button
- choose the Existing Documents index tab
- click on the Open a document not listed here button
- type the disk drive and file name (for example, a:\survey)
- choose open

Previewing a worksheet before printing

- choose Print Preview from the File menu or click on the Print Preview button

Printing a spreadsheet

- choose Print from the File menu (or click on the Print button)
- choose OK

Saving a spreadsheet document

- choose Save As from the File menu
- type the disk drive and file name (for example, a:\budget)
- choose OK

Selecting a cell

- point to the cell
- click the left mouse button

Selecting a group (range) of cells

- point to the first cell in the range (upper-left corner)
- hold down the mouse button and drag to the end of the range
- release the mouse button

WORD PROCESSING

Closing a word processing document

- choose Close from the File menu

Copying text

- select (highlight) the text
- choose Copy from the Edit menu (or click on the Copy button)
- position the insertion point at the new location
- choose Paste from the Edit menu (or click on the Paste button)

Creating a new (blank) word processing document
- choose New from the File menu (or click on the Task Launcher button)
- choose the Works Tools index tab
- choose the Word Processing button

Help, Getting
- click on the Shrink Help button
- choose a topic from the list

  or

  click on the Index button

  type a term in the text box and click on the related word in the list

Moving text
- select (highlight) the text
- choose Cut from the Edit menu (or click on the Cut button)
- position the insertion point at the new location
- choose Paste from the Edit menu (or click on the Paste button)

Opening a previously saved word processing document
- choose Open from the File menu
- type the disk drive and file name (for example, a:\letter)
- choose open

or

- click on the Task Launcher button
- choose the Existing Documents index tab
- click on the Open a document not listed here button
- type the disk drive and file name (for example, a:\letter)
- choose open

Previewing a word processing document before printing
- choose Print Preview from the File menu or click on the Print Preview button

Printing a word processing document
- choose Print from the File menu (or click on the Print button)
- choose OK

Saving a word processing document
- choose Save As from the File menu
- type the disk drive and file name (for example, a:\memo)
- choose OK

Selecting (highlighting) any text
- drag the pointer across the text

Selecting (highlighting) a word
- double-click on the word

Selecting (highlighting) an entire document
- choose Select All from the Edit menu

QR.1

Word Processing Toolbar

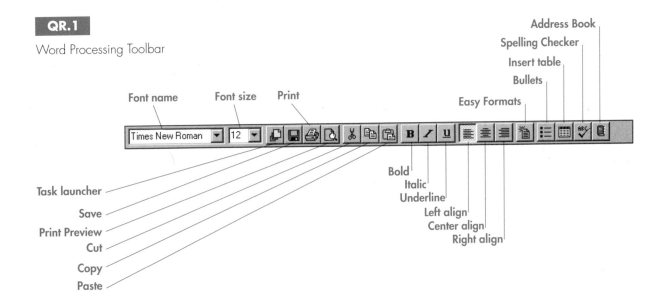

Font name   Font size   Print   Easy Formats   Bullets   Insert table   Spelling Checker   Address Book

Task launcher
Save
Print Preview
Cut
Copy
Paste

Bold
Italic
Underline
Left align
Center align
Right align

QR.2

Spreadsheet Toolbar

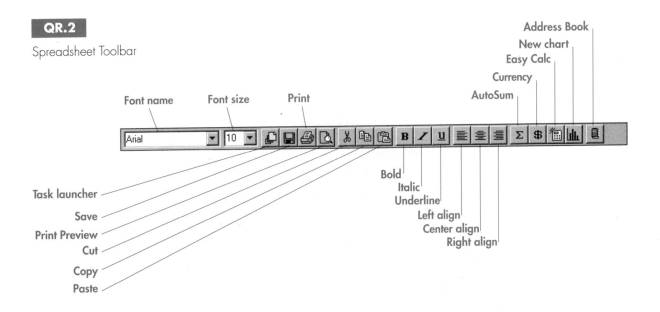

Font name   Font size   Print   AutoSum   Currency   Easy Calc   New chart   Address Book

Task launcher
Save
Print Preview
Cut
Copy
Paste

Bold
Italic
Underline
Left align
Center align
Right align

QR.3

Database Toolbar

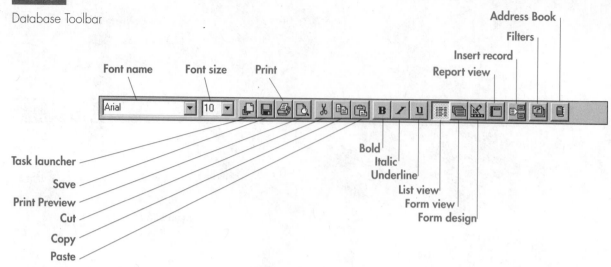

Font name Font size Print

Task launcher
Save
Print Preview
Cut
Copy
Paste

Bold
Italic
Underline
List view
Form view
Form design

Report view
Insert record
Filters
Address Book

QR.4

Chart Toolbar

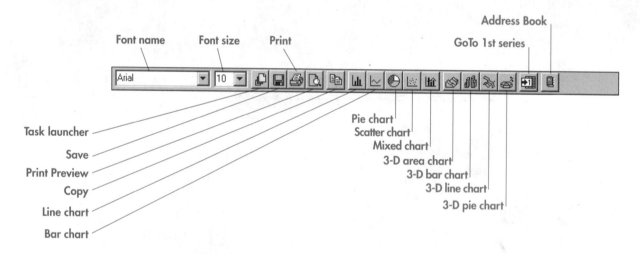

Font name Font size Print

GoTo 1st series
Address Book

Task launcher
Save
Print Preview
Copy
Line chart
Bar chart

Pie chart
Scatter chart
Mixed chart
3-D area chart
3-D bar chart
3-D line chart
3-D pie chart

Glossary

Absolute cell reference A cell address that will not change when it is used in a formula that is copied to another location.

Active cell The selected cell; the first cell selected in a block of cells.

Aligning data The process of determining the placement of data within a cell or across a range of cells. Data alignment can be left, right, centered within a cell, or centered across a selection of cells.

Aligning text The process of determining the placement of text in relation to the document margins. Text alignment can be left, right, center, or justified.

Antonyms Words with opposite meanings.

Ascending order A sort order from lowest to highest (0-9, A-Z).

AutoFormat command Allows you to apply one of several predefined styles for formatting data in a spreadsheet.

Automatic page break A break inserted by Works that causes text to print on the next page.

AutoSum button Inserts the SUM function into a cell.

Bar chart A graph that uses columns to represent and compare sets of numerical data.

Bold A type style that causes text to appear darker.

Border An outline surrounding a single cell or group of cells.

Bulleted list A list of items that are marked with symbols called bullets.

Cell The area of a spreadsheet where a row and column intersect.

Cell reference The unique reference that indicates the location of each cell in a spreadsheet.

Center across selection command Places data from a single cell across multiple columns of a spreadsheet.

Chart A graphical representation of the relationship between sets of numerical data.

ClipArt A collection of graphical images and symbols that comes with the Microsoft Works program.

Clipboard A holding area in the computer's memory for data that has been cut or copied.

Close button Closes a window and any open application or document that is displayed in that window.

Column labels The letters at the top of the spreadsheet page, beginning with A and ending with IV, that identify columns; they are used in connection with row labels to form cell references.

Column width The horizontal size of a column.

Combination chart A graph that uses both columns and lines to represent and compare numerical data.

Command An instruction that tells the Microsoft Works program to perform a particular task or operation.

Copy and paste The process of duplicating text or objects and placing them in another location within the same document or a different document.

Currency format A number format option that displays numbers with a dollar sign and two decimal places.

Cut and paste The process of moving text or objects and placing them in another location within the same document or in another document.

Data series The series of numbers used to create a chart.

Database A collection of related information such as a company's list of customers or employees.

Descending order A sort order from highest to lowest (9-0, Z-A).

Dialog box A box displayed onscreen in which the user gives instructions to the computer program. For example, the Save As dialog box allows the user to specify the disk drive and file name when saving a document.

Document A term used to refer to a file created by Microsoft Works spreadsheet or word processing tools.

Document window The window area onscreen in which a file is displayed.

Double-clicking Pressing the left mouse button twice in rapid succession.

Drag and drop The process of moving text or objects from one location in a document to another using the mouse.

Field A category of information used in constructing a database record, such as first name or phone number.

Field name The label assigned to each field that identifies the data in the field.

Filename A string of up to 255 allowed characters that identifies a file.

Fill The process whereby information in one cell is copied to another cell or, in the case of a series, the process whereby information in one cell is the basis of data that is automatically inserted into adjacent cells.

Filter A feature in Microsoft Works that allows you to select specific records to view or to include in reports.

Find command Allows you to search for specific text within a document.

Font A type design such as Times New Roman or Arial; also called a typeface.

Font size A measurement, usually designated as a point, indicating how large or small a type design will print or appear onscreen.

Footer   Text that is repeated at the bottom of each page of a document.

Form letter   A word processing document that is merged with information in a database to produce a finished letter.

Form view   A database view that displays database information one record at a time. Used to type information into fields on a form.

Formula bar   The line in the spreadsheet window that displays the data entry for the selected cell.

Functions   Preset formulas that perform mathematical operations on the values in a spreadsheet.

Graphics   Images and pictures placed in a Microsoft Works document that can be edited, resized, and moved.

Hanging indent   An indent where the first line of text extends to the left of the other lines in a paragraph. Used to set text apart, as in a bulleted list.

Header   Text that is repeated at the top of each page of a document.

Heading section   The area of the report definition that contains the information that will be displayed at the top of each column.

Help feature   A reference tool for learning how to use Microsoft Works.

Hide cells   A feature that allows you to selectively display worksheet cells.

I-beam pointer   The shape of the mouse indicator when it is placed anywhere within the text of a document. The I-beam pointer allows you to quickly move the insertion point from one location to another and to select text.

Insertion point   A line showing the location onscreen where the next keystroke will appear.

Italic   A type style that causes text to appear slanted to the right.

Landscape   The orientation of a document that will cause it to print horizontally (sideways).

Leaders   Characters that appear to the left of a tab stop (e.g., periods, dashes, and underscores).

Line   A partial outline appearing along one or more sides of a single cell or group of cells.

Line chart   A graph that uses a line to show the relationship between sets of numerical data.

Linking documents   The process of establishing a connection between two or more separate documents by sharing data.

List view   A screen that displays database information in a table format so that multiple records can be viewed onscreen simultaneously.

Mailing labels   A type of word processing document that prints multiple addresses on sheets of self-stick labels such as Avery labels.

Main document   A word processing document, such as a letter, that is merged with information in a database to produce a finished document.

Manual page break A break added to a Microsoft Works document to prevent inappropriate automatic page breaks, such as a break between a heading and its corresponding text.

Margins The white space between text and the edges of the paper.

Markers Small rectangular boxes that appear on a line chart to indicate each data point.

Maximize button Enlarges a window to the size of the screen.

Menu A list of functions, such as the File menu, that contains commands used in Microsoft Works.

Menu bar The area of a window that displays menu names and gives access to the program commands.

Microsoft Draw A Microsoft graphics program that allows you to create pictures and other graphical objects.

Microsoft Works for Windows 95 An integrated software program that includes four commonly used applications—word processing, spreadsheet database, and communications tools—and is used in the Windows 95 operating environment.

Minimize button Reduces the size of a window to an icon.

Number format Determines how numbers will be displayed (e.g., decimal places, currency, etc.).

Object An document or portion of a document, such as a drawing or chart, that is placed in a Microsoft Works document. Also refers to linked data, such as a spreadsheet, that is added to a word processing document.

Page buttons Used to move through a document, either one page at a time or directly to and from the first and last pages. Page buttons include first page, previous page, next page and last page.

Paragraph indent The process of moving text away from the left or right margin towards the center of the page to create white space around the paragraph.

Paragraph mark A non-printing symbol that is inserted into a document whenever the Enter key is pressed; used to divide text for formatting purposes.

Pattern Shading that is added to cells to draw attention to cell contents or to set them apart from other cells within a spreadsheet.

Percent format A number format option that displays numbers with decimal places and a percent sign.

Pie chart A graph that uses a circle divided into sections to represent the relationship of individual numbers to the total.

Placeholders A code that reserves a space within a word processing document for information from the indicated database field to be inserted when a merge is performed.

Points A measurement used for determining the size of fonts and spacing. There are 72 points in an inch.

Print Preview button Displays the document in the Print Preview screen.

Record A group of related information (fields) such as a person's name and address.

Record section The area of the report definition that contains the data records.

Replace command Searches for text or formatting and replaces it with alternate text or formatting.

Report A document that can display record information in various formats, including field groupings, and can provide additional data such as summary totals for numeric fields.

Report definition The design screen used to determine the contents and format of a report.

Restore button Returns a window to its previous size.

Row labels The numbers on the left edge of the spreadsheet page that identify each row and are used in connection with column labels to form cell references.

Ruler Used to set tab stops, create paragraph indents, and measure the placement of text and graphics on the page.

Scalable font Type styles that can be printed in virtually any point size.

Scroll bars Wide lines displayed below and to the right of the document window that are used for moving vertically and horizontally through a document using the mouse.

Sizing handles Small rectangular boxes that appear on the borders of a selected object and are used to resize the object.

Sort A feature that allows you to arrange records in a specified order (ascending or descending).

Spelling command Activates the spelling checker, a feature which looks for misspelled words in a document.

Spreadsheet A document that organizes data in rows and columns and is used for creating files that use numbers and mathematical calculations.

Start button Provides access to programs and files.

Status bar The bottom line of the Microsoft Works window that displays information about selected commands and keyboard functions.

sum function Used to add the values in one or more cells.

Summary section The area of the report definition that contains summary information, such as totals for numeric fields.

Synonyms Words that have similar meanings.

Table The structure, consisting of rows and columns, used for storing information in a database.

Tabs Preset positions across the page used for placing text in columns.

Taskbar Displays the Start button used to access applications within Windows 95 and shows which applications are currently running.

TaskWizards Self-guided templates used to create professional-looking documents like form letters, mailing labels, and other documents commonly used in business and home management. Users answer questions in a TaskWizard dialog box and the Works program creates and formats the document.

Thesaurus command Activates the thesaurus, a feature which provides antonyms, synonyms, and definitions of selected words.

Title bar The highlighted bar at the top of a window that identifies the program and/or the document displayed in the window.

Title section The area of the report definition that contains the information that appears on the first page of the document.

Toolbar A row of buttons beneath the title bar that are used as shortcuts in carrying out various functions.

Type size A measurement, usually designated as a point, indicating how large or small the text will print or appear onscreen.

Type style Determines the appearance of a font. Type styles include bold, italic, underline, and others.

What-if analysis The process of using a Microsoft Works spreadsheet to find out the results of different financial or numeric scenarios, such as the result of doubling income for one month.

Wildcards Characters used when searching for data that allow flexibility in the search string. For example, ? is used to represent a single character, and * is used to represent any number of characters.

Word processor An application that is used to create text-based documents such as letters, memos, newsletters, and announcements.

Word wrap A feature where the insertion point automatically moves from the end of a text line to the beginning of the next line.

WordArt A text-design program that comes with Microsoft Works.

Works Task Launcher The dialog box used to start one of the Microsoft Works tools, to open existing documents, or to create a new file automatically using TaskWizards.

X-axis The horizontal line of a column or line chart that usually displays a timeline or labels.

Y-axis The vertical line of a column or line chart that usually displays units of measurements.

Zoom command Allows you to adjust the amount of document data displayed onscreen.

Zoom buttons Used to quickly adjust the zoom percentage of the active document.